STRATEGIES OF
SLAVES & WOMEN

STRATEGIES
OF
SLAVES & WOMEN

Life-Stories from
East/Central Africa

WITHDRAW

by
MARCIA WRIGHT

LILIAN BARBER PRESS
New York

JAMES CURREY
London

First published in the United States of America in 1993

LILIAN BARBER PRESS, INC.
P.O. Box 232
New York, NY 10163

JAMES CURREY
54B Thornhill Square
Islington, London N1 1BE

Library of Congress Cataloging in Publication Data

Wright, Marcia.
    Strategies of slaves & women : life-stories from East/Central
Africa / by Marcia Wright.
        p.   cm.
    Includes bibliographical references and index.
    ISBN 0-936508-27-2 (cloth). — ISBN 0-936508-28-0
(paper)
        1. Slavery—Africa, East—History.   2. Women—Africa, East—
History.   I. Title.
HT1326.W75   1993
305.5'67'09676—dc20   91-32722
                                                                    CIP

British Library Cataloguing in Publication Data

Wright, Marcia
    Strategies of Slaves and Women:
    Life-Stories from East/Central Africa
    I. Title
    305.567082
    ISBN 0-85255-707-8 (Paper)

Typeset by Smith, Inc., New York
and printed in the United States of America

Contents

CREDITS

Part I, "Women in Peril" originally appeared as a separate volume under the same title published by the National Educational Company of Zambia in 1984. Reprinted with permission.

The "Commentary" in that volume, which also appears in this edition as "Prelude to Texts and Contexts" originally appeared in *African Social Research,* no. 20 (1975), published by the University of Zambia. Reprinted by permission.

"Grandmother Narwimba" and "Chisi-Ndjurisiye-Sichyajunga" originally appeared in *Stories of Old Times,* recorded, arranged, and translated into German by E. Kootz-Kretschmer, translated into English by M. Bryan (Sheldon Press, London, 1932).

"Msatulwa Mwachitete" was originally published as *Ways I Have Trodden* (Sheldon Press, London, 1932).

"Mama Meli" was originally translated from Mambwe by E. Sichilongo and B. Lea for *Women in Peril.*

"Justice, Women, and the Social Order in Abercorn, Northeastern Rhodesia, 1897–1903," originally appeared in Margaret Jean Hay and Marcia Wright, eds., *African Women and the Law: Historical Perspectives,* published in 1983 by Boston University African Papers (vol. 7). Reprinted by permission.

"Bwanikwa: Consciousness and Protest" originally appeared in C. Robertson and M. Klein, eds., *Women and Slaves in Africa,* published by the University of Wisconsin Press, 1983. Reprinted by permission.

Preface

Looking back over the twenty or more years since I began to appreciate the life stories of ex-slaves that form the core of this volume, it is very difficult to disentangle the threads of motivation and stimulus. The work is both an individual inquiry pursuing questions raised for me by prior reflection on the history of the Protestant churches in this region of East Central Africa and a product of the times, borne along on a widening stream of scholarly and general interest in the history of women and of slaves and slavery. To give credit where it is due is therefore a hard task, and the acknowledgments to be found here touch only on some main currents: feminism, with its insistence on retaining the personal and private within the consideration of power and social relations; African social history, with its increasing sophistication in treating popular consciousness; and lastly, the vigorous and undiminished interest in slavery as a theme in Africa's internal and external history.

"Women in Peril," which forms Part I of this volume, enjoyed instant success from the time the original draft of the commentary was presented at an M.A. seminar devoted to autobiography and biography at Sarah Lawrence College, directed by Gerda Lerner. As a neophyte in studies of empathetic texts, I still had much to learn about how to frame such narratives critically while still preserving the immediacy of the narrators' perspectives on their own experience. When the commentary was presented at a colloquium on African women's lives at the University of California at Los Angeles, the question arose as to whether sufficient numbers of texts of ex-slaves' lives existed to provide an adequate basis for generalizations about the conditions and consciousness of such women. The second part of this volume offers two responses to this pessimism by displaying additional lengthy texts from the same region and time and suggesting how they may be enlarged upon to generate new agendas of research drawing upon a diversity of sources. The diversity achieved in this volume is mainly in the documentary realm. Some sources, like early colonial court records, formed part of the process of re-defining and decommercializing property in women. Others are recollections of various distances. Where interviews are cited, they are from fieldwork in the region between 1970 and 1976, which I carried out in association with Emanuel Silanda and Ephraim Mgawe.

It is my contention that we, as historians, have only scratched the surface, and that literary and anthropological perspectives on this same material can also be applied with many returns. An excellent recent example of the rich rewards of feminist cooperation across disciplines, with special reference to the handling of biography, life stories, and autobiography, is to be found in *Interpreting Women's Lives* (Minnesota Personal Narratives Group 1989). My own contribution to that volume treats high-status women rather than ex-slaves, but the exchanges with members of the editorial collective, during visits to the University of Minnesota and elsewhere, provided encouragement, incisive criticism, and an invaluable sense of community of purpose, all of which carried over to my thinking about personal narratives, especially in the concluding chapter, "Tatu Mulondyelwa Recollected." Feminist studies flourish when there is exchange across disciplines, each of which must transcend its own reflexes. I look forward to the inevitable call from students of literature for greater attention to the problems of text transmission, translation, and exegesis.

Historians may be slow to commit themselves to self-scrutiny and lengthy deliberations on the subject of authorship and contexts shaping the creation of their documents. With social history's maturing effort to include the illiterate as well as those who are underrepresented in documents as actors and bearers of history, attention has necessarily turned to a range of questions about the creation of popularly received versions of the past, their embodiment in written chronicles and social charters, and their manipulation, restatement, and demise as social values change. In African historiography, discussions of the invention of tribalism, ethnicity, and custom have played havoc with the staples of an older anthropological literature. History thus practiced and abated by the new anthropology becomes at the extreme devoted to the study of the times and circumstances of the creation of texts, not the past events to which they allegedly refer. While agreeing with critics of this tendency that there are major limitations on the extent to which we can fully retrieve the processes by which communities became imagined and projected as historical entities, I am convinced that the questioning is indispensable as a preliminary to a positive statement of the nature of collective memory and to sharpen awareness of the ways in which ideological constructions take on the appearance of empirically determined facts.

As the introduction discusses the question of African slavery, it will suffice here to mention three edited volumes that reflect the great contemporary attention to the theme. In the first, *Slavery in Africa: Historical and Anthropological Perspectives* (Miers and Kopytoff 1977), the introduction argued that the domestic slavery of women dissolved within two generations, and suggested that the cultural norm of incorporation mitigated the harshness of slave status. The slavery of women emerged as a more central feature of nineteenth-century African conditions in *Women and Slavery in Africa* (Roberts and Klein 1983), but women largely receded from view in *The End of Slavery in Africa* (Miers and Roberts 1988), where the authors tended to reflect the disregard typical of colonial documents that focused on men as the labor force to be emancipated and redirected into "free" labor.

Beyond the company already mentioned, an array of other works and authors will be acknowledged as their contributions bear upon the interpretations to be offered from chapter to chapter.

More immediately, for their critical readings at formative moments, I wish to thank Ronald Grele, Elisabeth Hansot, Jean Scandlyn, Jay Spaulding, and Katya Skow, who also prepared the translation from German of the memoir of Tatu Mulondyelwa. For their commitment to the material and work in seeing it through publication in various forms and places, I am grateful to Eileen Haddon, Margaret Jean Hay, and Monde Sifuniso. Anne Dow has been a supportive and relentlessly demanding critic, especially at the outset in Zambia in the early 1970s and again when this volume was re-edited in 1989-90. Terry Walz and the Lilian Barber Press deserve the final acknowledgment for constancy of purpose, patience, and determination to make accessible the experiences of people whose voices are often lost, neglected, or relegated.

General Introduction

Individual lives in a specific region and period, a part of East Central Africa before and after 1900, occupy the foreground of this book. The discussion raises questions about the recurrent patterns, universality, betterment, and worsening of conditions for slave and ex-slave women. During times of stress — during times of transition and reconstruction not only in their own lives but also in the values ordering society — what were their strategies? What was the interplay of institutional or structural elements with situational, idiosyncratic actions? When does gender enter or become explanatory?

The lives of the six principal characters encountered in this volume — five women and one man — collectively extend from the mid nineteenth to the mid twentieth century. What is most revealing is the evidence of consciousness and changing circumstances in the decades before World War I as these people went from slavery to some sort of freedom. This alteration was not necessarily by a formal act of emancipation, but all the focus characters finally belonged to or were sheltered in a Christian community with a strong antislavery ideology and the capacity to provide a base for social reconstruction. The life stories contain much that verges on the mythic, and it will be a continuing challenge to apprehend the interplay of genuine historical forces and retrospective visions.

The narratives of ex-slaves, where they treat childhood circumstances of initial enslavement and subsequent tribulations and dangers, are filled with psychological drama. The terrors of cruelty were eclipsed by the terrors of abandonment. Passages expressing desperation at being lost in the wilderness, compelled to take the

1

risk of entering a settlement come what may, give evidence of this
deep fear of isolation. A complementary attitude – unwillingness
to accept freedom if it meant loss of protection – is well illustrated
by the autobiography of Goi, who as a Luba slave boy could not
distinguish redemption from purchase. The missionaries, after all,
had paid the few scarves that had been asked for him. As he put
it: "I could not understand what freedom meant, and I thought
I was now a slave of the white man. I did not want to be free, for
I would only be caught and sold again."[1]

There is very little to distinguish boys from girls in their
expressed need to be in a relationship with others. What begins
to make their careers divergent is how they are socialized and
put to work, groomed for their mature lives. Girls, as future concubines, mothers, and agriculturalists, were more universally
assimilable than were boys, who had to be occupied in some more
immediately productive way and whose marriage was problematic
in simple communities where a slave mode of production was not
established. Male slaves were difficult to absorb at the family level;
they tended to enter the service of important personages and become linked with commercial activities. Not only was Msatulwa,
a key figure in this volume, a slave responsible for the household
of a female provincial chief, he was also permitted to join caravans
and earn money. This scope for trusted slaves to range widely was
not unparalleled.[2] The divergence between male and female
career lines persisted and widened when the commercial economy
of the late nineteenth century merged into the colonial economy
of the early twentieth century. While men became employees with
the possibility of advancing in education, skill, and prestige in the
new order, women continued to be assigned reproductive roles
in the economic, biological, and cultural senses.

Ex-slaves who became Christians joined pace-setting communities in which they were encouraged to look upon themselves
as both redeemed from the atrocious slavery and brought into the
"light" of salvation. A sense of improvement surrounded the
carpenters, the tailors, the teachers who were likely to be the

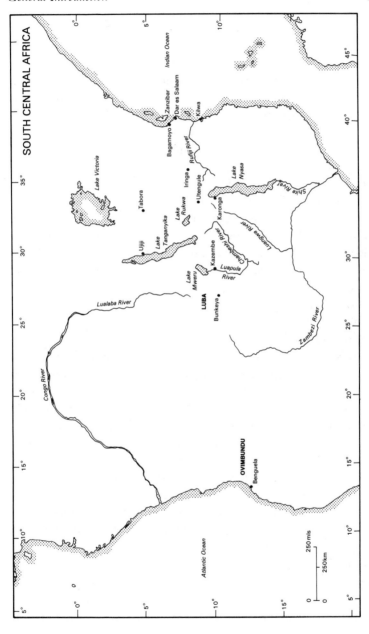

husbands, fiances, sons, and mentors of the women who are central to the analysis. Rarely did a woman risk violating norms of
deference. Bwanikwa, the subject of Chapter 7, was seen to be
exceptional for the equality she earned by working on her own
account: "Our friend Bwanikwa, indeed, fulfilled the requirements
of the Scripture, for she was pre-eminently and above all else,
diligent in business. She was a worker. . . , a diligent worker."[3]
A recent study of the Luapula Valley suggests that the cultural
environment of her diligence may have legitimated both the
solidarity and the individual initiative of women so evident in
her situation.[4] The matter of work, and work for the benefit of
whom, must be considered and reconsidered objectively and
subjectively in terms of perceived justice and injustice, in slavery
and freedom, within and without Christian communities, and in
light of the privileges and vulnerabilities associated with age and
life-cycle status. The optic of individual lives allows for the ordering of this massive agenda.

Violence of Enslavement

It is only in the middle of the nineteenth century that the historical setting for this study of slavery and postslavery crystallized
in the area of East Central Africa of concern to us. As the map
indicates, the area extends from the northwestern corner of Lake
Nyasa across to the southern end of Lake Tanganyika and westward to Lake Mweru, the Luapula River, and beyond to Katanga.
The explorer and hero of the antislavery movement, David
Livingstone, who was the first Westerner to describe parts of the
area, happened upon a crucial buildup of local power and economic restructuring for commercial purposes. He found at the
south end of Lake Tanganyika that the chiefs of the Lungu people
had adopted the policy of collaborating with long-distance traders
ultimately based in Zanzibar. While Livingstone was there, the
famous Afro-Arab merchant, Tippu Tip (Hamed bin Muhammad), having met resistance, called upon his local allies, the Lungu,
to help eliminate the Tabwa chief Nsama.[5] The Tabwa chief, in

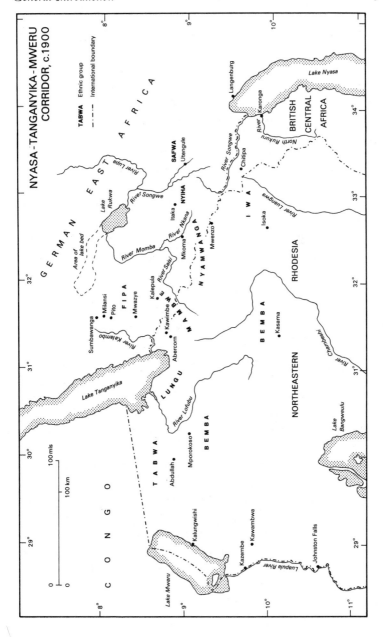

NYASA-TANGANYIKA-MWERU
CORRIDOR, c.1900

TABWA Ethnic group
–·–·– International boundary

successive episodes of friction with the Swahili, ended up virtually stripped of an important perquisite: one tusk of each pair taken from an elephant felled in his territory. Lungu commitment to long-distance traders implicated them in the slave trade, although Livingstone merely noted their self-righteousness in joining the assault on Nsama, as they contended he had "broken public law by attacking people who brought merchandise into the country."[6]

Chiefs enhanced their positions through the wealth gained from collaboration with long-distance traders. At mid century, they also developed new dimensions of coercive power, for the first time creating regular corps of armed enforcers. The military inspiration was derived from the Ngoni, immigrant warrior groups originally from southern Africa whose tactical innovations, aims, and discipline made an impression not only upon the Lungu but also throughout the whole area of East Central Africa from Lake Nyasa to Lake Tanganyika. By the late 1860s, the main groups of Ngoni had dispersed elsewhere, but scattered residual bands had remained behind and become notorious as brigands who "carried off very large numbers of the women, boys, girls, and children."[7] As they conscripted young men into enlarged contingents of armed guards, the Lungu and other chiefs copied the characteristic weapons, shields, and manner of the Ngoni. Livingstone moralized that the young men who affected the ways of Ngoni warriors ought instead to be at work in agriculture, but he was powerless to alter the trajectory of male prestige, opportunity, and obligation. The consequences of militarization, with its diversion of youth into defensive and destructive activities, deserve fuller study as a background to early colonial efforts to generate a wage labor force while also expecting to normalize agriculture. The definition of women's place in the fields and homesteads of the region bears the marks of precolonial as well as colonial diversion of men into the migrant labor force.

Not all areas were identically affected. In the late 1870s, throughout the 1880s, and into the 1890s, it was the Bemba who engaged most aggressively in organized military activities as well as more individualized and entrepreneurial brigandage, generating a flow of women and children who were often kept in villages, their disposability obscured until such time as they were needed and found themselves handed over to traders in exchange for goods. Insecurity in Bemba country itself and in areas better favored agriculturally into which the Bemba expanded or raided led to a growth of strategic settlements. Capital villages tended to swell and to be ever more heavily fortified. With an increased number of subjects and dependents directly under their control, chiefs could create economic focal points and at the same time provide protection.[8]

Slave raiding per se played a relatively small part in creating a pool of slaves. A listing of thirty-six women and children freed at the north end of Lake Nyasa in the early 1890s provides a catalog of how slavery was initiated.[9] The victims were most often kidnapped or taken in compensation for offenses by male relatives. Ngola, a Bemba woman, was captured in reprisal for her husband's adultery. Kapaso was commandeered as a "wife" by a chief, and when she remained faithful to her husband, she was sold. Mangala had been taken in a Bemba attack, the motive for which was unknown, and sold, together with her infant son. Kionga, a Bemba girl on a visit at a distance from her home, was seized by two Bemba youths who sold her for guns. A Lungu boy was kidnapped by passing Bemba and sold to traders for twelve yards of cloth. Another boy, originally of a Chishinga village, was a famine refugee when taken by "Arabs." Such victimization did not necessarily end in confirmed slavery. Sometimes the woman or child remained a pawn, to be redeemed when a debt could be settled by no other means. Only with repeated transfers and the passing of currencylike trade goods, and by coming into the possession of traders, did people finally become commodities.

Commercial Practice and the Asset-Value of Women, 1870-1900

The ever-extending frontier of the ivory trade in the late nineteenth century led to the existence of various commercial

provinces, one of which straddled the "corridor" running between
Lakes Nyasa, Tanganyika, and Mweru. Long-distance traders
operating in this area were generally called Arabs by their European competitors, who were also well aware of the wide differences among the organizing traders, who might be Baluchi, Afro-
Arabs, or Islamized, Swahili-speaking Africans. Africans, both
slaves and free communities of the area, more usually designated
the long-distance traders collectively as "Alungwana," a term
suggesting a Muslim religious identity and linkages with coast-
oriented commerce, but not necessarily with ancestry external to
Africa. In this appreciation of the common culture of trading
communities, the indigenous perception was generally accu-
rate.[10] The translation of texts by which "Alungwana" is rendered as "Arab" is therefore very misleading, although it is
significant as an example of how the antislavery rhetoric has
sometimes invaded the English or German versions of vernacular
understandings.

In addition to the Muslim traders, who for purposes of clarity
I will call "Swahili" after their lingua franca, there were also
Nyamwezi traders known in the region as Yeke. The orientation
of the Yeke was toward the north, to Tabora and Unyanyembe,
their homeland and entrepot. Nyamwezi traders also organized
major caravans from Tabora to the Indian Ocean and thus fully
participated in the overall Swahili commercial system.[11] Any
comprehensive view of the commercialization of East Central
Africa would also acknowledge the petty traders who belonged
to local societies and specialized in goods of local manufacture,
such as hoes and other iron wares. The equivalent of the Nyamwezi, but operating to the west from Katanga, were the Ovimbundu. While regional and local entrepreneurs had a role in the
overall penetration of commercial values and the exploitation of
indebtedness, they do not seem to have been accumulators of
slaves. The life stories of the women that occupy our foreground
have as a common denominator sale to long-distance traders, and
aspects of this situation therefore command attention.

Women were assets to traders in three main ways. Most immediately, they could constitute households for men who moved from place to place and might remain camped for a whole season in one spot. Major traders established permanent bases that served as supply and market centers for more petty operators as well as their own itinerant activities. In 1890, a commercial map would have shown two different networks of commercial outposts, one belonging to Swahili traders and one to the colonial African Lakes Company.

Swahili operations were also based in chiefs' capitals, reinforcing the mutual advantage of such alliances. A trader-in-residence drew upon the services of the chief's subjects, including women. Along the caravan routes, the chief's friend could count on local communities, which also had their own interest in earning cloth and beads in return for supplying provisions, entertainment, cooked food, and sex. It was upon the female realm that many of the demands were made. In this environment, acquisition of women, as pawns, whether as "wives" of chiefs, or as slave dependents of traders made very little functional difference since normative distinctions were easily breached when it suited the masters' convenience. Women moved into and out of these latent or active conditions of servility as their asset-value figured in disputes and in the extraction of fines from men.

Overview of the Chapters

The arrangement of the chapters generally follows the order of their composition. This sequence reveals an unfolding process of analysis, drawing upon an ever-expanding body of primary materials and the reconsideration of texts from different perspectives. In general, the focus of the chapters moves chronologically from precolonial to colonial times.

An attraction of the recorded lives of ex-slaves rests in the evidence they contain of struggle and resourcefulness in the face of dramatic adversity. The first-person accounts satisfy the late-twentieth-century desire for personal statements about the experience of past generations. They also provide points of entry into the wider, deeper, and more complex workings of community, economy, and society.

The steps in gathering data for a study of slavery as part of a commercial system began with the list of liberated slaves used above to exemplify the circumstances whereby people became detached from their homes and families. An examination of the early colonial record books for the districts of Northeastern Rhodesia, a semiautonomous colonial entity administered by the British South African Company, revealed that the bulk of cases of women or their kin applying for emancipation contained similar background elements of indebtedness or male malfeasance.

Before seeking to analyze the slave experience itself, it seemed necessary to identify the social and commercial attributes of the long-distance trading elements shaping relations in the "corridor." In an article entitled "Swahili Settlements in Northern Zambia and Malawi" Peter Lary and I explored the comparability of the Swahili and the missionary-commercial communities founded before the coming of formal colonial administration.[12] We also discussed how the African Lakes Company anticipated the final episodes in the conquest of the "Arabs." The conclusions were that while the African Lakes Company existed to serve the missionaries and had humanitarian backing, its rivalry for the ivory trade represented direct competition with the Swahili and a basis for symbiosis, since long-distance traders came to the company with ivory to resupply themselves for further trade in the region. Ivory and cloth linked the "legitimate" to the "illegitimate" slave trade.

Through a treatment of the lives of three women of successive generations and a man of the middle generation, Part I, "Women in Peril," takes on the question of the experiences of slavery. Two of the women, Narwimba and Chisi, and the man, Msatulwa, all wrote or had their life stories recorded at the Moravian mission station Utengule, near Mbeya, Tanzania, before World War I. This commentary, in a slightly revised form, was later published in a booklet also containing the texts themselves.[13] The availability of these texts, above all the story of Mama Meli, something of a prototype of Zambian womanhood linking precolonial to post-colonial times, made for the popularity of this Zambian publication. The confined circulation of the booklet and the enthusiasm of people of various backgrounds for the linkage of analysis with complete texts encouraged me to develop this technique further.

Issues of context had meanwhile been addressed in "Justice, Women, and the Social Order," which examined the records left behind by a certain magistrate who had been sent to the south end of Lake Tanganyika in 1893 to establish a strategic outpost on what Cecil Rhodes hoped would be the route from the Cape to Cairo. H. C. Marshall was chosen for his cool temperament: not only would he be the pillar of a civil administration, but he would also be a diplomatic presence coping with the neighboring German and Belgian officials as they sought to make effective the nominal partition of that part of Africa. From Marshall's carefully compiled record books has come an unusually detailed picture of an early colonial community. Although enlarged, Westernized, and backed by imperial resources, it was in many ways not different in kind from the Swahili and missionary settlements that went before, at least in the early years.

The Marshall era in the Tanganyika District went through three classic phases, from initial "strong point" — essentially a garrison but one situated in a complex and lively commercial zone, to colonial district capital — with its own community and sense of state-building, to peripheral imperial outpost as the larger apparatus and homogenizing ideologies of colonial rule became dominant. Because these phases coincided with an upsurge and then recession of activity in transport and employment in the Tanganyika District, they are particularly striking.[14] Of special interest is the fact that the middle phase saw a strong contract between the magistrate and women as persons often acting on their own initiative. In the third phase of normalization, the alliance shifted to become one with chiefs and elders determined to impose order through the control of women as a category. The outcome of this succession of involvements was the increasing effacement of women in the attendant records.

At the conclusion of Chapter 6 is the text of a decision by the High Court Judge of Northeastern Rhodesia in a case of child custody that reflects a process of weighing many different factors before deciding in favor of the mother, an ex-slave. It captures some of the evaporating alliance between women and early colonial court holders who were influenced both by the anti-slavery ideology of imperialism and by the conditions of mobility and susceptibility to exploitation that stimulated female initiative.

"Bwanikwa" moves the geographical focus westward, to the Katanga and the commercial state presided over by Msiri, a Nyamwezi merchant prince. In many ways, this treatment is the center of gravity of the volume, bringing to conclusion the process of juxtaposing text and context, and deploying court records and other contemporary documentation to embark on judgments about how representative a single life may be. There is no doubt that colonial and missionary records for the decade after 1900 convey the ideology of western agencies in respect to the approved form of control over women. Nevertheless, embedded in them, especially in the court records, is direct testimony of women's perceptions of the actuality and implications of slave status. From the standpoint of personal interactions, many compromises and accommodations certainly occurred, but a hardening of "tradition" and a strong disposition to enforce patriarchies were discernible among the main outlines of a settled colonial situation.

"Tatu Mulondyelwa Recollected" has been prepared specifically for this volume. Here the turn of the century, the middle phase of the transition from Swahili to colonial time, is seen to be one of varied opportunities, with alternative kinds of communities existing under the wing of secular colonial officials and missionaries. Last of the six ex-slaves, Tatu provides the springboard for this discussion. She is compared with the equally self-reliant Chisi, her elder by a generation in the missionary community at Utengule. But because the mediation of this life story poses such challenges, it can serve as the case study it is only because of the unusually dense body of Utengule texts taken directly by and from Africans and published in association with the ethnographic writings of the missionary Elise Kootz-Kretschmer.

Accounts by "intimate outsiders" become objects of critical examination in the case of Tatu's life story. Colonial literature in this genre often verges on fiction in that it enters imaginatively into the life circumstances of Africans — especially African women — and transgresses boundaries between the observer and the observed. When the ethnograph Oscar Baumann chose the "tale" instead of the reigning "objective" style of scientific communication, he did so to reach a wider audience and also to bring out the foibles and stereotypical thinking of German officers. His *Afrikanische Skizzen* (1900), published posthumously, may have been delayed and contained only muted criticism of German officials because of the hostile reaction earned by an earlier-published sketch that satirized the ignorance displayed and pointed up the consequent injustice of colonial military prosecutions and punishments in the early 1890s.[15]

When *Afrikanische Skizzen* was published, one of its key segments exposed the callousness of "white Arab" slave owners accorded the rank of gentlemen by explorers and colonial neophytes, who equated color and civilization and benefited from the generosity of well-situated collaborators. Baumann, in contrast, followed the fate of a slave woman removed arbitrarily from life with her slave husband to become one of the many concubines in a harem.[16] The editor touches lightly on the erotic features of the material. To a late-twentieth-century reader of this book, the term applies more to some of the photographs and thus to the eye of the photographer than it does to the written accounts, but male readers in Europe at the turn of the century may well have been led by popular stereotypes to expect the "erotic peoples" of Africa to satisfy their fantasies.[17]

Where they achieved social intimacy, male outsiders often did so through sexual partnership with African women, an experience not shared by colonial women, whose emotional standpoint depended upon their ability to extend their own identity to females. Magdalene von Prince and Elise Kootz-Kretschmer, the exemplars drawn upon in the final chapter, each took special note of the investment of pride by African women in dress and adornment.[18] They also provide a more global view of relations among women and their attitudes toward status, work, and economic self-reliance. Men, too, could appreciate such qualities, especially missionaries determined to reward evidence of a work ethic. Dugald Campbell applauded Bwanikwa's enterprise and community service and went on to acknowledge that she was "my wife's right hand and true helper, yea, more, a real companion and sister."[19]

Oscar Baumann's conviction that the empathetic tale captured dynamics of real life and revealed interactions that were erased in standard ethnographic formats does not seem to be a radical or highly dissident standpoint in the late twentieth century.[20] Anthropologists of the current generation have been busy deconstructing the central theoretical assumptions and the associated accumulation of "facts." The stress today is more likely to be on the ambiguity of categories as power relations are modified to accommodate new economic conditions. Closer studies of the roles of men and women in agriculture and trade have drawn attention away from lineage, genealogy, and inheritance, which is to say away from the elders and their ideologies. Citing Rodney Needham, the recent study of the Mambwe by Johan Pottier agrees that "quasi-technical terms like 'matrilineal' and 'patrilineal' denote polythetic classes of social facts and do not demand the presence of any special feature." Pottier adds, "I cannot comment, on the basis of my fieldwork, on the usefulness of the concept 'matrilineality,' but 'patrilineality' has most certainly a limited role to play in the local design of survival strategies."[21]

Inquiry must press forward, undeterred by the frowns of such scholars as Igor Kopytoff who, while seeming to advocate varieties of social relations, is too defensive against economic change and relies in the final analysis on a static conception of the structures of African society. Fred Cooper commented well on behalf of historians when he wrote: "The emphasis on the integrative nature of slavery may largely reflect the fact that with the removal of its coercive and exploitative dimensions — and above all its means of reproduction — the social dimension is all that is left."[22] Beyond the issue of selective recall, the question is: who is recalling? Kopytoff nowhere takes into account women as actors. For women, the texts presented here show that the opposite of slavery is not simply "belonging."[23] The present dissonance in anthropological theory at the very least casts doubt on the ranking of "ethnographic facts" that contain no specifics on women. On reexamination, the paradigms that guided the accumulation of empirical data are seen to be constructions of a normal, Western science, embodying evolutionist doctrines and suppositions about lineage control that do not stand the test of counterquestioning, especially by those who do not accept the segregation of the domestic and the politico-jural spheres.[24]

The decline of old male-oriented explanations has not yet been paralleled by the rise of a coherent new theoretical frame of reference. While women, women's work, and issues of economic control are being brought to the surface and will figure in an eventual restatement of a normal science in anthropology, some scholars are hesitant to subscribe even to the idea of a new synthesis, observing that attention to fluidity, manipulation, and adverse realities is often sacrificed when knowledge becomes a mainstream rendering of fact. Historians have been relatively well served in the 1980s, but there are still many avenues untried.[25]

This volume befits the present intellectual climate of creative difference of opinion, but it is on the side of those who inquire first about work and rights to retain the produce of labor, and treat inheritance as a subsidiary consideration. Work, marriage, and inheritance are of course linked in practice and ideology, as the experiences of women in slavery and postslavery demonstrate.

Questions of work and marriage touch the male youth in ways

that must have consequences for the status of women. Bride-service, the labor of a suitor for the parents of his future wife, figures prominently in the life stories of the Utengule community and prevailed elsewhere in the area covered in this volume. When wage labor made it possible and necessary, bridewealth became more usual. In the postmigrant era of the 1970s and 1980s, when the young men no longer had the money for a large, direct marriage payment, brideservice revived as an option among the Mambwe in Mama Meli's home area.[26]

Economic adjustment and manipulation of kinship also marked East Central Africa eighty to a hundred years ago. The presentation of life stories and the opening of questions of gender, life cycle, and historical contextualization to be undertaken in the following chapters will have succeeded if readers are emboldened and in some greater measure equipped to pursue new directions of analysis.

Notes

1 Dugald Campbell, "An African Autobiography: The Story of Goi," in *Blazing Trails in Bantuland* (London, 1934).

2 See M. Strobel, "Slavery and Reproductive Labor in Mombasa," in *Women and Slavery in Africa,* ed. C. Robertson and M. Klein (Madison, 1983).

3 D. Campbell, *Ten Times a Slave But Freed at Last: The Thrilling Story of Bwanikwa, a Central African Heroine* (Glasgow, 1916), 28.

4 K. O. Poewe, *Matrilineal Ideology: Male-Female Dynamics in Luapula,* Zambia (London, 1981), 11ff., 80.

5 D. Livingstone, *Last Journals,* 2 vols., ed. H. Waller (London, 1874), vol. 1, 222–23. See A. D. Roberts, "Livingstone's Value to the Historian of African Societies," in *David Livingstone and Africa, Proceedings of a Seminar . . . on the Occasion of the Centenary of the Death of David Livingstone* (Edinburgh, 1983).

6 *Ibid.,* 210.

7 *Ibid.,* 205.

8 See A. D. Roberts, *History of the Bemba: Political Growth and Change in Northeastern Zambia Before 1900* (Madison, 1973). "Bemba Warfare in the Nineteenth Century" was the subject of a special exhibit at the Museum of Mankind, London, 1985. The domestic economy of Bembaland in the nineteenth century awaits its historian.

9 Enclosure in Nauhaus to Committee, March 7, 1893, Berlin Mission Society (hereafter BM), 4.1.8b, Bd. 1.

10 The extent to which Islam defined the behavior of the Alungwana in the interior is highly debatable. In a controversial article, Carol Eastman contends that even on the coast, women were associated with non-Muslim practices while the men were the cultured Muslims. See Eastman, "Women, Slaves, and Foreigners: African Cultural Influences and Group Processes in the Formation of Northern Swahili Coast Society," *IJAHS* 21, no. 1 (1988).

11 A. D. Roberts, "Nyamwezi Trade," in *Pre-Colonial African Trade in East and Central Africa* (London, 1970).

12 M. Wright and P. H. Lary, "Swahili Settlements in Northern Zambia and Malawi," *IJAHS* 4, no. 3 (1971).

13 M. Wright, "Women in Peril: A Commentary on the Life Stories of Captives in Nineteenth-Century East-Central Africa," *African Social Research* 20 (1975); and *Women in Peril: Life Histories of Four Captives* (Lusaka, 1984).

14 See S. Morrow, "Policy and Practice: The Economic Role of the London Missionary Society in Northern Rhodesia to 1914," *Zambia Journal of History* 1 (1981).

15 N. Haberlandt, "Dr. Oskar Baumann, Ein Nachruf," *Abhandlungen des Kaiserliche Geographischen Gesellschaft in Wien*, Bd. 2 (1900), 15.

16 O. Baumann, "Salama," in *Afrikanische Skizzen* (Berlin, 1900).

17 *Ibid.*, 2–3.

18 M. von Prince, *Eine Deutsche Frau im Innern Deutsch-Ostafrikas* (Berlin, 1903), 79, and E. Kootz-Kretschmer, "Tatu, The Kidnapped Mbemba Child," in Chap. 8, p. 195 below.

19 Campbell, *Ten Times,* 28.

20 For a review of the feminist contribution to this shift, see H. Moore, *Feminism and Anthropology* (Cambridge, 1988), in particular, Chap. 3, "Kinship, Labour and Household: Understanding Women's Work."

21 J. Pottier, *Migrants No More: Settlement and Survival in Mambwe Villages, Zambia* (Manchester, 1988), 180. See also Poewe.

22 F. Cooper, "The Problem of Slavery in African Studies," *Journal of African History* (hereafter *JAH*) 20, 1 (1979), 111; I. Kopytoff, "The Cultural Context of African Abolition," in *The End of Slavery in Africa*, eds. S. Miers and R. Roberts (Madison, 1988), 490ff., seeks to rebut his critics including myself in Chap. 7 below, by tarring them as "Western" as opposed to his own perspective, taken from the interior of African culture. I submit that interior cannot be segregated from exterior in such a simplistic fashion. These reservations do not, however, diminish the value of many of the points made in the chapter and also in the essay, "African Slavery as an Institution of Marginality," which opens S. Miers and I. Kopytoff, eds., *Slavery in Africa: Historical and Anthropological Perspectives* (Madison, 1977).

23 Miers and Kopytoff, 17.

24 Moore, 60.

25 See especially *Women and Slavery in Africa*, eds., C. C. Robertson and M. A. Klein (Madison, 1983). Martin Klein's long record of research and publication on many aspects of slavery in Senegal deserves special note. For an indication that women slaves and ex-slaves are entering the mainstream, see P. Lovejoy, "Concubinage and the Status of Slaves in Early Colonial Northern Nigeria," *JAH* 29, no. 2 (1988), which makes up for neglect evident in his *Transformation in Slavery* (Cambridge, 1983).

26 Pottier, 180.

PART I
Women in Peril

ONE

Prelude to Texts and Contexts *

To be born in the region between Lake Nyasa and Lake Tanganyika in East Central Africa in the second half of the nineteenth century was to be put down in a fluid world of economic change, social dislocation and regrouping, armed conflict, and striving for security.[1] These pressures affected the status of women, who had perennially been exchanged among lineages through marriages and transfers made to balance debt relations but who had, in this period, become more vulnerable to arbitrary transfer.

The corridor of highland country comprising some twenty thousand square miles running between the lakes is an area of ancient settlement.[2] It supports a diversified economy that in the nineteenth century included cattle and small livestock, a wide spectrum of crops, varied agricultural systems, craft specialization, and regional trade in such items as salt, iron wares, tobacco and

---

*Note on the orthography. Modern renderings are used in the commentary, but their original forms are used in the texts of the life stories. For example, the reader will have to see Sangu and Sango as the same ethnic group, and Kyungu and Chungu as the same chief of Ngonde. Konde may refer not only to Ngonde but also to the land of the Nyakyusa directly north of Lake Nyasa. Namwanga is the Zambian and Nyamwanga the Tanzanian name for the same people.

Prefixes of place include Lu-, Bu-, and U-; uRambya and Ulambya are identical. Ki- and Ci- (Chi-) are prefixes of language. Wi- is a plural prefix, occasionally written simply I-. Modern usage is to have the prefix capitalized and the stem following in lowercase.

indigenously woven cloth. The societies occupying the corridor all speak languages of the Bantu family but belong to three distinct dialect groups: the Fipa-Mambwe-Nyamwanga in the west and west-center being mutually intelligible; the Nyiha-Safwa-Lambya in the east-center forming another cluster; and the Ngonde and Nyakyusa in the east belonging to yet another group. The Nyiha-Safwa-Lambya of the east-center lived in the most mountainous and least productive parts and organized themselves in fragmentary polities. Among the Fipa-Mambwe-Nyamwanga, the ideological base for centralized authority existed, although in practice kingship often remained more ideal than real. The only consistently effective kingships in the corridor during the late nineteenth century were those of the Nyamwanga rulers who became entitled Mkoma, and the Ngonde rulers hereditarily known as Kyungu.[3]

From the middle of the century, increasing trade with Indian Ocean entrepots brought the corridor into contact with new horizons of exchange. Commercial activity intensified in both regional and export spheres. Units of value became more standardized and arranged relative to one another, larger units being ivory, cows, women, and guns. Women, especially if young, seem to have been the most widely acceptable. But just as there were generalizing effects, so there were differential ones depending upon the kind of production, proximity to trade routes or trade settlements, and political responses. Certain features of political organization became exaggerated, with a strong polity like that of the Nyamwanga becoming still stronger while others were subordinated or otherwise reduced.[4] Much attention is devoted, in oral and documentary sources, to the personalities and deeds of leaders in this period. That their status was imprecise and altering emerges clearly from the life stories of vulnerable individuals. Personal resilience and powers of decision among men and women alike became more important relative to formal or structural factors in that time of rapid change.

To measure the degree of instability in the corridor and to weigh all the contributing factors is no easy task. For even a simple sketch of the factors it is necessary to recall the dislocation of productive activities and persons and their consequent effect upon the Ngoni dispersals from Ufipa at mid century, the northward expansion of the Bemba in the same period, and the somewhat later pressure of the Sangu from the northeast.[5] The increased presence of Swahili-speaking Muslim traders, peaking about 1890, the European commercial and missionary communities established in the 1890s, and the advent, also in the 1890s, of military and administrative colonialism led to the creation of new, polyethnic communities where physical security was offset by alien values. Between 1888 and 1894, a combination of drought and locust plagues compounded man-made distress, culminating in a general crisis. The terms of reconstruction were dictated by the colonial authorities in the years after 1895, when pacification came to mean immobilization of populations, reinforcement of ethnicity, and greater rigidity of social definition.

Autobiographical narratives by survivors of these times evoke the period as no other kind of source can.[6] Narwimba, Chisi, and Meli, the three women to be discussed here, were all uprooted from their home villages as small girls; had a succession of protectors, husbands, and masters; traveled considerable distances; and ended up as Christians attached to Christian communities. The texts were combined biography-autobiographies, compiled when the women were grandmothers. Narwimba and Chisi told their stories to Elise Kootz-Kretschmer, a Moravian missionary and ethnographer living in Utengule in the Mbeya District of present-day Tanzania. Kootz-Kretschmer was a woman of enormous talent, prepared through her own background in the Moravian community to look upon souls in an extremely humane and egalitarian way. Women had far greater recognition within the Moravian community in Germany than they did in the bourgeois society from which many Lutheran missionaries came.[7] Furthermore, the Moravian view of spiritual progress involved the entire career of a member, who was encouraged to write his or her autobiography to demonstrate the working of the Lord.

Their testimonies would be read out at their funeral. It is important both to understand that in this instance the brand of Christianity being propagated did not despise the pre-Christian life of such persons, and to appreciate that the autobiographies were not initially elicited for purposes of missionary propaganda.

Elise Kootz-Kretschmer had gone with her husband to German East Africa in 1894 to work in the newly established Moravian mission. After a short time in Nyakyusa country, they moved to Utengule near Mbeya. It was only after the removal of the Sangu overlords, and her development of a firm command of KiSafwa, that Kootz-Kretschmer began to gain access to the kind of life stories reproduced here. Indeed, the gathering of oral data was a team effort, in which Msatulwa Mwachitete, whose autobiography is also included here, played a major role. Between 1908 and 1914, his position as a spiritual and community leader in the churches of Utengule parish allowed him many opportunites to elicit narratives. The activity gradually gained in popularity, and people sought him out to hear their stories. Msavuje-Mugara later joined the team, specializing in the recording of sayings and fables. In this way, Kootz-Kretschmer acquired an abundance of texts to be used for ethnographic purposes as well as to perpetuate the evangelical biographical tradition. Unfortunately, through her detention and deportation in World War I, the vernacular versions of many narratives were lost.[8]

One check upon the representative quality of the texts is to be found in the civil court cases from Northeastern Rhodesia involving fifty women seeking their freedom from alleged slavery. These provide corroboration by non-Christian women involved in similar domestic and general conditions spanning the period from the 1880s through the first decade of the twentieth century.[9]

Narwimba and Chisi, although baptized, reflect in their stories the desire for security within a "traditional" home where they would manage and execute agricultural production, care for children and grandchildren, contribute food, and cook for the head of the household. In neither case was conversion a radical social act. The residence of their old age, Utengule, was neither a center of agricultural innovation nor a strictly regulated community. It had formerly been the capital of the Sangu overlord Merere, where missionaries had settled as barely tolerated observers. When Merere moved his capital to the east, Moravian missionaries occupied his niche as the leaders of the community of Safwa, Nyiha, and other subjugated people who had gathered there.[10] No marked introduction of Western institutions occurred. Economic and family life went on within a pattern of African culture already experienced in adapting to changing conditions.

The story of Meli was written down by her son and edited for publication in the vernacular by a grandson. There is a special quality in this biography of a woman famous among her own people, who must have recounted her tale many times.[11] The process of reinforcing identity through a tracing of clan background is very evident in the material prefixed by her son, a well-to-do farmer and former teacher, and her grandson, the principal of a secondary school in the urban Copperbelt. Yet there is candor and simplicity in Meli's story, and it has much the same quality as the Narwimba and Chisi texts.

The quality comes from acceptance of the conventional roles of women and a certain fatalism about adversity. Regardless of finer variations in social practice, in all societies a woman remained in legal terms a perpetual dependent. Without a husband, uncle, brother, or father to represent her, she lacked access to the judicial process. A woman's status was secured through progress into marriage, motherhood, and grandmotherhood. Sometimes marriage took place not through exchange of bridewealth or the giving of brideservice but through the transfer of the girl as payment for debt.[12] In such a case, already detached from her own lineage, a woman would be married to either a relative, client, or suitor offering the equivalent of bridewealth or brideservice. The disposition to construe relationships as familial and to impute kinship was instrumental in assimiliating outsiders, especially females, into domestic society and economy. The same process of absorption applied to captives and refugees, who likewise were isolated from their kin group. Such persons were at the mercy of officials and guardian masters. Slaves who were bought and sold knew the callousness of society more than others, yet when they were settled into a domestic unit, they were embraced by the kinship idiom.

The fortunes of men and women varied along sex lines. In raids, women and children were ordinarily captured and men killed. Boys growing up as slaves could never be absorbed into a lineage; they remained social outsiders, founding separate and "inferior" lineages. To them, however, new occupations opened as economic systems expanded: they could rise to positions of trust and access to wealth by virtue of their very immunity to the pressures of kin interest groups. More will be said later about the widening horizons of men and the persistent domestic confines of women. It is sufficient to note here that while women in these circumstances had exceedingly limited life chances, their life expectancy was much longer than that of their men.

The three women will be presented separately, with occasional comparative interjections. Msatulwa Mwachitete's own story has been included, for he was a stepson of Narwimba, of an age with Meli, and while clearly an especially able person, he nevertheless can be taken as an example of some contrasting male roles and male experiences when caught in the same uprooting. For the women, selected elements have been stressed, namely status of families both extended and nuclear, and of individuals transferred between domestic units and polities. Comparison is limited in some respects because the women belong to successive generations, but there are advantages in having a range of ages among those recalling the time of the general crisis, 1888–94.

Narwimba was born about the middle of the nineteenth century into the family of a lesser Lambya chief. We are told nothing of the mother. While she was still a small girl, she and her family fled from Ngoni attacks and moved eastward until they found refuge with Kyungu, the paramount chief of the Ngonde people.

There she grew to adolescence, married a Lambya man, and bore six children, of whom one survived (p. 47).

The marriage occurred after the usual service by her suitor, who also gave her parents token gifts. Brideservice among the Lambya, Nyiha, and Safwa entailed labor until the parents were satisfied, often for two or more years.

The suitor would cultivate a field, usually of cereal or grain, and build a house or out-building for his prospective parents-in-law. The social ramifications of this marriage contract remained limited, for the benefits accrued mainly to the parents. Neither the suitor's family nor the bride's family was mobilized to raise or share significantly in the exchange of bridewealth; hence the stakes in the success and prosperity of the marriage were not high beyond the nuclear families.

Sometime around 1880, Narwimba's first husband died in battle. "Now I was a widow, and had to see which of my husband's relatives would take me to wife — for my husband had no brother, or I should have become his wife." The dead husband's sister, a wife of a Lambya chief, had a son, Mirambo, who appeared before Chief Kyungu as heir and successor. He was instructed to assume responsibility for Narwimba and her child. This judgment was heartily approved by Narwimba herself: "And I, on my part, begged him to take me to wife, so that we might be protected" (p. 48). In the course of this marriage, she had six children of whom four died.

Mirambo's status as prince and potential heir to the chiefship did not exempt him and his dependents from physical danger. As enemies again forced the militarily weak Lambya to scatter, the family sheltered with various neighboring chiefs, having "to beg or we should have starved" (p. 49). When times became more peaceful, Mirambo returned and rebuilt his village. He subsequently succeeded to the chiefship as Mirambo Mwachitete, and so began a new period in his life. His acquisition of chiefly office was marked by the taking of a new and younger wife, who was installed as the royal, senior wife whose children would be the

princes and princesses of the next generation. There were implications for all the women of the household, and Narwimba rather
poignantly commented upon the emotional as well as the formal
aspect of this adjustment. Her own declining status in the royal
household was attributed in part to the fact that "I was one of the
older ones, and he had not wooed me" (p. 40). Mirambo became
a big man; Narwimba was an aging dependent whose situation
was more and more akin to that of one refugee among many in
a royal household swollen by the need for protection and the role
of chiefs as concentrators and redistributors of wealth. Women
were received into the town for a variety of other reasons—a
client's desire to ingratiate, the need to pay court fees or compensation, and so forth. On the other hand, the chief was responsible
to his people for their security and came under great pressure in
times of general crisis, as during the famine of the late 1880s.

Chief Mkoma of the Nyamwanga may have had added
incentive in the famine time to attack Mirambo Mwachitete, with
whom he had a standing feud. The victorious Nyamwanga took
many women and children with them back to their own country
(p. 40), among them Narwimba, who was now over forty and
aware of the disadvantage of her advanced age: "Things fared ill
with me, for I was old and could not do much work" (p. 50). She
suffered the indignity of being unsuccessfully peddled as a slave,
beaten and threatened with execution, and then walked northward
to the main thoroughfare of commerce where she would be sold
at a cheap price. At this point she ran away, and after some days
she found her way to a Nyamwanga settlement. There she was
again saved from a headman's threat of execution—this time by
the intercession of a royal woman—and was eventually allowed
to escape and rejoin her own people and husband at his capital
(p. 51).

Some comment upon the political system of the Nyamwanga
may help to explain Narwimba's eventual return home. The Nyamwanga king was very strong in part because of a kind of dual
representation in the outlying divisions of the country (p. 50).[13]

The king recognized headmen as the active administrators and posted sisters as royal representatives and censors. When a royal representative died, she would be succeeded by a sister of the reigning king, thereby renewing the personal quality of the link between the center and the peripheries. Two different royal sisters had objected to plans to kill Narwimba and she was therefore spared. The lucky beneficiary did not understand the structure of Nyamwanga government, which was much more formal than that of the Lambya, and believed that her deliverance had been prompted solely by special sympathy for a member of a chief's family, albeit in a foreign land (p. 51). It is true that political considerations could sway the Nyamwanga king. Another of Mirambo's wives had been released by Mkoma to return to her father when he learned that she was the daughter of an ally. Such a dispensation, however, did not extend to her children, the off-spring of Mirambo, who remained enslaved (p. 49). Whatever consideration was given in Narwimba's case because she was a chief's wife, it would not be of the same explanatory order as the institutional role of royal censors in curbing the arbitrary power of headmen. Narwimba, however, continued to attribute her good fortune to her good connections (p. 51).

It is all too clear that, try as she might to maintain her position in an aristocracy, ugly realities accrued as Narwimba grew older. In fact, the connections were not even good enough to constitute security, the measure of which lies not merely in her own situation but in that of her children and grandchildren.

Narwimba's daughter apparently ran away with a man who did not give either service or gifts to regularize the marriage. That no one pursued the matter reflects a social indifference on the part of the men who should have been complainants in such a case. Evidently she did not belong in a clear enough way to the royal family either as kin or as property to inspire the usual vigilance. The uncertain status of dependents falling between full lineage members and slaves, it becomes evident, created a pool of expend-able persons. Without rather intimate details about the lives of those involved, the criteria for selecting or neglecting persons for exchange remains puzzling. Meli, for example, noted an apparent breach of family solidarity in Bembaland: "Chief Nkula himself took his own child and sold it instead of a slave." In the case of Narwimba's daughter the ambiguity had to be resolved when the girl returned to the capital with her infant, fleeing from accusations of witchcraft and repeated poison ordeals. At that point, Mirambo Mwachitete gave her as a wife to a trusted functionary, a slave who had been found as a small child in the wake of a passing caravan (p. 53). Given the circumstances, such a match with an important retainer was a respectable solution to the stepdaughter's dilemma.

It is in Narwimba's granddaughter, however, that vulnerability culminated: she was regarded by the chief as an appropriate pawn to compensate villagers who had been attacked because of a dispute between himself and Mkoma. Learning of the impending loss of this grandchild, Narwimba took her and ran to her son, who, as the progeny of the chief, was able to provide sanctuary. The stratagem, we infer, afforded not only physical but also social shelter. Although Narwimba returned home, it is plain that the child was perceived as a valued pawn in local disputes (p. 54). In a quarrel over Mirambo's physical abuse of the girl, the grandmother herself was struck by her husband-master-chief. The situation had so deteriorated that, forced now to recognize that Mirambo Mwachitete was no longer an effective protector of herself and her progeny, Narwimba set out for her original village. There is an independent witness to Mirambo's increasing arbitrariness. Msatulwa Mwachitete, his son by another wife, also emigrated from the chiefdom, asserting that his father was drunken and capricious (p. 76). He could find employment as an individual, while Narwimba needed support within a domestic unit. In her home village she was tolerated and given shelter but could not be self-supporting because she lacked a man to break out the earth to establish fields. Finally, feeling unable to ask the headman to pay tax on her house, Narwimba followed her son, who had settled at the Utengule mission station.

At Utengule, she would have encountered Chisi, who had also come to the settlement because a son had found employment and land there. Apart from this, they had little in common, being a generation apart in age and of very different social outlook. Whereas Narwimba expected the support of a family, Chisi knew from childhood that she had to be self-reliant. Having an early experience of slavery, she was without illusions about what to expect from society and succeeded in establishing a viable position by practicality and hard work. It will be noted that her life was spent in small-scale settlements or homesteads, where a person was more quickly and completely absorbed in familial terms despite persisting judicial vulnerability as a refugee or slave.

Chisi was born in Bisaland sometime around 1870. Her mother died when she was small and her father, who apparently had no other wives, took care of the children himself, except for a baby who went to a grandmother. Overcoming objections, Chisi managed to get permission to visit and remain with a sister who was about to give birth to her first child (p. 81). Very soon after her arrival, a Bemba party raided the village and captured the women and children, among them Chisi and her pregnant sister. While marching toward Bembaland, the sister delivered twins. Her principal captor was solicitous since he anticipated making her a wife. A companion laid claim to Chisi, but as she was his first captive, she was owed to the chief (p. 82).

Chisi remained in the chief's household for three years, until she was sent away with traders euphemistically presented as "relatives." Not only was the kinship idiom employed to mask the transaction, a bundle of food was carefully prepared as if for an ordinary visit to relatives.

Throughout the region, slavery was not institutionalized: the slave trade was covert—the transaction taking place in the evening and the transfer of persons occurring at a later time and with a minimum of fuss—in order not to arouse the community at large.[14] Only upon joining other slaves did Chisi recognize her situation (p. 83). In the manner of itinerant traders, travel in the caravan was not continuous, and the party remained several years in Nyamwanga country before moving on toward the coast. Life in these trading bands seems to have been characterized by some gentleness in interpersonal relations and, as is plain from Meli's life story, a process of inculcating Swahili ways was undertaken. The commercial aspect of the slave trade had apparently receded in the girls' awareness for they were shocked to observe, after one of their number was told to remain with the trader's "relatives" in Safwa country, a new tusk of ivory (p. 83). The jolt made Chisi and another girl attempt an escape. Chisi, on her own, made straight for a Safwa settlement and threw herself upon the mercy of the people. The chief agreed to let her remain on a provisional basis, at first hidden completely and then at greater liberty. The Safwa headman had to be circumspect, owing to their position of subjugation by the Sangu, who were closely linked with Swahili traders. At the end of her period of hiding, the chief awarded rights over her to the head of the household where she had been lodged, saying that the man was authorized to accept brideservice when she married. This foster father opted to marry her himself, and soon after puberty she bore him a son (p. 85).

Times became difficult during the 1893–94 famine and tensions mounted in the joint family. While Chisi worked in distant fields and stayed with some relatives of her husband, the senior wife attempted to arouse suspicion: "Your wife, this runaway slave, will stay away until her son is grown. Then he will come and kill you, who are his father, and return with his mother to her home" (p. 85). Such a comment reflected Safwa social patterns. In common practice, women and their children in those times constituted relatively autonomous domestic and productive units. Men achieved greater security by dispersing their fields and families. But there is also abundant evidence of women dissolving marriages and contracting new ones without severe social penalty. A refugee such as Chisi, by acting in the Safwa pattern, put her master's stake in her at risk. The senior wife could well play on the insecurity of patriarchal authority in this situation.[15]

The substance of Chisi's freedom became obvious, however, when upon her return home her husband abused her, drew blood, and was recognized as guilty and unreasonable by the villagers. As she put it, she had no male relative to receive compensation and had to endure in silence (p. 86). She bore another child, after which she refused to move with the joint family to a place more directly ruled by the Sangu. Although able to assert her own right to remain behind, she lost the two children who were indisputably the property of the man. Both returned to her eventually, the boy by running away and the girl by resisting separation and making life uncomfortable in her father's family. Chisi did not repudiate her status as the wife of this man, even though she lived alone. On his death, she established a similar relationship by marrying an itinerant trader or artisan, who did not live with her continuously. She was then in her late twenties.

While in this situation of semi-independence, Chisi took in two youths whose mother had died. Their claimed relationship, as mother's sister's sons, must be reckoned in terms of Chisi's Safwa family of adoption (p. 88). Chisi, as their guardian and a householder in the neighborhood, had assumed a male role and was liable for their actions, including the offense committed by one of them. Although she seems to have been able to subsist, the fine was beyond her resources. She had to move away: "I was afraid that the Zambi people would kill me, for I was poor and had nothing to give to atone for the crime" (p. 88). She went to another chiefdom where her second husband was counted a subject; as his wife, she gained sanctuary. There was an added source of social support in this community: some relatives of her first husband lived there and recognized her children as of their clan: "When they saw [the children] they took good care of me" (p. 88). Chisi was indeed skillful in establishing and maintaining a good social position, notwithstanding intrinsic status vulnerabilities.

A certain practicality continued to characterize her social priorities. After receiving brideservice from a suitor for three years and thus seeing her daughter properly married, Chisi went to the

Utengule mission station and "cooked for" her son while he undertook his own brideservice (p. 89). This son had various difficulties before settling down, but when he did, his mother set up her own house and gardens within the mission community. She maintained her role as mother and grandmother, going to her daughter when she herself was critically ill and remaining there until she recovered. When a granddaughter contracted an infectious disease, she took her away to an isolated place and kept her there for a year. It is clear that although attracted by the Christian teachings, Chisi did not change her life-style or social expectations when she converted.[16]

The contrast between Narwimba and Chisi lies in both personality and social milieu. That Chisi was a willful person even in childhood is indicated in her account of a stubborn insistence upon making that fateful visit to her sister. As a refugee in Safwa country, she knew well the disadvantages of an unconnected foreigner, sized up the realities of her position, and strove to achieve a degree of economic autonomy, always with a recognition of the need for attachment to a man with jural and social status. The tendency in Safwa society toward mother-focused households favored her success, yet she nevertheless had to be resourceful in transcending the condition of a refugee slave to achieve the comparative independence of a local free woman.

The factor of age must figure in any comparison of the experiences of Meli, who was a juvenile throughout the period of difficulty that dominated the life situations of the others. She might have been of an age with a child of Chisi and a grandchild of Narwimba. Although it occurred when she was quite young, her enslavement is probably so vividly told because Meli became a missionary protégée and was encouraged to recount it. The London missionaries at Kawimbe gave special attention to the bright young girl whose epic story of slavery and liberation legitimized their antislavery traditions and proud references to Livingstone as the inspiration for the endeavors. The narration was probably well rehearsed by the time of World War I, when the autobiographies of Narwimba and Chisi were recorded.

Not only was Meli still young while a slave, she also changed hands a number of times, and on each occasion she began to adapt to her social situation as if it were to become permanent. Meli (Mary) is only the last of a succession of names, renaming being part of the process of incorporation whereby alienness was to some extent masked.[17] Names given at birth reflected circumstances at the time, and persons were free to choose names for themselves later on in life. Narwimba reported how, in order to disguise her origins, she assumed a name common in Nyamwanga country when she came back there as a runaway (p. 51). Meli is retained throughout this discussion because that was the identity of the narrator when the text was crystallized.

Meli was born in a frontier zone between Mambwe and Bemba. More correctly, it was an area of Bemba expansion where the Mambwe accepted the power realities and in turn were given a share in the government by the succession to a subordinate chiefship of a leader of mixed Bemba and Mambwe parentage. Meli's family was of the maternal clan of this chief, Changala. The attempt at resolution of conflict and regularization of dominance by the succession to a subordinate chiefship of a leader with mixed Bemba and Mambwe parentage seems to have been only partially successful, for the Mambwe to the north remained free and provided refuge for dissidents. Meli's father, a headman under Changala, earned the displeasure of the senior Bemba chief when a kinsman allegedly committed adultery with one of the chief's wives. Adultery was subject to clan jurisdiction when the woman was attached to a commoner's household, but it became a matter of political consequence if she belonged to the chief. The penalty in the latter case was always heavy, often calling for the surrender of another woman.[18] There may well have been other political motives for teaching the subject Mambwe clan a lesson, but in this case the charge of adultery became the pretext for war.

The Bemba raid in which Meli was captured, then, had the character of a punitive expedition. The people expected it and many had dispersed in anticipation (p. 94). Meli, who must have been about five, was at home with her sick mother, doing various chores, when the attack came. She and other women were captured and taken to the capital of the vengeful chief, where the older women soon attempted an escape, one carrying the little girl. They were overtaken, however, and on the next opportunity, although tied in pairs to logs, the grown-ups succeeded in getting away. The small girls left behind were distributed to different households for care.

A mixture of familial warmth and danger is reflected in the account of life in the Bemba household to which Meli was attached. When everything went well, the kinship idiom obtained, but when one was in trouble, its limits became evident. The first crisis came when through carelessness she burned down a temporary shelter. Both master and mistress expressed extreme anger and Meli was about to be literally burned herself when the woman intervened, suggesting that the girl's family was important and there might be reprisals if she died: "Don't you know that this person belongs to a chief's family?" (p. 99). Among the possible interpretations of this consciousness of high status elsewhere is the appreciation that Meli remained to some extent a political prisoner and was not merely an anonymous female to be absorbed into a family. Although she was spared after her blunder, she was turned out of doors when seriously ill and only taken in again when she recovered.

When a Swahili elephant hunter came to buy slaves, Meli was among those sold: "I was kept totally in the dark about this. Only later did I see them bring *mpande* [conus shells]" (p. 99). Once she was sold, her background became a matter of increasing indifference to those who controlled her fate, but she was still close enough to home to meet passersby who had knowledge of her family. From one, she learned of the death of her father and became aware that she was orphaned (p. 100). This interjection may well be a kind of apology for the ensuing episodes in which Meli tried hard to become absorbed into the families of traders. Her new master moved to another Bemba chief's village, where they settled for a while. She received a Swahili name, had her nose pierced in the fashion of Muslim society, but became sickly — a bad investment, in effect (p. 100). A Nyamwezi trader bought her, now for ivory, and was remembered as generous with clothing and food. When she did not stay well, this master also sold her: "Let her go and die elsewhere" (p. 101). The price this time was paid in cloth, possibly suggesting a lower value. Again she received some cloth for herself and was renamed. The trading party she now joined was a joint Nyamwezi-Arab one, intent upon continuing the slave trade despite the newly established colonial frontier posts deployed to arrest it. The caravan was eventually intercepted in Nyamwanga country. The setting of the ambush confused the children, who could not identify with either side, and they hid and scattered, returning to the scene only when all became quiet. White officials took charge of the "liberated" children and women and repatriated all who knew their home villages. Meli, now about ten, and some other orphaned girls, went to live at Kawimbe on the petition of the missionaries (p. 104).

At Kawimbe, an unexpected process began. Meli saw familiar-looking people; mutual recognition followed. A woman asked her name and took the news to an uncle that Mwenya, the daughter of the dead headman, Mumembe, had been sighted. He in turn reported to the Mambwe-Bemba chief Changala, who sent one of Meli's sisters to make certain of the identification. The next step in retrieval by the clan was to dispatch a delegation of three male relatives: "He told them that if they found that it was truly I, they should tell the white men to allow me to return with them" (p. 106). The missionaries demanded a steep compensation for surrendering the girl and Changala claimed he did not have the cattle they specified, so Meli remained at Kawimbe where she could be visited by relatives and was promised the opportunity to return to them when she grew up.

Meli's family lived in the Bembaized area that she refers to as Bembaland, but it is uncertain how far they went in culturally

accommodating their matrilinear overrulers. At the level of agricultural methods, there was no great difficulty, since the forest
Mambwe cultivate as the Bemba do by lopping and burning
branches, a system called citemene.[19] The northern or grasslands
Mambwe who had remained free were distinct in their practice
of cultivation, a matter of some importance in Meli's story (p.
107). A brother was sent to stay with her at Kawimbe, apparently
as a representative of the family's claims. After a year, however,
he returned to the forest area, being unable to adjust to the
grassland agricultural methods, with its mounding, deep hoeing,
and demands for more continuous attention. The social retreat of
the family, symbolized by the departure of her brother, which was
explained by Meli as his inability to adapt, may very well have
been brought about by her own success in adaptation and assimi-
lation into the Kawimbe community.

At the turn of the century, Meli found a suitor named Silanda,
a young Mambwe carpenter working for the mission. His over-
tures were made to the missionaries who in due course acted in
the place of her family, receiving bridewealth, arranging the
marriage celebration, and helping the couple to get a start in their
life together. Care was taken to apprise the families of both bride
and groom of the arrangements and to draw them into the ritual
and celebration. There is no mention of any protest or challenge
of the right of Mrs. May to act as if she were Meli's mother, and
the Kawimbe African community is portrayed as cooperating fully
in the simulation of a traditional ceremony.

The match did not please Silanda's maternal uncle, who was
taken to be the head of his family. He objected, "because the girl
is lazy and does not know how to prepare *nsima*" (p. 108). Meli
felt the continuing disapproval of the influential in-law quite
keenly and may for that reason have been especially happy after
her wedding when Silanda's father came forward to condemn the
uncle for keeping his son's marriage from him. The father insisted
upon replicating the ceremony, which guaranteed Meli recognition in his own family and reasserted lineage rights over his son

and his son's prospective offspring. In the context of the second wedding cermony, Meli confessed her domestic shortcomings, recording her dismay at being given millet to grind as part of the ritual: "How shall I grind all this millet, a thing I have never done. . .?" (p. 113). The difficulty was surmounted by paying another woman to do the task. As her husband's family intended to incorporate, not alienate, her, goodwill seems to have been the main prerequisite.

By her marriage, Meli became connected with two families that rivaled one another in claiming Silanda. His father's family comes across as the weaker one. At one point in the second two-day ceremony, one of her new sisters-in-law took her aside to identify the members of the immediate family. "The next morning my sister-in-law Namukale brought me a small hoe from Lunda. It was very well decorated and beautiful. When presenting me with her gift, she advised, 'My sister-in-law, look at me. In my family we are not many — we are only three, with the youngest one seated over there. Even though they are present at your wedding, we do not acknowledge the others'" (p. 113).

In contrast to the increasing complexity of Silanda's family situation, Meli's was simplified by her marriage, because the parental role of the missionaries became confirmed and Kawimbe was established as the home to which she could retreat when in need of familial support. Plainly, although the whites themselves may not have fathomed the difference between the ceremony of marriage and the social meaning of incorporation into larger families, the missionaries and the African Christian families composing the nuclear community at Kawimbe were perceived *in loco parentis* in a fully Africanized way. The lack of overt conflict between African and missionary culture reflects the conditions and reconstruction prevailing in the last decades of the nineteenth century.

Missionaries unconsciously as well as consciously adapted, and were accepted by the Mambwe as a part of their environment. Even before the beginning of formal colonialism, those at

Kawimbe had eclipsed local leaders in material power. After 1895, they superseded impoverished chiefs as concentrators and distributors of wealth. The young couple benefited substantially, as Silanda's family doubtless anticipated they would. The missionaries and African Christians built and furnished a house for them at Kawimbe. Then, when Silanda completed his bridewealth payments, the whites made a grand gesture against the system they had resolved to uphold by returning to him the entire sum, with interest: He was then given back all that he had paid, plus a cow, which he called *Acisi kwa mene cili uku milimo ya Mambwe,* which meant "white men did not care about wealth as the Mambwe do" (p. 114). So the family fortunes were founded.

Meli was baptized in 1910 and undertook various journeys with her husband, who, aside from prospering as a cattle farmer and trader, sometimes took employment in various colonial establishments. Upon his death in 1919, the struggle between the maternal and paternal families erupted once again, with that of his father prevailing (p. 119). Meli acquiesced to custom in agreeing to be inherited along with her husband's other property, but only on condition that the household be monogamous. Her objection on these grounds to the man who stepped forward caused the family to withdraw, acquiescing to her dictate (p. 119). Clearly, both the cultural premises of her missionary foster parents and the life-style she had maintained with her husband had confirmed her early disengagement from the imperatives of a settled Mambwe milieu. She had, in the Kawimbe community, an alternative network of social support.

Her conditional willingness, as a widow of presumed wealth, to follow tradition represented a temptation for her husband's heir, who discarded his other wife, took Meli into his house, and began to administer the estate. In Meli's terms, he squandered the wealth and inadequately supported the children of his deceased brother (p. 119). She left him, earning her keep for several years by work around the house of the African family at Kawimbe that, when she had first married, had pledged to help in time of need. She then took another husband, a kinsman of Silanda on the maternal side, only to discover upon reaching the provincial capital with him that he had misrepresented himself as unmarried. At that point, Meli resigned herself once again to the force of circumstances and remained in this plural household until his death. During this nine-year period, she achieved some occupational and economic autonomy by training in and practicing midwifery. After 1934, she sought work in various places, but always returned to home base at Kawimbe, where she eventually became a community worker and church elder.

Comparing Narwimba and Meli, two people who regarded themselves as well-born, we find one continuously sensing decline and the other springing back from adversity, enabled to benefit from the changing social milieu. The explanation of why Narwimba was let down by her people while Meli was prized has a good deal to do with their respective ages. The world of Narwimba's mature years was one of repeated crises while Meli's was one of pacification and reconstruction. As part of the Christian community, Meli belonged throughout adulthood to an innovative social group that was regarded as neither alien, in that the Kawimbe elite were accepted as pacemakers among the modernizing Mambwe, nor antisocial. The kinship idiom continued to soften the realities of differentiation.

Men separated from kin groups became reattached to communities as clients or through definition in occupational rather than familial categories. Narwimba's son-in-law was a functionary under Kyungu, her son a worker at Utengule. Although many motives may be found among men who took work or became followers of strong leaders in both traditionalist and polyethnic communities, the appropriate comparison in the present context is with those directly involved in dislocation and involuntary servitude. Such a person is exemplified by Msatulwa Mwachitete.

Msatulwa, Mirambo's son who was then perhaps eight or nine, went as a captive to Mkoma's town in 1891. Given into the custody of a family where he was ill-used by being overtly reminded of his slave status and in having to do women's work, Msatulwa was initially most unhappy (p. 65). Then he was transferred to the household of a royal woman and led a more normal child's life. In about 1896, he became major-domo for another royal sister as she was installed into office at Iwawa in the western part of Nyamwanga country. He managed the princess's household and in time received permission to earn cloth for himself by joining caravans traveling to the south end of Lake Tanganyika and to the Karonga on Lake Nyasa. Persistent temptations to stay at one or another of the trading settlements were recorded (p. 70). To explain returning to his mistress, Msatulwa stressed loyalty to his ailing brother, who preferred to remain with the Nyamwanga. Eventually, after meeting some men from Mirambo's village and persuading his brother to escape, Msatulwa returned home. The adjustment to life in a small-scale, poor, and arbitrarily governed polity, however, proved to be impossible, and after entertaining the idea of returning to the Nyamwanga, he chose instead to follow another brother who had settled at Utengule.

Male slaves, groomed for occupations in war, trade, government or the crafts rather than in homes and fields, were not thought of as an integral part of domestic productive units. As commerce became complex and foreign agencies assumed prominence, new kinds of employment opened for both free and unfree men, and the constraints upon the unfree diminished. Economic diversification enhanced the options of all men, and those already in service probably acted faster than men belonging to lineage groups in responding to new opportunities.

The narratives of the women and the man underscore the necessity of taking a more dynamic view of deprived status than is suggested by a simple slave-free or slave-pawn-free formulation. Abstract notions of freedom lose meaning in light of their lives. Chisi, the most "liberated" of the women, was the most astute and active in making the most of her chances. She seems to have been fortunate in her intermittent relations with extended families. For the others, Narwimba and Meli, the economic consequences of impoverishment through raids, famine, and changing values accompanying enlarged trade seem to have been profound. Property in the form of persons during times of dislocation and reconstruction became more important and women — as multipliers of the population, as laborers, as inheritable and disposable units — were at a premium. Unless, of course, they were beyond childbearing age and agricultural work.

Although their fates tended to fluctuate with their value as assets or liabilities, certain women seemed to adopt strategies of survival within the social systems and realities of their time, some more effectively than others. Often, however, true situations remained obscure. The kinship idiom cut both ways: it could give comfort to the woman who knew her vulnerability as a slave or refugee, or it could obscure the peril of one who regarded herself as at home. A hypothesis suggested by these narratives, worthy of further consideration, is that in times of extreme crisis, men raised capital by disposing of low-status women. Hence it becomes important to study the processes at work in generating a reservoir of disposable persons, rather than seeking hard and fast conditions for freedom, pawnship or slavery itself.

To be born a woman and to be dislodged from a conventional social setting in the late nineteenth century was to be exposed to the raw fact of negotiability. Hence the quest for protectors, the expressions of gratitude toward those who were merciful, and the strong pressure for conformity and minimization of the cost to the head of the household or other man responsible for a woman. A parallel preoccupation with the family, defined narrowly as the woman and her progeny, comes to the fore. Such a sense of family must be placed alongside that of the extended family and the household or domestic unit as we delve more deeply into the social history of this part of Africa and women in general.

Notes

1 This commentary draws on a few of the many sources for study of that region. It is slightly revised from the article that appeared separately in *African Social Research,* no. 20 (1975).

2 See map, p. 5. The usage of "corridor" is modern, reflecting the development of lake transport and overland links between lakes. Earlier trade did not have the same orientation. See M. Wright and P. H. Lary, "Swahili Settlements in Northern Zambia and Malawi," *IJAHS* 4, no. 3 (1971).

3 Fundamental work on the economy has been done by Andrew Roberts in "Pre-Colonial Trade in Zambia," *African Social Research,* no. 10 (1970) and "Firearms in North-eastern Zambia before 1900," *Trans-African Journal of History* 1, no. 2 (1971). Ethnographic materials include Monica Wilson, *The Peoples of the Nyasa-Tanganyika Corridor* (Capetown, 1958), and Friedrich Fuelleborn, *Das Deutsche Njassa und Ruwuma-Gebiet* (Berlin: 1906). See also G. Wilson, "The Constitution of Ngonde," *Rhodes-Livingstone Papers* 3 (1939), and W. Watson, *Tribal Cohesion in a Money Economy* (Manchester, 1959).

4 The Nyamwanga occupy the center of the corridor and a central position in the reconstruction of my forthcoming book, provisionally entitled: "Lords and People in South Rukwa, 1870–1930." Oral tradition; missionary accounts by Scottish Prebyterians; English nonconformists of the London Missionary Society, and French Roman Catholics; and official and unofficial documents of the colonial period — all are drawn upon for these generalizations and will be fully evaluated and cited here.

5 A general interpretation of these factors has been presented in M. Wright, *German Missions in Tanganyika* (Oxford, 1971).

6 Two texts were published in English in a single pamphlet entitled *Stories of Old Times,* M. A. Bryan, ed. and trans. (London, 1932). The German version of Chisi's story is *Sichyajunga, ein Leben in Unruhe* (Herrnhut, 1938), comp. and trans. E. Kootz-Kretschmer. M.A. Bryan likewise prepared the English version of Msatulwa Mwachitete's narrative, as *Ways I Have Trodden* (London, 1936). Meli's narrative was published in Cimambwe by H.E. Silanda, *Uzya Wakwe Mama Meli* (Lusaka, 1954).

7 See Wright, *German Missions,* Chap. 1.

8 E. Kootz-Kretschmer, *Die Safwa, ein ostafrikanischer Volkstamm, in seinem Leben und Denken,* 3 vols. (Berlin, 1926–29), 1, 7–9.

9 For a brief example from this kind of source, consider Kisani, who testified as follows: "Has always been Kasoma's slave wife. He paid a debt of her mother's. She does not want to leave Kasoma but wants to be redeemed by her brother and then let Kasoma marry her by dowry so that she is not a slave wife." National Archives of Zambia, Case 32, 30 March 1906. KDF 4/1/1.

10 Wright, *German Missions,* Chap. 3.

11 A slightly varied version was recorded by Newton Silavwe. See "The Story of Mama Mary," radio script, preserved in the Ethnography Collections, National Museum, Livingstone, Zambia. A daughter's recitation of the story was heard at Kawimbe on 21 April 1971.

12 This practice, reflected in the narratives, is more fully documented in court records of the early colonial period and confirmed by African authorities on customary law throughout the corridor. See also M. Douglas, "Matriliny and Pawnship in Central Africa," *Africa* 34, no. 4 (1964).

13 Waitwika, interview, 12 April 1972.

14 Moses Sikazwe, interview, 3 February 1972.

15 See "Family, Community and Women as Reflected in *Die Safwa* by Elise Kootz-Kretschmer," in *Vision and Service: Papers in Honour of Barbo Johansson,* ed. B. Sundkler and P.A. Wahlstrom (Uppsala, 1977).

16 A quite similar pattern is to be found in the autobiography of an Amerindian woman. See Nancy Oestreich Lurie, ed., *Mountain Wolf Woman* (Ann Arbor, University of Michigan Press, 1966). I am grateful to Gerda Lerner for directing me to this source.

17 In his radio text (p. 8) Silavwe makes a major point of the renaming.

18 British officials noted the difference and respected it as customary law.

19 See Watson, Chap. 2.

TWO

Grandmother Narwimba

Childhood

My father was Chief Sirwimba, "The Great and Mighty Song," and I was called Narwimba, "The Mother of Song," after him. I was born in a village on the Songwe in the land of uRambya. While I was still a little child terror came upon our land, for the Ngoni attacked our village and we fled before this terrible enemy to Karonga in the Konde country. Chief Chungu, who was then a very powerful chief, allowed my parents to settle in his land. We lived there in peace for a number of years.

Marriage

When I was grown a man came to woo me. He had to work for my parents. He tilled a large field of millet for some years during the rainy season; he brought many presents and he built them a new hut. When my father was satisfied, the man was allowed to take me to his hut and I became his wife. My husband's name was Sambi Simuchimba. Six children were born to us in the Konde country. Five of them died in infancy and we were left with one daughter named Chifuwa. This name means "Death," and we gave it to her because our other children had died. When she grew up she took a name that pleased her better.

After some years, the Ngoni, those robbers and murderers, came to the Konde country and made war upon us. In the battle with them my husband fell. Nor could our great Chief Chungu defend himself against the enemy.

Widowhood

Now I was a widow, and I had to see which of my husband's relations would take me to wife, for my husband had no brother, or I should have become his wife.

In the Nyika country, some days' journey from where I now live, dwelt my husband's only sister, who was the wife of Mwachitete, the chief of that land. She had one son, named Mirambo. After my husband's death she sent this son, the nearest relation of her dead brother, to the Konde country to greet our chief, Chungu, for that is the custom among our people. Chungu told Mirambo what had happened in the battle in which my husband lost his life.

After he had told the tale, Chungu said to Mirambo, "Son of Mwachitete! You have come here to mourn for your uncle who was slain by the enemy. But before you go back to your home I want to ask you what is to happen to the wife and child whom your brother left. Who is to look after them now? You are the only relation here, so you should be responsible for Narwimba and the child and inherit them from your uncle Sambi." Thus the chief spoke with Mirambo, and I, on my part, begged him to take me to wife so that we might be protected.

I Marry Mirambo

Mirambo would not give an answer at once, but went back to his own land and talked over the question of inheritance with his mother. When he had obtained her consent he took me and my child to Chitete and I became his wife.

I bore Mirambo six children — three boys and three girls; of these four died. Do you know what it is like? I have mourned so many times. When they laid my children in the ground I have lamented and wept myself hoarse until I could weep no more.

War

Alas! there was no peace in our country. The Ngoni, who live on Lake Nyasa, went far and wide through the land plundering and murdering. They burned the harvests in the field or mowed down what was too green to burn. All who fell into their hands were slaughtered or taken into slavery. Sometimes the enemy stayed a year, sometimes two. When they had laid waste to the land they went back to their own country.

My husband and I fled before them. We sought shelter with different chiefs and had to beg or we should have starved. Not until the enemy left the country could we return to Chitete, build up the ruined huts, and, when the rains came, till the fields.

Mirambo Becomes Chief

Then the old chief Mwachitete died, and after a time the elders and councillors chose Mirambo, my husband, to succeed him. So he entered into his father's inheritance.

Mirambo had several other wives beside me. I was one of the older ones, and he had not wooed me, but only inherited me. According to the custom of the land; when he became chief he had to take another wife, a young woman who should be "crowned" with him.

Then came another time of hoeing and another dry season. The years passed and the Ngoni did not return.

The Inamwanga

In the neighboring country of Inamwanga, where the great Mkoma was chief, famine had broken out, so many of the people fled to other lands and begged for food that they might not die. Some came to our land. Among them were spies who wished to see the country that they might betray us to their chief.

At last the warriors of Chief Mkoma came upon us. They attacked our village, shot into it with their guns, hurled their spears at us, set fire to the huts. I was taken captive in the battle and dragged off to Inamwanga with many other women and children. I had one daughter with me, my tenth child, but she was separated from me, and I never saw her again from that day to this. Perhaps Chief Mkoma sacrificed her at the grave of his ancestors, when he prayed for rain that his land might not be visited by famine.

Slavery

Alas! Things fared ill with me, for I was old and could not do much work. The man who had taken me captive offered me to slave traders, but when they saw me they would have none of me, saying I was only an old woman. My master beat me because he could not get rid of me. At last he bound me in a tall sheaf of grass and would have burned me had not a woman, a sister of the chief, said to him, "The right to kill a person belongs only to the chief. If you kill this woman, the chief will punish you."

Then the man let me alone. But he said, "Very well, I will take her to that part of the country through which slave traders from the coast pass to and fro. I can get rid of her there." He bound my hands together behind my back and drove me before him.

We traveled a long way and came to the country of Chief Kapara on Lake Rukwa. When I saw where we were I said to myself, "Now all is over for me. I am far away in a strange land. I shall never see my own country again."

Flight

The sun set, and we spent the night in the wilderness. Whether we could not reach a village, or whether the robber was avoiding villages, I do not know. In the night, when all slept, I crept away quietly. It was very dark, and in the darkness I climbed a mountain, crouched in the underbrush and fell asleep. At dawn I looked around me, but did not know where I was. I wandered this way and that, but could not find my way. For five days I stayed on the mountain, without food or water.

At last I saw smoke rising in the distance and said to myself, "I will go there and die!" I followed the smoke and came to a fire. As I drew near I knew I was in the country of the Inamwanga. What should I do? If I turned back I should die of hunger and thirst; if I went on they would kill me. Then I cried out, "Well, if I die, I die! I cannot go on living like this!"

I went toward the smoke and found a girl sitting by a fire. Her mother was at the stream with the other women, gathering grass to dry and burn in order to get the salt from the ashes. I begged the girl for some water, but when I tried to drink it I could not swallow, so faint with thirst was I.

The girl ran to the stream and called the women. They asked me whence I came and I told them. Then they knew me and said, "This is one of the women whom our warriors captured from Mwachitete." Then they asked me my name, but I did not tell them my name, not the name of my family, nor the name of my husband, but called myself Namira, which means "That I Might Drink." For I thought, "If I tell them the name of our village and of my husband they will say, 'Of a truth this is an enemy.'" On the other hand, the name Namira was not strange to them, for many women bore that name in their country.

They talked together, and at last they said, "We will not take her back to Chief Mkoma, but only to our chief in the village."

First, they set water on the fire and heated it, and gave it to me, saying, "You must take this, for your throat is dry. When the warm water has rinsed away the dry spittle that blocks your throat you will be able to drink." When I had quenched my thirst they took me to the village and hid me in a hut. They said to the village chief, "We have found an old woman in the bush who was nearly dead of hunger." The chief said, "Let her be killed." But the chief's daughter said to him, "You want to kill the woman? Have you forgotten that in this land no one may be killed except by the order of Chief Mkoma?" I bless this woman. When we fled from the Ngoni we had found shelter in her village. Now she saved my life. She knew that I was one of the wives of Mwachitete, and therefore she wished to prevent the village chief from killing me.

They kept me in the village for several days, then I crept away one night and made my way back to my own people. They all rejoiced greatly and welcomed me and embraced me, saying, "Praise and thanksgiving that you have escaped from the enemy!"

I spent a year in peace in Chitete with my husband, Chief Mirambo Mwachitete.

My Children

Of my twelve children only one daughter, Chifuwa, and one son, Ngwara, lived to grow up. When Ngwara was about sixteen years old, he wished to go away. He had seen that many people from his father's village went to the English who had settled on Lake Nyasa and who went up and down through the land. Some of them were traders and others had schools where they taught people to read and write. In Ngerenge there was a mission station, and my son wanted to go there and earn material for clothing.

When he had gone I went to my daughter, Chifuwa, who was married to Nyondo. But Nyondo was not a good man. He had taken my daughter to wife without giving a single gift, and he had made her drink the poisoned drink, so that she nearly died, for the villagers had called my daughter a witch. Nyondo would not allow this disgrace to rest upon himself and his family, so he said that his wife should be judged by the gods by drinking the poisoned drink to prove that she was no witch.

When she had drunk the poison she threw it up again, and this was the proof that she had worked no magic. Now no one dared accuse her. I said to my daughter, "Come back with me to Chitete, and never return to the wicked man who almost poisoned you." My daughter listened to me, and lived in my hut with her little girl.

My Grandchild

She had borne Nyondo this little girl, and called her Musamarire —that is to say, "It Is Not Yet at an End," meaning the quarrel over the child. Nyondo had given no gift for my daughter, so he had no right to the child. She and her mother now belonged to the family of the chief. But there was to be much quarreling over this granddaughter of mine.

Chief Mwachitete had a slave, Mwandarirwa. To this man he

gave my daughter Chifuwa to wife. This slave had been lost by the Arabs. After they had passed through Mwachitete's land with a caravan, the little boy was found, lying in the tall grass. His mother must have been one of the women whom the Arabs were taking to the coast for sale. Perhaps she fell ill and had no more strength to carry the child, or perhaps she had died. The boy stayed with the chief and was brought up by one of his wives until he could look after himself. Now he was grown up, and my daughter was given to him for a wife. Two children were born to them. But my granddaughter Musamarire remained with me in my hut, and I looked after her, for I loved her dearly.

Now there was strife in the land, and I had to give up my grandchild. This was the cause. When the great Chief Mkoma had made war on our land, two men of our village had fallen in battle. The relations of these men now came to Mwachitete, saying, "O chief, you must atone for the loss of our relations, for it was in your village they were killed. You are to blame for the death of these men, and you must give us a girl to atone for it."

At last, for the sake of peace, the chief was going to give my grandchild Musamarire. But I took the child and fled with her to my son Ngwara. He was greatly startled to see me, and after I had rested a few days, he said, "Mother, you must not stay here. What can you live on here? Come, let us go back to my father." And he went on talking to me until I consented to go back. When he had taken us back to Chitete, he returned to his work with the English.

About a year later I was told that my son had gone to Utengule in uSafwa with a German missionary and his wife, and was working for the white people as a cook. My heart was sore that my son had not stayed with me. I thought to myself, "Mwachitete will need another girl to pay for some wrong, and he will take my granddaughter again, and there is no one to protect us."

The brother of my husband, the chief, had taken into his hut a wife whom another man had already wooed. The first man was very angry and demanded payment. Because he did not receive it quickly he helped himself according to the custom of the land. When we were working in the fields one day, he seized my granddaughter Musamarire and carried her off to a village in wiNamwanga, the country of our enemies. So my granddaughter came to the same land in which I had been a slave while I sat in Chitete and mourned for her. Later, the quarrel was settled, and the child was brought back to me.

Once again I sorrowed because of that child! One day, when he was drunk, my lord Mwachitete struck her. I was very angry, and said, "My lord, why did you strike the girl Musamarire? What has she done that is wrong?" I tried to snatch the girl from him, so he struck me, too, with his stick.

When he let me go, I ran to my hut, fetched my skin and bound it on my back, then took my granddaughter and fled with her. We went to uRambya, the home of my youth, and I was allowed to stay in one of the villages. But I had no one to look after me. Who would till the field for me in the rainy season? Who would build me a new hut when the old one fell down?

A Quarrel

My daughter was now a widow, for her husband had lost his life in the service of his master. The quarrel which caused his death was not his quarrel nor his master's but the affair of two other men, one of whom was a subject of Mwachitete and lived in his land. This man's name was Papatara. The other man was called Halinga and lived in the country of Nsunda, where he was one of the chief councillors of the chief. These two men quarreled. Papatara was in debt to Halinga, but did not pay his debt. Because Papatara lived in the land of Chief Mwachitete the quarrel was Mwachitete's quarrel.

A man named Namusechi passed through the land with his little son and came to the village where Halinga lived. When Halinga saw Namusechi with the child, he seized the boy, hid him in his hut, and said to the father, "I shall keep your child captive until Papatara has paid his debt to me. Go and tell him that, and when he has paid it I shall give your child back to you."

Namusechi came to Chitete, to the chief village of Mwachitete, and said to Halinga's debtor, "You, Papatara! Halinga has seized my child because of your quarrel with him. Give me what you owe him, quickly. I will take it and redeem my child!" But Papatara would not hear of it, and he said he owed Halinga nothing. Then the man went to the chief, but he got no help from him.

At last he was helped by the German government. The district judge came from Langenburg and traveled through the land. When the great white man reached Chitete, Namusechi went to him and said, "Great chief! Help me against Halinga, who has stolen my child for no reason." The district judge sent for my lord Mwachitete and asked him about it, and Mwachitete answered, "Yes, sir, it is so. Namusechi is not to blame for the quarrel between Halinga and Papatara."

When the white man heard this, he sent three of his askari to Halinga's village to discuss the matter with Halinga, and to demand the return of the stolen child. When the askari approached the village, Halinga's people took arms and spears and fought them. The soldiers were very angry at this but did not defend themselves, for they had no orders to fight for their master, but only to bring back the child. They took Halinga's cattle and herds and drove then away before them. Then Halinga's people came out of their village, waylaid them, and shot at them. They hit one of the soldiers and broke his leg, and they shot my son-in-law, whom Mwachitete had given them as guide, through the head so that he died. The soldier also died later of his wound.

The soldiers seized their guns and wounded one of the attackers. The district judge heard the shots in the distance, called for Mwachitete, and said to him, "Do you hear the shots? Halinga is fighting the askari! Call your people together speedily, and let us go to their help." When the soldiers reached Halinga's village, the villagers shot at them. The district judge ordered the askari to return the fire. One man was killed and the rest fled and left all the goods in the village. The district judge gave Mwachitete ten goats of the livestock that was taken, and said, "Here, take these goats for your man who was shot."

Whether Papatara's quarrel with Halinga is settled now I do not know, but it was through this quarrel that my daughter lost her husband and the chief his slave. Neither of them was to blame; they had to suffer for the fault of others.

I Go to Utengule

So there was warfare and no peace. I ought to have gone back to Chitete, but I did not, for I thought, "If the chief has to pay another debt tomorrow, will he not take my granddaughter again?" I was so tired of all the trouble over the child, I thought I would go to the Konde country to see if my relations who were still there would take me in.

But before I could leave came the tax. The government demanded four shillings a year for every hut, and the chief of the village had to see that every man paid his tax. Who was to pay for me? I was far from my husband, Chief Mwachitete, and my son-in-law was dead. The village chief should have come forward for me, but I said he should not have trouble because of me, so I went to Utengule to my son, Ngwara.

In Utengule my son built me a hut and tilled a field for me and we had food to eat. My son was no longer called Ngwara, but he was now called Muganomgorofu. He had gone to school and had been taught by the missionary, and had asked for baptism. When he was baptized, the missionary said to him, "Ngwara, you have often told lies, but now you will become a new man and bear a new name, you shall henceforth be called Muganomgorofu — 'He Who Loves Truth.'" So my son is now called Muganomgorofu, but they generally just call him Gorofu, "The Upright."

After a time my daughter, Chifuwa, came to us in Utengule and brought her two children to me. Soon afterward she fell ill and died. She lies buried in Utengule, so I have three grandchildren to look after.

After a time I went to be taught by the missionary, but I was so old that I could not understand much of what he said. When I had been taught for some years I was baptized and given the name Musundjirirwa — that is, "You Are Cared For." My granddaughter is a Christian too, and is called Mukumburirwa, "You Are Thought Of," or "Jesus Has Thought of You and Not Forgotten You."

THREE

Msatulwa Mwachitete

These are my memories of the ways I have trodden and the work that I have done, of the good and also of the evil. My father's house is the house of the chief of Chitete in East Africa. The families of the rulers of Chitete and of Inamwanga were related, and our customs are still the same today, but the families have been enemies for some time.

My father had twelve wives, one of whom is my mother. Now my mother is old.

We Are Attacked by the Inamwanga

Mkoma, the chief of the Inamwanga, attacked Chitete. He killed some of the people, carried off women and children, cattle, and anything else he could find, and set fire to the village.

After this we had peace for a year, but in the second year Mkoma attacked Ntembo, where my father lived.

This was the cause of the war. There was famine in the country of Inamwanga, and the people fled from the great hunger and came to Chitete. Among them there was a man named Ruamba, who had two wives and two daughters. This man could find nothing to eat, so he came to our village and spoke to my father saying, "Give me some corn. I have a charm which I will give you for it." My father replied, "I have no corn to spare; I also am in want, and my wives are likely to die of hunger. Be off! I have nothing for you."

But the man would not believe that my father spoke the truth, and came again and again, repeating that he would give a charm in return for food. At last my father grew weary of him, so he called his elders together and told them of the stranger who offered a charm for corn. When the elders had listened to my father's words, they said, "Lord, give the man corn, if there is any, in return for his charm." The chief replied, "I have no corn." But afterwards he thought better of it and fetched some corn from his brother, and gave the stranger three baskets full; for he himself had but little. But when his brother heard of this he went to the stranger and took the corn from him.

Then the stranger hastened to my father and said, "O Chief! Your brother has taken away the corn which you gave me." My father, knowing well that it was his, answered, "Let him take it. But I cannot give you more." Then the stranger renewed his entreaties, saying, "I beseech you, give me some corn, and I will bring you my charm at once." My father thought the matter over and said, "This man bothers me so I shall have to give him something." He brought some corn from his granary and gave it to the stranger, who took it to his hut. Later the stranger came for more, and again my father fed him, for it was the dry season and there was little food in the land.

After a time my father's councillors asked, "O Chief, did not this stranger from Inamwanga promise you a charm? Has he brought it? Where is it? Tell him that he must bring it, for he has promised it often." Then my father sent for the man and said to him, "Bring me the charm which you said you would give me." But the charm which the man had spoken of was his child. He brought the girl to my father and said, "Here is the charm which I promised." My father was taken aback and asked, "Your child is your charm?" The man answered, "Yes, Chief." My father said, "As you will; think it over first and then tell me what you decide." He gave the man a hoe and some clothing in payment, and the girl stayed in my father's hut.

Of the Death of the Stranger

When the stranger saw that the maize was once more ripening in the fields, he stole his daughter and left the country. When the people told my father, he said, "He may go for all I care. He has not taken my power from me. And if I did give him corn, what does it matter? I can cut some more."

But the stranger never reached his home. For a month he remained hidden in the bush, then he lost his way. In the second month he was found by the people of the chief's son. They asked him, "Where do you come from?" He answered, "I am of this country." (That is to say, "I am not a spy.") They said to him, "If you are of this country, what are you doing in the bush with two women and two children? You must be an enemy come to spy out our land; for you are an Inamwanga, and they are our enemies." The man denied it and said, "I am no enemy, and I have not come to spy out your land."

Then the people recognized him, and said, "This is the man who was given corn over and over again by our chief, and gave his daughter in payment for it."

The chief's son sent the man and his wives and children to the chief, with word about how he had found them. My father said, "I know this man; it is he who tricked me, who begged for corn and promised me his charm for it. I cared for him through all the days of the famine. He gave me his child; for a month she slept in my hut, then he stole her away. When the people told me he had run away, I said, 'I do not care.' He knew that the time of want was over. But before, when he was hungry, what a beggar he was."

Then my father called his chief men and told them the whole story. They said, "O Chief, you know that this creature is an Inamwanga, and that the Inamwanga are our enemies. They have made war upon our land, even upon your own village. Let us kill this man. He must die, O Chief!" But my father would not allow it. He said, "No; let us take his children, but do not kill him." The councillors replied, "If you let him go free he will lead the enemy into our land. Do you not know, O Chief, that this wretch is a deceiver? He will bring the Inamwanga, and our land will be laid waste." Finally, the elders persuaded him that the man should die.

At that time we were living out in the fields with my mother, but my father slept in the village. He sent a messenger to tell us to return, and summoned all his other wives as well. We started very early and reached the village in the morning. There we found the man bound, and also one of his wives, the mother of the girl whom he had given to my father. All were talking about this man, and all said that he should die. So the elders took the man and his wife outside the village and slew them. They were hanged, and their bodies were left as food for the hyenas.

War

Four months later the Inamwanga attacked our village. I think it was in the year 1891. On the day of the attack we were taken by surprise and were filled with dismay, for there was beer in the village, and there was not a man who had not drunk of it. No one had seen the approach of the enemy.

When the enemy were upon us they fired shots, and fear filled our hearts. Men seized their spears and fought, but they were overpowered, and the enemy pressed in on all sides. They killed two old men. The others, among them my father, fled, but I, my brother, my mother, and the other wives of my father, and the wives of the village people, were taken prisoner, as were all the children who were in the village. The women were bound with cords, loaded with what the enemy had stolen, and forced to carry it away. My mother took me on her back, for I was still small and could not walk far. Sometimes the man who had captured us carried me.

We left our country and came to the land of the Wiva. There we spent the night. At night the enemy bound my father's wives and the other women with cords so that they should not escape. The next morning we set out once more. One of the old women could go no further. So the enemy took sticks and beat her and threw stones at her until she lay as one dead. After we had passed on she recovered and returned to my father. I saw her later on, when I came back from slavery.

As we drew near to Tschindi, the women of the village came out singing songs, the men fired their guns and joined in the singing, and there was much beating of drums. The rejoicing over the return of the victors was great.

How I Become a Slave and Am Parted from My Mother

Very early the next morning our captors went to Chief Mkoma. They said to him, "We have returned from Chitete. We conquered the enemy, destroyed the village, and captured the people who were in it." The chief commanded them, saying, "Bring all your captives to me, that I may see them." Now, the men of Tschindi took only the old women to Mkoma, and they hid the boys and girls in their huts. They sold a few of the children to the people of another tribe who traded in slaves with the Arabs. My brother was one of those who was sold. The man who had captured my mother and me hid me in his hut; he took my mother to the chief.

When the chief saw the old women he said to his people, "Did you not capture any young women? Were there no children there? Have you taken no boys and girls?" The men answered, "No, Chief; we only captured these old women; we found no children in the village." Then Mkoma asked the old women who were my father's wives, "Have you old women borne no children?" And they answered, "We had children, both boys and girls, but they have been left in Tschindi." And my mother said, "I have two children—two boys who are left behind there."

When Mkoma heard this he was very angry, and upbraided his people, saying, "Bring me all those whom you have captured in Chitete, and do not hide any of them. If you hide any, be they boys or girls, you shall pay for them with your own children. This is my country, and I am master here. When you set out to fight against the enemy at Chitete you went in my power, for you came from my land." When they saw that Mkoma was very angry, they took us to him.

The man who had captured my mother and me took his spear and wanted to kill me, for he was angry that Mkoma had commanded all slaves to be brought to him. But the others warned him saying, "If you kill the child you will have trouble with the chief."

So we came to Mkoma's village. I was taken into the chief's hut, and my captor said, "Here, O Chief, I have brought you the little boy who is my prisoner." Mkoma said to me, "Stand up!" So I stood up, and all laughed at me. Mkoma called his brother and said, "Take this boy; he shall live in your hut and carry your gun for you. When he is grown I will take him into my hut." In this way he divided all the children, taking some of the boys and girls for himself and putting the others in the huts of his wives.

As my brother had already been sold to the coast people, Mkoma sent men after the traders, taking the goods they had received in payment, which they were to return, and to bring back the boy. On the third day the messengers overtook the traders and found my brother. On the way back they beat him sorely and brought him to Mkoma, who put him in his hut, where he had to remain.

That year Mkoma went to a new village. When he had moved he sent for my mother and said to her, "I know you; you are a daughter of a chief. I will let you go free, and send you back to him." Then he commanded a few men to take her to her father — for my mother's father was an old friend of Chief Mkoma's. But my mother began to plead with Mkoma, saying, "Let my children also go free, that I may return home with them." This Mkoma refused.

So my mother made ready to return to our home. Seeing her preparations, I knew she was going away. She gave me some porridge and said, "Don't cry, my child; farewell! I am going to the fields and I shall come back again." When I heard these words I wept bitterly, for my heart was sad. And when my mother saw me weeping, she wept also.

Then I said to her, "Go, my mother. I know all." So she went out weeping, and I remained behind, weeping. As for the porridge she had given me, I threw it away, because I could not eat it.

My Sufferings in My Master's Hut

The year in which my mother returned home I spent in the hut of the Inamwanga man, Mitanto. I had no peace there, and was very sorrowful — I wept daily. Mitanto was fond of me, but his wife was a very bad woman. She was forever scolding me and saying, "Slave, you shall be sold to the coast people." This was the work I had to do in the hut of my sorrow — I had to cut firewood, grind corn for porridge, cook vegetables, look after the woman's children, hoe her field, fetch water, and carry everything for her. It was the woman who gave me all this work, not the man.

In 1892 I had a bad wound on my leg, for I had burnt myself in the fire while asleep in the hut. No one cared for me, and I nearly died. When the woman in whose hut I was saw the state I was in, she hated me the more, and threw my food to me as though I were a dog. Sometimes I had to catch it like a ball. I could not stay in her hut and had to go into the compound.

At last the elders who advised the chief went to him and said, "Put the boy in another hut. He has a bad wound, is near death, and has nothing to eat. The woman is a bad woman; she does not look after the boy." So Mkoma took me away from Mitanto's hut and put me in the hut of his sister, whose name was Nandwara. I had been in Mitanto's hut three years.

Peace in the House of Nandwara

In Nandwara's hut I had peace; there was no sorrow and suffering there. I was received kindly and lovingly. The man, his wife, and the children treated me as though they were my relations. The man bathed and tended the wound and was not revolted by the stink of it. And the woman fed me; I no longer went hungry. For a month they tended my wound until it healed, and I began to feel again that I was a human being.

In Nandwara's hut there were her own three children, an orphan boy, and a slave girl. I was the sixth. They loved me like one of their own children. Their eldest son and I were very fond of each other, and we were always together. I looked after the goats and sheep, and I hoed the fields with the other children. In this hut I did not work in sorrow, but in joy.

But the two strange children in the hut were bad; they stole. And when they saw how beloved I was, they hated me. When they had stolen something and our mother asked us about it, they lied and said, "No, we have not stolen anything, perhaps that stranger took it." One day when all denied it, and no one would confess, the woman cut the meat into a small number of pieces, counted them, put them in the pot, and placed the pot on the fire. Then she said to me, "Stay in the hut, don't go out, and watch the meat on the fire." She went to the fields, and I stayed in the hut. When she came in from the fields she looked at the meat, and it was all there. The next day she did the same and made the others stay behind. When we came in, in the evening, she counted the pieces and some were missing. And on the third day she did the same again and some were missing. So she said, "Now I know. It is you who steal the food in my house, and then call this strange boy a liar. I have found out your tricks."

I Go to Muenisungu

For three years I worked in the hut of the chief's sister, Nandwara. When the three years were over and I was nearly full grown, Mkoma took me away from this hut and put me in that of his sister, Muenisungu, whom he had made chieftainess over part of his land. He sent for me and made me her *migave,* which means a man who is chosen and "crowned" with the chief. Such a man is given the title of *migave.* Mkoma sent us from his village to the village of Iwawa. He gave the land to his sister, Muenisungu, and said, "The people who live in this district are yours, and shall work for you."

When we moved into Iwawa, a great number of people came out to welcome Muenisungu. They began to fire their guns and waged mimic warfare for joy over their new ruler. The elders spoke to the people, saying, "Mkoma has given you your ruler; obey her commands; harken to her words and do not rebel."

When the elders had spoken we withdrew with them and Muenisungu into the hut. Then they advised me, saying, "Boy, watch your mistress and take care of her; never leave her alone, and when she speaks sit near her and listen to all that she says. Your work is to protect your mistress, for you are the *Migave*."

In Muenisungu's Hut

When I went to Muenisungu I was a well-grown boy. I lived at peace in Muenisungu's hut. My mistress was kind to me and was very fond of me. I knew how to do all kinds of work and did my work gladly. I took care of everything in the hut, counted her sheep and goats, brought her food and beer, sent for people she wished to see, accompanied her on her journeys, waited on her, and directed the boys and girls who were in her hut. There were six boys and five girls in the household, and her own four children, two boys and two girls — fifteen children in all.

Longings for Home

Though I had pleasant work in Muenisungu's hut, I did not cease thinking, "I will escape and run away, and go back to my home and to my people." But I could not carry out my plan, for I had forgotten the way home. I had been only a child when they brought me to this country. I had forgotten the custom of my people; I only knew the customs of the Inamwanga. And I clung to my brother, who lived in Mkoma's compound, and said to myself, "If I run away now, and leave my brother in this country, Mkoma will be very angry. He will think, 'If one of them has run away, the other will run away too.' And if I run away he will kill my brother or sell him to the coast people." It was these thoughts of my elder brother that kept me from running away; for all the people knew that we were brothers and had grown up together, and were sons of one mother. My brother was much older than I and therefore remembered all about our home; he knew our relations and remembered their names. But I knew neither my parents nor many relations. When relations from our home came to the country my brother recognized them, but I did not.

Some people from our country came to Mkoma's village when I was there with my mistress on a visit to the chief. They belonged to the caravan of a white man. It happened that I was sitting on the veranda of the hut where my mistress was staying, and one of the girls who worked with me in my mistress's hut was sitting by me, when two men from Chitete came up. They had cloth with them which they wanted to exchange for meal. They said to me, "We want to buy some grain. Have you any?" But I cursed them, saying, "Sons of dogs! Who told you that we sell grain? Be off at once!" At this they both ran away. Alas! I had cursed my relations, though at the time I did not know them.

The Customs of the Land

The thought of returning home had taken hold of me, but my brother was content to remain. He said that we knew this country, and he did not think of leaving it. But I knew that though we lived in peace in this land I did not love it; I thought, "Here are we, two slaves, alone in this country. My brothers and sisters and relations have all been sold. Some of them have been sacrificed to the ancestors on the graves of chiefs. Why should we stay in this country?" And then I thought, "One day Mkoma will die, and they will come and kill us, that we may die with him. We shall be sacrificed, for there are no other slaves. We alone are left." For it is a custom among the Inamwanga on the death of the chief to bury four people with him: one of the elders, one of his wives, and two slaves—a man and a woman. They are strangled and their throats cut so that the blood flows into the grave, in which they are all buried with the dead chief. The body of the chief is placed on the knee of the wife, and she holds him in her arms. These people are to look after the chief and to serve him in the land of the shadows. The grave is not filled with earth, but beams are laid upon it and the earth is sprinkled on them. A hut is built over the grave, and one who served the chief when he was alive sweeps it out daily and lights a fire in it.

There are other sacrifices, too. When a new chief comes to the throne and goes to pray at the grave of the dead chief, another man is sacrificed. He is killed on the grave like a sheep or an ox, and his blood flows into the grave of his dead lord. This is the sacrifice to ancestors.

The chief has many wives, perhaps a hundred, perhaps two hundred. They are like slaves; they live in fear. If one of these wives has been unfaithful, the chief has her put to death. The man is also put to death; or, if she is not put to death, she has both her hands, her nose, her ears, and her lips cut off, and the man has his eyes put out. The parents of the woman must give the chief another daughter and must thank him for punishing her who has been unfaithful. If they do not do this, they are punished for approving of their daughter's sin.

Girls are sometimes given in payment for quite small offenses. For example, if the chief calls his people together to work in the fields, and one of them does not come, he may have to pay for his absence with his daughter. If a man is forbidden by Mkoma to set the grass of the pastures on fire and does it, perhaps by accident, he may have to give his daughter. If anyone has taken the poison ordeal and has not thrown up the poison, he pays the chief for the deed for which he had to take the poisoned drink with his daughter. If he refuses, he dies. If he dies of the poison, his heir must undertake to pay the penalty.

The poisoned drink is often given. I have twice taken it, but the affairs for which I had to drink it were not mine. Once it was a quarrel between the chief and his brother. The chief accused his brother of planning to make war on him. His brother denied it. So Mkoma gave me the poisoned drink; but I threw it up, so Mkoma said, "My brother is innocent; the poison denies his guilt." The second time I drank poison was on account of one of the chief's wives who was accused of unfaithfulness. She denied it, so the chief gave me the poison to drink. I threw it up, so the chief said, "No, she did not sin." I knew these and other customs of the land, and though we were at peace, I longed to go.

Journeys with Caravans

I said to my mistress, Muenisungu, "I should like to go to the caravan of the white men to get some stuff for clothing." My mistress gave me permission, and I traveled to Lake Tanganyika. I wanted to stay there, but the thought of my brother made me return.

I went with a second caravan to Karonga, on Lake Nyasa. And once more my heart said, "I will stay here," and again the thought of my brother made me return.

One day I heard that a white man had settled in Chitete, which was distant two days' journey. When I heard this my heart beat fast.

Another time I went to Saisi, a river south of Lake Tanganyika, with white men who were measuring the land. Some of them were English and some German. Once again I returned to Iwawa.

With a fourth caravan I went to Sakariro, southwest of Lake Tanganyika. The caravan belonged to a Greek who traded in rubber. On this journey I met my brother on the road. He told me that a man from Chitete had come to Nonda and had asked why he did not visit his father and mother who were both living. The man also told him that our elder brother was still alive, but he had moved to Utengule, to the mission station in the Sawfa country, and had married and had a child.

When my brother told me that my parents were still alive, and that my elder brother was also alive and had gone to the white man in Utengule, I thought deeply, and then I said to him, "Brother! It is for your sake I stay in this land. If I were alone I should run away from this country and go home." And I added, "Now I am on a journey with white men, but my heart is not here. I long to go home. If I cannot do this I will go to the white men and find work, for the white men are not like our masters; they reward their people with clothing." Then I said to my brother, "What do you think? What does your heart say?" He answered, "Nothing. What should I think?" I said, "Don't you know that we are the only two slaves left in this country, you and I—that all the others are dead? Why is it we are the only slaves? Where are the others? When the day of Mkoma's death comes, what slaves will they take and kill if not us?"

When we had reached Sakariro, the white man with whom I had gone gave us our payment, and I returned to my mistress.

I Meet My Own People

That month my mistress said to me, "Come, let us go to Nonda to visit Chief Mkoma." We set out. The people who went with us carried beer, which we took as a present to the chief.

We arrived at Nonda and greeted Chief Mkoma. We meant to stay there for three days. On the second day a caravan of white traders came to Nonda. It came from Chitete, and the porters were our people. Among them was my father's brother. The caravan camped outside the village, in the rest camp that Mkoma had built. In the evening the people of Chitete came into the village with their flutes and played them, and the Inamwanga gave them good food. Then the strangers returned to their camp.

In this way I met my father's brother. He saw me sitting with my friend and a girl, and began to talk to us. He said jokingly, "Give me your sister, and I will give you things from the white men for her." And he laughed, but I was very angry and said, "You are a liar. Is the white man your father, that you say he will give you goods?" I did not know then who he was, nor did he know me.

Later in the evening my brother said to me, "I know the people who came with the white man. One is our father's brother, and the other is a slave of our father's." When I heard this I was silent and could not speak. I said to myself, "What shall I do? Tomorrow I am to go back with my mistress to Iwawa." And I thought, "I will go to the people in their camp." The thought made me dizzy. It was as though I were drunk. At night I left the village. No one saw me. I said nothing, even to my brother, about going to the camp to see the people from the country.

When I got to the camp I found them sitting and talking. I

went up to them silently, for I could not speak. Then they spoke to me, saying, "What is it, you Inamwanga? What do you want here at night in our camp?" I answered, "I have only come for entertainment. I want to see the flute on which you play." They said, "Come play on our flute." But I said, "I can't; only let me watch you." So they said no more.

As I sat there I began to wonder how I should begin to talk to them. I did not know them, and if I began to speak, perhaps they would seize me, take me to Mkoma, and say, "This man came to us in the night and wanted to speak to us." But I thought, "Well, come what may, let it come!" And I said, "Do you not know me?" And they said, "No, we do not know you. *Who* are you? Tell us your name." They all spoke at once, with many empty words, so that I did not dare begin.

When they saw that I was very unhappy they said again, "Now tell us, who are you?" So I told them my name. Then they crowded round me and asked me again. "Who are you?" I repeated my name and said, "The enemy Inamwanga stole me from Chitete." Then they called my father's brother and said, "Question this boy more closely." He asked me many questions, all of which I answered.

Then they knew I spoke the truth. And my uncle and the others said, "Come, let us run away and go home at once, for it is night." But I said, "No, not now. First I will go back to the village and speak to my brother. If he is ready to come, we shall return. But if he will not come, neither shall I." When they heard this they said, "Then neither of you will come. Let us take him and go off with him." But I called out, "If you hold me, I will cry for help." So they let me go, and I returned to the village.

Flight

I called my brother out of the hut, and said, "Brother, I have come from the camp of the men from Chitete who are with the white men. I have spoken to those from our home. They knew me when I told them my name and the names of our parents, and they asked me to escape with them. But I wanted to speak to you first, and said, 'First I will go to my brother; if he is willing to escape we shall come tonight, otherwise I will not go.' Come, let us set out now, for it is night, and tomorrow I shall have to go with my mistress to Iwawa. If you will not come, say so, for I know that you are not strong, and I know you are content. But if you refuse to escape with me tonight we shall have nothing more to do with each other." Then he agreed and said, "Let us go."

We considered what we should take with us, but I said, "If we try to take a gun or anything like that, our escape will be unsuccessful. What do things matter? Let us take nothing." Then we went to the hut where we slept, and lay down. I was determined to keep awake. When I saw that all the others slept I rose quietly and made up the fire so that it burnt brightly. It warmed them all thoroughly, and they slept deeply. If they had been cold, one or other of them might have wakened, and we could not have escaped. I roused my brother, and said, "Let us go." We took two spears, two knives, and an umbrella, and went out of the hut.

The village was a large one and had five gates. My brother was to go out through one gate and I through another. As I was going toward a gate I saw some of the villagers coming toward me. I was wearing a white loincloth, and when I heard them talking I hid behind a huge basket. But they had seen me and called out, "Who are you? Where have you come from in the middle of the night?" I answered, "Where have you come from?" They said, "We were gossiping in the village." And I said, "I wanted to follow you and talk with you." They asked, "Why did you hide behind the basket?" I answered, "I wanted to frighten you, and to make you think a wild beast was after you." So we all laughed and went back together to the hut. My brother had heard our voices and he, too, came back to the hut. He crouched by the wall so no one saw him, for the hut was a very big one.

The others lay down to sleep, and when they were sound asleep we left the hut for a second time, and reached the camp which the people of Chitete had made. They slept, for it was now the dead of night. I woke them and said, "I have come with my brother, of whom I told you; now let us go." They were very glad and said, "That is good; we will go. What do our wages as carriers matter? Let us leave the white man." So my father's brother and his slave set out with us in the night.

The Journey

About an hour's journey from the village we came to the burying ground of the ancestors of the chief. There we halted and prayed, saying, "O Lords of the land, be with us, that we may go speedily on our way. Let us return to our home, for we have done no harm in this your land. We worked well in the hut of Mkoma, your relation. Be not angry with us. We have done no wrong. We ask but one thing, to return to our own land, to our own home. O ancestors of this land, hold not our feet as we go on our way. Bring no harm upon us; grant that we may go swiftly, that Mkoma's people may not find us." When we had prayed thus at the graves of Mkoma's ancestors we went on, and it was night. When morning came we still journeyed on. But as the sun rose higher I became very weary, for my eyes had known no sleep the whole night through. And hunger overcame me. I could walk no further, so they carried me on their backs.

But I said, "I weary you, and we all need sleep. Let us leave the path, and let us sleep in the tall grass." So we turned aside and lay down in the grass.

When I awoke, I was too weak to walk, for I was very hungry, and there was no food by the way, for no people lived there. Again they carried me, and again I tried to walk a little. The sun was high when we came to a village on the border of Mkoma's land. There we asked for food, and the villagers gave us meal and cooked soup for us. I drank the soup, and soon my strength returned. The people gave us porridge also, and I walked again.

We passed through many villages, greeted the people, and continued our journey till we reached our own land. When we drew near my father's village my uncle went on as fast as he could, and said to my father, "We have brought the children whom the Inamwanga once captured."

Our Welcome

At this news all the people came out of the village. My father began to run, and so did his wives and the other villagers. When we met, my father embraced me and kissed me, and the women danced and sang songs. There was a great feast of rejoicing because we had come home.

I could not say, "That is my father," for I did not know him. And I could not say, "That is my mother," for I did not know her. Only when a woman embraced me warmly I thought to myself, "That is my mother." But I had not yet found my mother, for she had gone to her father. My father sent a messenger after her and told her that her children had come home. The next morning she arrived. When we met, we embraced and greeted each other, and wept.

Such was our homecoming. I had spent nine and a half years in Inamwanga. I had worked three and a half years in the house of my mistress, Muenisungu. The year in which I escaped from slavery and returned to our home was the year 1900, and it was in the month of May.

Mkoma's Vain Efforts

Chief Mkoma went to the white men whom we had left behind and said, "O white men! My two slaves have run away and gone back to Chitete. I bought them with ivory. And now I would like you to write a letter to the white man who has settled in Chitete, so that he may capture my slaves."

When we had been two days in Chitete two messengers from Mkoma came with the letter which the white man had written for him. They went through my father's village to the white man's house, but he was not at home. He had gone away to buy rubber, but he had left a man in charge of his house. This man asked Mkoma's people, "Why has your master sent you here?" They answered, "His slaves have run away." He asked them, "With what did he buy his slaves? Did he make war on this land and capture them?" They answered, "We do not know." So the man replied, "Wait here till he returns, then you can tell him what Mkoma sent you for." But in the night the two messengers ran away.

When the white man came back he said, "Who brought this letter? Call the messengers. I want to hear what they have to tell." The man explained, "The messengers have gone home." So the white man asked, "Where are the two slaves?" He replied, "They are with their father." We came with my father and my mother. Then he asked us, "Why did you run away from Mkoma? You are his slaves; he bought you with ivory." We replied, "No, sir, that is a lie; he did not buy us with ivory. He made war upon our land and took us captive. And now that we are grown up we decided to go back to our father and our home. Chief Mkoma did not buy us; that is a lie." And the white man turned to my father, and asked him, "Is this the truth? Are these your children?" and he answered, "Yes, these are my children, and this is their mother." So the white man said, "Then you are not to blame," and he said to us, "Go home with your father." So we went home.

I Go to Utengule

Though I had run away and returned to my home, my heart was not in this land, and I began to long to go back to Inamwanga. I said to myself, "Perhaps I will go to the English and settle there."

I thought these thoughts when my father had drunk beer and talked senseless words. I could not settle in my father's house. I wanted to be again in the other land; I longed for its customs and its talk. These things I thought when I was with my parents.

I had been there three and a half months when my brother from Utengule came to Chitete, for he had heard that I had come back. We greeted each other and spent a month together. One day the chief, my father, had drunk beer and began to beat me. My heart blazed with anger, and I said, "Now I am going to Inam-wanga." I set out and spent the night in a village. But my brother sent a messenger after me to say, "Have we had enough of each other already? No, no; come back to me." On hearing these words I turned and went back to Chitete.

After a time my brother said, "Now I have been here long enough; I shall return to Utengule." I said, "I will go with you." My brother asked my father who said, "Yes, take him, and when he has been some time in Utengule, he shall come back to me." So we went to Utengule in September 1900.

In Utengule I asked the missionary for work. After I had worked two months for him I fell ill with fever. When I had recovered I herded my brother's cattle and the cattle of the other villagers. For when they saw that I herded the cattle well, they brought their cattle to me. Now I began to know Utengule and wished to settle there. I said, "I will stay here in Utengule and will not go back to Chitete."

I Learn and Am Baptized

When I came to Utengule I knew nothing of God's word and did not know about the school. All that the missionary said in the church passed me by. I did not take it in at all. And I did not think of learning anything. I only said, "What does the white man keep talking on about?" And although my brother told me that I ought to go to school, I did not go. I said to myself, "There is no one here who can teach me all those funny little scribbles they write on paper, those little partridges" (for scribbles on paper look like tracks of partridges in the sand).

During 1901 I began to understand more. One day four of us were herding cattle out in the pastures. One of my companions had taken his paper to the pastures. It had letters and words on it. He said, "I am going to learn while we are herding the cattle."

At the pastures one of them began teaching another to write, and I watched them idly. After a while I began to think about what they were learning, and said, "I, too, am going to try to put something down on paper." They said, "Yes, come and try." By and by I wrote many letters on paper. And at last my teacher said,

"These are all the letters. You have finished." That day my love of learning began.

The next day I went to the missionary and said to him, "I should like to learn the word of God and go to school." He said, "Come in the morning when I ring the bell." In that year I began to learn about God and school learning. But school learning came first for me — the other came later.

In my first month of school I learnt all the letters and some words. Then I began to teach some of my companions and the children in the school.

In the same year the missionary taught me God's word, and on December 25, 1901, I was baptized and given the name of the Liberated One. From that time on I said, "Now I belong to Utengule. My father cannot take me away, and if he tries I shall refuse to go."

My Marriage

After my baptism my elder brother said to me, "We shall court a girl for you in the country of the Usafwa." But I refused, saying, "No, I do not want to court a girl from Usafwa, I want to court one from our home, Chitete." My brother answered, "It is a long way to Chitete." After much persuasion I yielded, and they courted a girl for me. This was in September 1902. Then I left off herding cattle and worked in my father-in-law's field.

I Become a Teacher

In the year 1901, when the missionary had gone to Europe to rest from his work and another had taken his place, I began to teach the children in the school. The next year the missionary said to me, "Would you like to go to the higher school?" I was eager to go, and on October 24th, 1903, I went over the hills to Konde, where I stayed until 1905. That ended my time in school.

On December 21st I left school and reached Utengule on January 1st, 1906. In that year I taught the schoolchildren and began to translate the New Testament into the language of Safwa.

Conclusion

I have written of the darkness in Mkoma's land. I believe that in his heart Mkoma is afraid. If Mkoma knew about Jesus it would be a good thing. In 1907, I wrote him a letter of greeting. I said but little of what I should like to have said. When this letter reached Mkoma's house great fear entered his heart, for he thought I wanted to remind him of his deeds in the war and of the terrible work we had to do, so great fear seized him. After reading my letter, he said to his people, "The teacher shall come in peace to see me, if he likes. He need not be afraid. Then we can talk things over together in my hut." I have but one wish in my heart: that this chief may be blessed and may realize the evil in his household while he is yet alive.

These are recollections of the ways I have trodden, of my sufferings in the land of slavery and of my work there, as far as I can remember.

Now I have finished.

FOUR

Chisi-Ndjurisiye-Sichyajunga

Childhood

My home was in the Biza country, for we are Chawa. I do not
know my family, for enemies carried me off when I was still a
child. The name of my father was Sichyajunga, and the name of
my mother was Ntundu.

I can just remember the death of my mother. I was a very little
child and sat beside her before the door of our hut. My mother
fed the baby with gruel while I held its hands. Suddenly a lion
sprang upon us, seized my mother and tore her with its teeth, and
scratched my leg with its claws. People drove off the lion and
rescued my mother, but she died of her wounds. Near our home
there were many lions. The lion which killed my mother had also
killed two of my mother's sisters, my aunts.

After my mother's death we were alone with my father, who
looked after us. My grandmother cared for the baby.

My older sister, Nsigwa, lived with her husband in another
village. She sent a messenger to my father who said, "Your daughter wishes you to know that she is with child." When my father
heard this he called my brother and told him to go and see how
my sister was. Then I began to cry and said, "Father, let me go,
too." But my father replied, "No, you cannot walk so far. You must
stay here. Your brother shall go alone." I screamed, "I will go with
him." At last my father said, "Go, if you must."

My brother and I set out. Part of the way he carried me,
part of the way I walked. When we came to the village where
my sister lived we found it was as the messenger had said. My
brother did not spend the night there, but set out for home

the same day, and I stayed with my sister.

Stolen from Home

Our land lies near the borders of the Bemba country, and the Bemba are our enemies. They are always making war on our land. That very night, as dawn was breaking while I lay asleep with my sister in her hut, the Bemba attacked the village.

There had been a beer drink the day before, so that everyone was drunk. The enemy killed all the men; not one escaped. Then they cut off their heads, put them in baskets, and carried them off to their own land to show to their chief.

Two of the enemy burst into our hut, seized my sister and me, and set out with us for luBemba. We spent the night on the way, and during the night my sister gave birth to twins, both girls.

The next morning my sister could not walk. The man who had taken her said to his companion, "What shall I do now?" His companion replied, "You dare not kill her, for the chief has forbidden the killing of women. If you are going to leave her behind, leave her alive." But the man said, "No, I will not leave her behind, for I have no other wife at home. I will look after her, and when she is better she will be my wife. Let the girl stay behind with me, too, so that she can look after her sister, and later I will give her back to you." The other agreed to this and went on alone, leaving me with my sister. We camped in that place for one more night.

The next day at dawn the man said to my sister, "Come along. We shall travel slowly and I will care for you." My sister set out, carrying one of the children, while the man carried the other. We traveled very slowly and spent ten nights on the way. At last we reached luBemba with both children safe and well.

In luBemba the chief said to my captor, "This is the first person you have taken in a raid, so she belongs to me, for it is the custom that the first person taken belongs to the chief." So it came to pass that my sister stayed in the hut of the man who had stolen her and became his wife, but that I was given to the chief.

Slavery

I stayed in luBemba for three years until I was ten or eleven years old. I must have been seven or eight years of age when I was stolen by the enemy. Then four coast people, an Arab and three black men, came to luBemba. After the chief had spoken with them in secret he brought them to the hut where I was and said, "Chisi, these men are my relations. You are to go home with them and stay with them. You shall return with me after a time when I go to visit them." Then he gave me meat and fish saying, "Eat this while you are with my relations."

I wept bitterly, but it was of no avail. The coast people took me to their hut, and there I met four boys and two girls. The coast people put food before me. I would not eat, but screamed and cried. At sunset we started our journey and traveled by night, for the moon was shining. We went toward wiNamwanga and were a long time on the way.

In wiNamwanga the Arab became so ill that he could not travel, and we stayed there for two and a half years.

When the Arab was somewhat better we set out once more and reached the village of Chief Zambi in uSafwa. We stayed there for three days. There the coast people said to one of the girls who was about my age, "You are to stay here with our relations until we come back and fetch you." But we found ivory in the hut and exclaimed, "Where did that come from? That was not here before! You have sold your sister for ivory!"

We left Zambi and traveled toward Intente. When we got there it was raining heavily and we were numb with cold. The coast people sat down and ate some honey. They said to my companion and me, "Go on, we shall catch up with you." The boys stayed with the men.

Escape

As we walked on, the other girl, who was bigger than I, said, "Child, let us run away and hide in the tall grass, for these coast people will kill us. One of us has already been left behind in

Zambi. She has been sold for the ivory they are carrying. They will sell us, too. Come along, let us hide in the grass and later we will make our way home." I answered, "It is all very well for you, my friend, for you are big and can run faster than I. You will go ahead and leave me behind, for I am small and very cold." But she said, "No, I promise not to leave you. Come on, let us be off."

She put down the Arab's cooking pot which she carried and we plunged into the high grass and fled. My companion ran quickly and I soon fell behind, so I turned aside and went down to the stream and hid in a cave in the bank. I heard my companion call, "Hurry up, child, come to me." But I did not want to follow her, and stayed in the cave.

The coast people came along the road and found the cooking pot. They followed our tracks through the grass, but they lost mine where I had turned aside to the stream. They followed the other girl, and I have never heard whether they caught her or not.

The water began to rise in the cave where I was hidden, for much rain had fallen that day. I crawled out and looked around. Nearby were fields of the Safwa of Itende. I went toward the fields and came on some boys who had been weeding and taken shelter from the rain. I stood still and thought, "The Safwa will find me in their fields and will call out, 'Thief, you are stealing our maize!'" So I went on toward a hut with smoke rising from it. I was shivering with cold and thought, "I will go to that hut and there I shall die."

Marriage

I went up to the hut, which belonged to Ndeye. He was not there, but his sister was in the hut. She looked up and said in Safwa, "Where do you come from?" But I did not understand Safwa and the woman could not speak Biza. I tried to explain with signs that another girl and I had run away from the coast people, but that I did not know where she was. Then the woman signaled me to come to the fire, and I drew near and warmed myself.

Ndeye's wife came in and found me there, and asked, "Where

does this girl come from?" Ndeye's sister answered, "Just think, she was traveling with the coast people and she had run away from them with another girl. Where the other is I know not. This one came into the hut suddenly."

The wife of Ndeye went to the chief and said, "A girl has come to my hut. She says she was traveling with the coast people and ran away from them." When the chief heard this he said, "Do not let her leave the hut. Keep her hidden there until Ndeye comes back."

When Ndeye came back and heard the whole story, he said, "It is well; my ancestors have sent this girl to my hut." So I stayed in the hut of Ndeye.

After a year the chief sent for Ndeye and said to him, "Bring the girl to me. I want to see her." Ndeye led me before the chief, who said, "Look after the girl as though she were your own child. Let men woo her, and he who wants her must work for her." But Ndeye replied, "Not so, O Chief, if I keep this girl she shall be my wife." So I stayed in the hut of Ndeye and grew up there.

After four years, when I was fully grown, I became the wife of Ndeye and bore him a son, Mbindijeriye.

Ill-Treatment

A year later there was a great famine in the land. I said to my husband, "I am going to the fields to hoe the maize and beans." My husband agreed. When the beans were ripe I cooked them, and my husband and child and I ate them.

Later I went again to gather beans, and as I wished to finish shelling them, I stayed there for two days with some of my husband's relations who lived near. Then Ndeye's other wife spoke evil of me to Ndeye, our husband, saying, "Your wife, this runaway slave, will stay away until her son is grown. Then he will come and kill you, who are his father, and return with his mother to her home."

After shelling the beans I went home. The relations with whom I had stayed had given me some wild pig's meat, and I returned carrying beans, maize, and meat. When I got back I shared all I had with the woman. I cooked meat and porridge and gave it to my husband, and he ate. After he had eaten and night had fallen, he said no hard words to me, and I lay down in my hut and slept.

But later he came while I slept and told me to let him in. I got up and opened the door. He struck me with his stick. I exclaimed, "Why do you beat me?" He gave no answer, but insulted me, saying, "You ugly, indecent blight," and struck me again. I seized the stick and threw it into the dark hut. Then he took a spear and struck off my ear. When I saw my ear was cut off I began to scream and call out, "Woe is me that I have no relations. I am done to death for some sin which I know not." I picked up my sleeping child and tied him to my back. The blood flowed from my ear. The people of the village who had been awakened by my cries came into my hut and asked Ndeye, "Why do you beat your wife? Why have you struck off her ear? For what sin do you wish to kill her? What does this mean?" When Ndeye saw the blood he trembled and did not wish to answer them. At last he said, "This is what happened. I beat my wife because my chief wife spoke evil of her and complained to me about her. It is true that if this woman had relations I should have to atone for the ear I have struck off." I was silent, for I had no relations to whom I could complain. For this reason I stayed with Ndeye and cooked for him.

The Sango from Itende attacked us, and we fled from them into the woods. Later we left the woods and went to the village of Ikuti, which is toward Itende. I gave birth to a girl in Ikuti. Her name was Sacharonga. She was Ndeye's child. I bore another child in Ikuti, but it died in its sleep.

After the death of this child, my husband Ndeye went with his first wife to luWiwa in uSango, for the father of that wife lived there. Ndeye said to me, "Come with us to uSango." But I did not wish to go, and said, "No, for you cut off my ear." So I stayed with my children in Ikuti, and Ndeye went with his wife to luWiwa.

Ndeye came from luWiwa and said to me, "Let us move together to luWiwa." I refused again and said, "I will not go to luWiwa and live there." Ndeye said, "Well, I shall take my children to luWiwa." I replied, "Take your children and go; I will not hinder you." Then he went away, but he left the children with me.

Later he sent his son Menzya to get my children. Menzya came to me and said, "My father has sent me for the children." When I heard this I gave them to him, and said to them, "Go to your father in luWiwa." I stayed alone in Ikuti.

The children went to their father, but his wife did not give them enough to eat. When my son was hungry he ran away and came back to me. I said to him, "Child, how is this? Who brought you?" He replied, "I came alone. My father's wife let me go hungry." His sister Sacharonga wept bitterly when she found her brother had run away to me. Then my husband's wife brought my daughter also.

Death of My Husband

In luWiwa my husband and his wife sought a wife for their son Menzya, and the son worked for the maiden whom his parents had chosen. But when the girl was grown she would not have him.

One evening this girl and her companions were talking together in a hut. Her betrothed, Menzya, came up. Night had fallen. When the girl saw Menzya she went out of the hut and ran away. In the darkness she fell into a pit, broke her arm, and died. The girl thought Menzya had come to take her by force to his hut.

The girl's parents blamed Menzya and declared, "You chased our daughter." Menzya denied this, and said, "No, I did not chase her; she ran away alone." But they seized Menzya and his father, and gave them *mwamfi* — the ordeal mixture — to drink, but both got rid of it. They gave it to them a second time, and again both Ndeye and Menzya got rid of it. Then the Sango said, "We have twice given them *mwamfi*, and both times they have gotten rid of it. Now if we let them go they will bring our enemies, the Kinga, to our village, and we shall have war. Therefore, it is best to kill them. Both father and son shall die." So they killed them.

That year I had left Ikuti and had gone to Zambi, to my mother's sister, for the Kinga had come into our land and had burnt all the standing corn. A man came to me in Zambi and said, "The Sango have killed your husband and his son on account of the girl he courted. She killed herself, but the Sango said that Menzya killed her."

I Marry Again

While I was in Zambi a man called Nzavira came from Marema. He took me and I became his wife. I bore him a child, a girl, who died when she was four years old. My husband Nzavira did not stay in one place, but wandered here and there, and I had to cultivate the field alone.

Now my mother's sister died in Zambi. When she was dead I took her two sons, Senga and Tanganyika, to my hut and cared for them.

The Sin of Senga

When Senga was a man he had intercourse with another man's wife. I heard of his sin and said to Senga, "Listen to me: Have you had intercourse with another man's wife?" He denied it, and said, "No, that is a lie." But others said to me, "Chisi, your son Senga has really had intercourse with a strange woman."

I was afraid the Zambi people would kill me, for I was poor and had nothing to give to atone for this crime. So I took my two children, Mbindijeriye and Sacharonga, and fled with them to the country of Chief Marema, to the village of Isukumavere. There I found my husband Nzavira. Chief Marema said, "Whence do you come?" I answered, "I come from Zambi; I fled from there on account of the sin of my son, who had had intercourse with a strange woman." The chief gave me a hut and said, "You may stay here." In Marema lived the relations of Ndeye, my first husband. When they saw Mbindijeriye and Sacharonga they took good care of me.

Utengule

We had lived a year in Marema when the chief died. After his death my son Mbindijeiye went to Utengule to the mission station to work. He wished to settle in Utengule, and the missionary said to him, "If you are really of age, go home, get your axe, and come build yourself a hut." Mbindijeriye came back to Marema and told me the words of the white man. Then he took his axe, went to Utengule, and built himself a hut there.

A man of uSongwe courted my daughter Sacharonga and worked for me for three years. Then Mbindijeriye came to me and said, "Mother, I am courting a girl. Come, let us live together, and you can cook for me while I work for the girl." This seemed good to me, and I said, "Yes, I will come gladly." In 1901 I went with him, and he built me a hut. But my daughter Sacharonga I left behind in uSongwe with her husband. I cooked for my son and he worked for the girl's parents, and then he married his wife.

In 1906 my son ran away with a girl who had a husband already, and he had to give her back. When this sin was atoned for, Mbindijeriye built a hut in chiZungu, where the white people are, and I went there, too.

In 1908 I was very ill and my daughter Sacharonga came and took me home with her. I grew worse and had to spend a whole year with her before I could go back to Utengule.

In 1910 my son's wife died. She left a little girl. This grand-child fell ill with an infectious illness, and I lived with her in an isolated hut and cared for her for a year until she was better. Then we went back to Utengule. Meanwhile, Mbindijeriye courted another girl. He worked for her parents for two years and married her in 1912.

Baptism

After I came to Utengule I learned the words of Jesus. But I did not hear with my ears, I only sat in the house in which the teaching was given. All I understood was the name, Jesus Christ from above. Later the missionary taught us in the house of God.

But there, too, I only understood the name — Jesus Christ. For five years I learnt, going to the teaching early each morning when the bell called us. Then I asked for baptism, and when the missionary enquired why I wished to be baptized, I said, "I want Jesus to give me a new heart, and so I come to Him." I was baptized on August 1, 1914.

I have finished.

FIVE

Mama Meli

*Background to Meli's Account**

About sixty years before Meli's birth, the Bemba expanded north-ward into Mambwe country. After taking the southern districts of Mpanda or Chinga, they attacked Chief Nsokolo, the senior Mambwe chief. Meli's forebears, the Silwamba, were uprooted. A group of them became reconciled to Bemba hegemony and lived in Bembaland where they became known as the Nsofus. Some of the Nsofu-Silwamba achieved fame as soldiers, particularly the brothers Kavwinta and Mulama, whose beautiful sister attracted the attention of the Bemba chief, Makasa. They married and had a son named Changala. Meanwhile, Kavwinta also had a son, and he named him Mulama, like his brother. This Mulama grew up to be an important soldier and commander under Makasa, fighting against the Mambwe and the Tuti, as the Ngoni were called.

Chief Makasa settled Mulama and his six sons on land at Luwingu near Kayambi. After Kavwinta's death, they moved to Ndaela and founded a village that became so large that Makasa advised Mulama to delegate responsibilities to his sons. Mulama's eldest son, Mumembe, Meli's father, took charge of Nkulumwe village, which was a stronghold of the Sikazwes, his mother's

---

*The introduction was prepared by H. E. Silanda, the grandson of Mama Meli, drawing upon family traditions known to his father and others. It is shortened and restated in order to clarify events and relationships. The following narrative was translated from Cimambwe by M. Sichilongo and Barbara Lea.—Ed.

family. At first, Mumembe encountered difficulty establishing himself because his wife was inattentive and neglected visitors unless admonished by her husband. She was withdrawn and did not voluntarily enter conversation. Furthermore, she managed food stores badly and ran out of millet early in October before the rains. The people therefore called her *NyinaSimulyancani,* "Mother-What-Can-One-Eat." Especially during the rains before the harvest, Mumembe's home was one of suffering and hunger. Mumembe was disliked. The villagers felt that he did not protect them from hunger as headmen elsewhere did, all because of the bad conduct of his wife. Mumembe knew of the people's complaints and shared them. One day he gathered the elders and asked their advice about what to do with his negligent wife. The old men listened, considered and then agreed that it was unfitting for their headman to work for others in order to get food. They feared that he might even be driven to stealing or become a loafer.

A friend stepped forward, offering to help Mumembe find a better wife at Yanda, where his own wife had originated. They went together to Yanda where they found Chitalu, who had separated from her husband, an accused witch. This man had been required to take the poison ordeal but had been judged innocent by it. His relatives demanded compensation for the false charges and were eventually paid by the accusers. Chitalu, however, remained convinced of his witchcraft, which she claimed she had observed. Popular opinion supported her and people suggested that the ordeal had not been effective. Chief Changala defended the correctness of the ordeal but allowed Chitalu to leave her husband. She had been all alone for a year before Mumembe reached Yanda. The match was arranged by his companion, who was also Chitalu's brother-in-law. After the marriage, her former husband demanded and eventually received a compensation in ivory to make up for the bridewealth he had paid her family.

Chitalu changed Mumembe's life. He looked respectable, had plenty of food, and pleased his uncles the Sikazwes and the rest of the Nkulumwe villagers. They asked him to move his home to Nkulumwe, which he did, although his land was still at Ndaela.

While his first wife had two healthy children, Chitalu's children died in early childhood. The people said they were bewitched by the jealous senior wife. One day Chitalu discovered her co-wife in the act of performing witchcraft and accused her of harming the children. The senior wife denied the charge, saying that she had come to Chitalu's house for a drink of water and to get a brand to kindle her fire. A quarrel ensued. People attracted by the noise saw medicine in the baby's calabash and joined in the accusation. The senior wife then left the village and remarried elsewhere.

Meanwhile, Changala had become the military leader in charge of defense against the Ngoni, and as his prestige grew, so did that of the Nsofu-Silwamba, who were his mother's family. Mumembe's status rose not only with Changala's, but also because his own children, three sons and three daughters, were well and healthy. The youngest of them was Meli Mwenya, who tells her story here.

It was just after 1890 when the events leading to Meli's capture took place. At that time, Chief Ponde Kapalakasya was particularly aggressive toward the Mambwe and the Lungu. Mumembe's sons were frequently called upon to fight. When Ponde's wives ran away from him and were returned, one of them was found to be pregnant. Ponde demanded to know the man and Mumembe's eldest son, Meli's brother, was named. The chief refused compensation and made known his intention to take retribution by blinding the youth and destroying Ndaela. A visiting chief intervened and took the young man to his own place. Learning that Ponde was in pursuit, Mumembe arranged that his son be hidden in Mambwe country at Penza's village. There he was safe even though Ponde continued to threaten the family.

In 1894, a year after this escape, Chief Ponde was at war with the Mambwe chief, Fwambo. When the refugee youth heard of the action, he escaped from hiding to fight for Ponde, supposing that if he distinguished himself, the chief would forgive him.

Ponde's forces, however, did not win easily, for Fwambo was well fortified. The Mambwe were accustomed to the cold and counterattacked while the Bemba were trying to warm themselves. D. P. Jones, the missionary at Kawimbe, sent his armed men to help Fwambo. Penza also dispatched men, who arrived in time to pursue the retreating Bemba.

In seeking to distinguish himself, Meli's brother had killed a Mambwe defender, but his deed failed to satisfy Ponde, who was still determined to destroy Mumembe's villages. Some of the people, anticipating an attack, were planning to flee to the Kawimbe mission to be protected by the white men. Others unsuspectingly collected *masuku,* a fruit that had ripened in the countryside. Ponde's men advanced and began killing.

Meli's Account

When we were at Nkulumwe I was only a small girl. Whenever the elders were seated together they talked about Ponde's warriors. Men at the *insaka* [the village meeting place] and women in small groups, near their homes, used to say, "Friends, can we not flee and seek refuge with the white people at Kawimbe? There we can live in real safety."

One day early in the morning people scattered, some going to get *masuku* in the bush because it was the period when *masuku* are ripe and fall from trees. Others had simply fled. Father had accompanied Mulama to Ndaela. My mother and I were still in bed because mother had a bad sore on her lower back. At dawn, mother sent me to the house of Museo, Namwezi's grandmother, to ask for water. I took a cup. When I entered the house I found it empty and in disarray. *Masuku* fruit was scattered about, the bed mats were torn up, and flies were buzzing all around. Then I thought to myself, "Where would the people of this house have gone?" I searched the place and then ran back to tell my mother all I had seen. She said to me, maybe they have gone to pick *masuku.* But I said it seemed strange that they would have destroyed their bed mats and scattered the *masuku* they had gathered only the morning before. Mother could not imagine where they had gone. As we were speaking, my elder brother's wife, Mulenga, came and beckoned to me. I went out and she whispered to me, "Tell my mother-in-law I would like to go into the bush and pick *masuku*." Mother agreed on condition that she first draw some water from the stream for us. Mulenga refused by shaking her shoulders and head, for it was not customary to speak to one's mother-in-law. Mother said, "Well, you may go, but come back early. Mwenya will fetch the water when the sun comes up."

Later I picked up a gourd and went to Melu and said to her, "Let us go to the stream to fetch water." Because her house was nearer to the river, my friend poured the water into an *nsembo* [water pot] and returned to the river without me. By the time I came out of our gateway I saw my friend returning from the river. I told her, "My friend, why did you leave me behind?" Without answering my question, she said, "Hurry up, go and fetch your water, you will find me here." I ran quickly and drew some water. When I had partly filled my gourd, I heard shots. I lifted the gourd and ran up the bank. I heard my friend shout, "Mwenya, hurry up! Be quick, let's go!" I thought perhaps she had seen a python. I became frightened and thought it might catch me. I had gone a little way when Melu said, "Mwenya, hurry up! It's an army, run lest we die." We fled following the little stream until we reached the place where it joins the Nkulumwe River. We went into an abandoned village. As we were about to hide in the thick elephant grass we saw three warriors running after us. My friend said, "Let us run." We heard these people shout, "Halt! Halt or we will shoot you down." We stopped and they captured us. When they saw people fleeing from the village they stood and watched. I thought these men were only scaring us. I did not know who they really were. Among the people fleeing the village, because they were at a distance, I only recognized Kazata, who once lived at Mpande Lyapa, and one woman, the wife of Nkunkulusya. This woman surrendered herself to the warriors because they had already killed her child. When she reached them she said, "Go ahead, kill me, too! I want to follow my child." But they only pushed her forward saying, "Move! You dog!" Then they took us to the village where my mother was detained.

When we came to where they had left my mother we found she had escaped. For this they said to themselves, "Let her go, with such a terrible wound she cannot walk far." When I heard that, I realized that they were talking about my mother. I became very upset and put my hand over my mouth. We reached the gate. When I looked around I saw that the wife of my uncle Swata had been struck in her neck and killed. Her lameness must have been the reason. That is when I fully realized that these men were our enemies! When I looked over my shoulder I saw the severed head of my uncle Kasinte nearby. I shouted, "Ow! that is my uncle's head!"

Captured as Slaves

Just then they rushed, herding us together. They were wearing quivers at their sides. Some were wearing skins. They took pots and chickens from the village as loot and tied them up with bark string. The adults among us had to carry them. We went as far as the village where Namuzewo, the wife of Kasengele, lived. It was deserted. We crossed the Sambwe stream and reached Simutowe's village at Cimbili where Mpande, now the village headman at Chipundu, lived.

When we reached the foot of a small hill, mothers became completely exhausted because they were carrying heavy loads and at the same time had babies on their backs. Our captors then separated the babies from their mothers, tied them into bundles like maize, and hung them up on trees. Babies remained crying hysterically while their mothers were led away. We then climbed another hill and came to the place chosen for our overnight rest. Hunger said, "[I'll be] wherever you go!" Our captors wondered how to feed such a large crowd. Their leader said, "Roast maize for them to chew." They roasted the maize and beans but gave us only beans. You should have heard the sounds that we made:

kukutu, kukutu, kukutu. We sounded like goats chewing maize. After we finished eating our beans, thirst also said, "[I'll be] wherever you go!" We asked for water from our captors. They said, "Where have you seen water? You may as well drink your own urine." We spent the night with dry throats.

Next day with the sun almost above our heads, we reached Chief Ponde's village. That was when hunger nearly devoured us. The only food they gave us was made of boiled leaves of beans. One night, three days later, the older ones amongst us started to plan an escape. I started to cry and appealed, "You're not going to leave me behind are you?" Ntawa said, "I will carry you on my back." Before cockcrow, Ntawa tied me to her back, and we slipped away. When day broke one of our captors found the house empty. He shouted, "The people have escaped!" They followed our trail and no sooner had we reached the thick bush than they caught up with us and threatened, "If you try to run we will shoot you!" We stopped still with nothing to say. Ntawa put me down. At this point they put all the older ones in yokes, with the exception of Zongoli and me, because we were young. They took us back to the village.

Two days later we were taken from the house where we had been held and put in a big house that had no veranda. It was very dirty, untidy, and infested with bugs. It was horrible! All those confined in yokes were forced to sleep with them attached to their necks. Since two persons were held by a single yoke it was very hard for them to turn at night. Whenever one needed to go outside, the other had to go as well, even if he did not want to go.

During the next two days the adults planned another escape, and we children wanted to go with them. They disapproved saying that it was our presence that had caused them to be recaptured. When we heard them say this we cried uncontrollably. I begged Ntawa, "My older sister, are you going to leave me behind?" She told me sadly, "Yes, I wouldn't have the energy to carry you and the grass is very tall." My friend Zongoli was slightly bigger, but she was ill and could not travel with them.

Then they realized how difficult it was to move with yokes around their necks, and began to ask each other what to do. Ntawa said, "It is not difficult, I will show you what to do." Just as the cock crowed, they left. Ntawa helped them put the poles of the yokes on their shoulders and they formed a single line. With Ntawa carrying the yoke of the last person, they left, walking tiptoe like thieves fearing detection in the night. When we tried to follow, they chased us back and we went into the house sobbing helplessly.

Three of us were left behind: Zongoli, Ntawa, and me. At daybreak, our captors came and asked us where our people were. We simply told them, "They have left." The command was given to go after them. The chief said, "If you find them, kill them all!" The men picked up their spears, and bows and arrows, and they started to run. As they were leaving, they talked among themselves about the possible places where our people might be found. But in the evening they returned empty-handed.

Early the next day they divided us up among their people. We were absolutely famished. Unable to withstand the hunger, Zongoli picked up someone's excrement to eat. From that point on, I do not know what became of Zongoli.

I Burn a Hut

When *katila* [a type of early millet] ripened, the man looking after me, with his wife, three children, and myself as the sixth person, moved to the gardens where we lived in huts. My job was to frighten away the monkeys. During that time of year it rained continuously. One day one of the children gave me the task of drying the *katila* near the fireplace. Because of the severe cold brought on by the constant rain, I put more wood on the fire to warm myself. The hut was small and it suddenly caught fire. I shouted, "Help! The hut is on fire!" The woman and the husband were furious and they scolded me very strongly. The husband, mad with rage, seized me and almost threw me into the fire. But, thank God, the woman objected strongly, saying, "Do not bring evil upon us. Don't you know that this person belongs to a chief's family?" The man said, "You have been saved! But from now on you will eat only wild things you find yourself." Soon after that I became very sick. When I became worse they took me and threw me into a pit, leaving me to die. After I had been there for two days a little boy bought me bits of pumpkin to eat. When I recovered they came and took me out of the pit.

After reaping the millet, the villagers started harvesting peanuts. I was left home to fetch water because I was not strong enough to go to the distant gardens. Every day I went to the stream I saw a leopard, although I did not know what it was. I thought it was just an ordinary animal. I admired it and said to myself, "What a beautiful animal, if only one could get the skin for wearing." Then one day the woman who looked after me went to the stream with a small dog, which the leopard caught. When the dog yelped, the people went and chased the leopard away. That is when I told the elders, "I always find an animal at this same place and it has very beautiful spots." They said, "You are lucky to be alive, you could have been attacked." We finally stored all the harvest and went back to the village.

I Am Sold to the Arabs

One day there came a large crowd of people from Chona Maluti's place. This Chona Maluti was a *lungwana* [Swahili trader] settled in Bembaland. He used to kill elephants and buy slaves. People called him Chona Maluti [Spender of Gunpowder] because he used a gun that made an exploding sound whenever he shot elephants.

He sent his people to look for slaves. When they came to where we were they inquired in the village if there were any slaves for sale. My keeper told them, "I have a small slave girl, if you like her, you may buy her." I was kept totally in the dark about this. Only later did I see them bring *mpande* [conus shells] in a basket. Although I am uncertain how many *mpande* there were, there were not more than four. They bought many other slaves and early the next morning they took us to Chona Maluti. It was during the dry season, soon after the grass had been burned.

One day Chona Maluti and his people went out hunting and found and shot an elephant. But the elephant seized Chona, threw him down, and trampled him to death. His men fled for their lives and then ran to tell the villagers. The people went to retrieve the body. The elephant, when trampling over him, had torn off one of his arms; it was found a little way from the rest of the body.

After a few days some people came and reported the death of my father. I cried very much but those who owned me stopped me, saying, "Did you think he was still your father?"

At the end of the dry season, they took us to the *Lungwanas* in Chief Nkula's area. We stayed for the whole rainy season. The *Lungwanas* pierced my nose and renamed me Naumesyatu.

During the rainy season I became very sickly and skinny. My owners complained, "She has cost us money for nothing. This little person will not benefit us at all." That same rainy season the Yeke [Nyamezi] came with ivory looking for slaves to buy. One of them bought me. After buying me he cut a piece of cloth for me to wear, because when he bought me, I was clothed only in a small *mwele* [a strip of cloth suspended from a string tied around the waist, covering one's private parts]. This man showed some kindness; he fed me well. I noticed an improvement in my health as I put on weight. Mulama, my cousin, was also in this village. When he recognized me he told me, "One day I shall escape with you and take you back home." Upon hearing this I was over-whelmed with joy. Each time we went to fetch firewood from the forest I would ask him, "When, if ever, shall we escape?" He would say in answer, "Patience! We will have to wait for the end of the rainy season. At the moment rivers are very full and we could drown." Yet whenever he found any food he shared it with me. Those were days of hunger.

Before we could make an escape my owners took me away into unfamiliar country, eastward, until we eventually reached a very big river. I thought that it was Luangwa River because the people we found there spoke a strange language that I did not understand. Also the people used the word *akencembele* as a word for maize, rather that the word *cisaka* as it is in my language. They were cultivating *nkona* [sorghum]. At harvest time we went back to the village in Nkula's country. The white man had about then established a *boma* [government post] at Kawa [Fife].

The Whites Save Us from the Arabs

Upon our return at harvest time, we heard of the order issued by the whites that there must be no more buying of slaves. But even then some people called Nyanyembe [Nyamwezi], from Tabora, had come from their home and resolved, "Whatever the problems, we shall find our way unnoticed past the white man until we reach Bembaland to buy slaves." These Nyanyembe were accompanied by two Arabs and had a little boy called Nasolo with them. One of the Arabs had along a pregnant wife. They went to Chief Chitimbwa's area and bought some slaves, and eventually came to Chief Nkula's, where we were. Chief Nkula himself took his own child and sold it instead of a slave. We, too, were sold, for cloth. Because I had been ill for some time, they were pleased to get rid of me, saying, "Let her go and die elsewhere." After being bought I was given a new piece of cloth to cover myself and they gave me a new name, Mauwa, and I was never again called Naumesyatu.

After the sale, we spent the night in their grass shelters. Early the next day, just as the sun was about to rise, we left and walked until it was time to sleep. On the third day one Arab killed a buffalo. We spent a day there to prepare the meat. That day, a man whose child they had bought when they left Nkula told the Arabs, "I will show you the safe way to go because the white people have forbidden the buying of slaves. Otherwise you may pass near them and be caught." This man then went on to say, "Remain here drying meat. Let me go and spy because we are about to reach the white men's place." He got up and went to the white people at Ikomba and informed them that the Arabs had come with slaves bought in Bemba and Lungu country.

Upon hearing this, the white men were pleased and sent word to Kawa where the white commander of the askaris Mr. Bell, lived. Our guide, the brave man, said, "I shall come with the caravan. You make your preparations." As we relaxed in the evening, we saw him come back and start to lie to the Arabs about what he had seen. He lied, "I have spotted a very safe path that we shall use."

Meanwhile, Mr. Bell and his askaris approached Ikomba and his fellow whites and told him everything the man had said. Mr. Bell was very delighted and the askaris began to take their positions.

We left and went past the road from Ikomba to Ikawa. This same man told the Arabs, "This is the road from Ikomba. Now that we have gone past this road we are out of danger. We are heading for Mwenzo." When the whites realized we were near, they went to Chitete ahead of us to lay a trap. When the evening came this man said, "Let me go and scout the way again." He went and found the whites and the askaris and reached Chitete. The man came back late in the evening. We left. We reached the village and the Arabs decided that we would pitch camp outside the village because it was crowded with people. One of the Arabs went to the village gate, but no one told him his enemies were inside. The villagers came to see us, and even asked the Arabs if they were willing to buy slaves. The Arabs agreed, not knowing that they were being deceived.

On that journey we had been divided into six groups. My group was in the lead. We crossed a stream called Chitete and heard the signal to make camp. We started to prepare shelters. We, the younger ones, carried branches of trees by the elders. Our shelter was near an anthill. The Arabs had donkeys which brayed every night, but not on this particular one.

Early the next morning the horn sounded telling us to tie up our bundles. The second horn was sounded, signifying departure time. One Arab took a child from his mother, telling her to dress so that we could leave. After a short while we heard gunshots.

Everybody was scared and jumped and scattered into the bush. What confusion! The Arab holding the child had nowhere to put it and he kept jumping to and fro with it. I went to the anthill where I found a little boy, hidden. He said, "Hide your head in the elephant grass. Get down. Don't let them see us." As I was stooping, another child joined us.

Then gunfire shattered the silence. The shooting was continuous. Armed men were running toward the anthill where we were hiding. We thought perhaps they had spotted us. We were already running when we saw that the child had been shot in one leg and was crying out in pain. A woman, too, had been shot in the back. She asked for help. In response I showed her my left arm where *nkololwe* [a thorny plant] had scratched me and blood was oozing. I lied and answered, "Look I have also been shot." Then I ran away to an anthill with the two little boys following me. The gunfire ceased and all was quiet. We whispered to each other saying, "Perhaps they have now gone." There were a few more shots. When one of the boys climbed to the top of an anthill to spy he saw no one. Then everything became silent.

Because we had been running to and fro, we lost our sense of direction. When we asked one another where we had come from, one of us suggested that we should surrender ourselves to the people firing guns because otherwise we would be lost. I did not know where the Arabs and the rest of the people had gone. When the sun was over our heads, we began to feel very hungry. We forgot all about the soldiers and were concerned only about where we might eat. When we looked about, we saw only trees and because we were all children, we invoked our fathers. "What shall we do?" We asked each other, "Have you been shot?" The other boy said, "No." I said, "I was only scratched by a thorn." One of my companions said, "When I was coming here I found they had killed an Arab's wife." At that point, I told my friends, "Let us find a place to go, or are we going to spend the night here?" We then left the anthill, moving furtively.

After a short while we heard the drums summoning the

soldiers back to their camp. The sound of drums came from where we had camped. We followed the sound, which stopped after a short time. We found a small path and hoped it would lead us to the place. It only led us into gardens. Since we were so hungry we plucked and ate the millet like goats. We went on into a field of sorghum and ate that, too. One boy noticed peanuts and called us to that place. We ran there and began eating. Thirst also overcame us. When we were full we followed a path and after going a little distance found soldiers' tracks and then a village where people were sitting on an anthill. They saw us and said, "Look, there are some children coming." When we got near we realized that they were in fact the people on the white man's side. An order had been made forbidding any person to leave the village; that is why they were keeping watch on the anthills. They came and led us to where the whites were.

The White Men Send Us to Kawimbe

Thereafter they took us into the village, I noticed that the donkey used by the Arabs was tied to a stake: its foreleg was broken. They gave us food. Early the next day they took us to Ikomba. All of us who had been caught were sent to Kawa and on the way we met an askari who was coming from there. He had been sent to announce that we were free again, and all those who knew where they came from were free to return to their homes.

Everyone who knew, went, but we went on to Ikomba, where I saw people from Chitimbwa. These were people the whites said we should live with.

After some days a letter came from Kawimbe inquiring about the girls who had been rescued from the Arabs. The white man at Ikomba told the Chitimbwa people, "Take these girls with you and leave them at Kawimbe because they are small children and cannot go alone." The girls with me were Maci [Maggie], the daughter of Musindo; Zini [Jean], the wife of Malombola; and others whose names I cannot remember. We spent four days on the way and on the fifth we reached Lombe, Nzika's village. Nzika was the younger brother of Chief Fwambo, who was building a village at Mulanda in 1899. Early the next day we reached Kawimbe and found people roofing the church.

As we arrived, we saw Mama Purves sitting, sewing something. She was reclining with her legs crossed. We went up to her, greeted her, and sat nearby. She asked, "Have you come from Bwana Bell?" We said we had. She said, "That is fine, we are very happy that you have arrived safely." As she talked to us I noticed that she had no toes. I drew Maci's attention and said, "Oh, look, she has no toes! Her foot is all smooth and round." My friend said, "Yes! Even those who sent us here had similar feet." Shortly after, the husband came and greeted us; he, too, had no toes! We then wondered how these people were made. Of course we realized later that they wore shoes. After a short while they took us to a house. They put my friends in one room, and I was put among the boys. The next morning they named me Jim. Later I told them I was not a boy and they exclaimed, "Oh, all along we did not know that you were a girl!" They decided to rename me Mary [Meli] and put me with my girlfriends. The people I stayed with were Maci from Yendwe, Nele, Kasulambeka's daughter, Mutawa, and the wife of Mulanda. All together there were seven of us, although I have forgotten some names.

I Am Identified by My Relatives

We settled at Kawimbe where people built their houses surrounding the white men. The whites' village was fenced. One day I happened to stroll with my friends around the village. When I looked around I saw my uncle Kapempe and the sister-in-law of Museo who was the grandmother of David Namwezi, and many other relatives of mine. When I first saw them, I thought that they were other people whom I had just mistaken for my relatives, because our home was far away and there was no reason for them to come here.

One day I went out and as I was leaving the white man's gate I met Cinyanje. She looked at me closely and asked, "Young girl, who are you?" I answered, "I am Mwenya." She then replied, "Mwenya the daughter of Mumembe?" I agreed. She left, apparently satisfied with her inquiry and told Uncle Kapempe, "Do you know I have seen Mwenya?" My uncle replied, "Where have you seen her? The child was lost a long time ago! Is she likely to reappear now? No, you have only seen some other person who resembles her." But she insisted, "No! It must have been she. I have even asked for her name and she told me she was Mwenya the daughter of Mumembe. She passes near here every day." Then one day they came to the gate and saw me walking. Chinyanje said to my uncle, "Here she comes!" When I arrived where they were, they embraced me and began to cry. My uncle also cried and before long we were all crying. The next morning they sent word to Chief Changala in Bembaland. They sent for my elder sister, the mother of Mulenga Chisani, to come and identify me conclusively. When she came my uncle fetched me. When Mulenga's mother saw me she said, "Yes, she is definitely the one." She then asked me about how I had been captured, sold, moved about, and suffered. I told her everything. She was very amazed but at the same time rejoiced at seeing me. For the two days she spent with me, we sat looking at each other. The following day she went back to Bembaland.

When she got there all my relatives heard that I was alive, and Chief Changala was told the story. The chief then sent three of my elder brothers, Mupemba, Ntindi Lubanda, and Chilumwa Mulendo, to verify the story. He told them that if they found that it was truly I, they should tell the white men to allow me to return with them to Bembaland.

Indeed, they found I was the one. They asked the white men for permission from them to take me. The whites said, "This person was brought to us. We therefore cannot let you take her. If you really recognize her as one of your family, go and tell Chief Changala himself to come and bring a cow with him to redeem her." My brothers were very sad to hear that they refused to let me go. They went back and told Chief Changala, who said, "Oh, dear, what a difficult condition. Where shall we find a cow? In Bembaland, too, the situation is the same. There are no cows."

After a long time the chief sent my brothers to the white men with the message that as he had no cow with which to redeem the child, would they not just let the girl go without seeking payment? The chief had continued, "Other people are identifying and freely taking their relatives. Why shouldn't I?" The whites said, "True enough, you have identified your relative, but you may not take her now because she is very hardworking in the house and at school. Perhaps the best you can do is to come and visit her here occasionally and when she marries, she will then come to your home with her husband." They agreed. One of them decided to remain at Kawimbe, saying, "I will stay and keep an eye on this child." He stayed a year but because he was used to *citemene* as opposed to digging the soil, he gave up and went back to Bembaland. Despite his absence, Kawimbe village was still crowded with my relatives.

I Become Engaged

When my brother returned to Bembaland, I remained with the whites, doing domestic work and learning in school. In 1900, Bwana Purves went to Mbereshi, leaving me in the care of Mama May. He went to Mbereshi with a young carpenter called Jones Changolo, the son of Mutota Simusokwe. In 1901, Jones Changolo sent word to Bwana Govan Robertson to say that he intended to become engaged to me and sent a *nsalamu* [token payment to indicate interest in marriage]. Bwana Robertson called the elders and asked them how engagement ceremonies are conducted under Mambwe custom. The elders then told him how it was done. They then asked him, "Who is the young man who wants to become engaged to Meli?" He replied, "It is Jones Changolo." They answered, "Oh, is that so? We know him well. He is the nephew of Chileye Sichikandawa." The whites said, "Well, we shall hear what his uncle has to say because the girl has already agreed." They then called Chileya and asked him. He refused and said, "I cannot agree because the girl is lazy and does not even know how to cook and prepare *nsima* [stiff porridge]." The white man informed Jones that I had agreed but that his uncle Chileya had refused, saying the girl was lazy and did not know how to cook or prepare nsima. Upon hearing this Jones was very upset and sent word that he would marry the girl even if she did not know how to cook. She would learn when she grew older. He further said, "I do not like small women. I want one with a big body."

The white man sent for the elders a second time and informed them that the young man still wanted to become engaged to the same plump girl. The elders agreed. The white men then asked, "What do you pay in order to seal an engagement, *nsambo* [bracelets] or beads?" They answered, "If the girl agrees and the father has given his blessing, one also pays *icumalui* [a token payment to request admission to the girl's home, meaning a knocking fee], a hoe striped with lines drawn out of white lime. After all these tokens are accepted the boy makes nsambo for the girl to wear on her legs. Finally, a bridewealth of ten sheep (an installment) is paid."

The whites, upon hearing all this, sent word to Jones saying that the girl had agreed and the elders had explained the traditional things to be carried out and the dowry that he would deliver. He should therefore come back in the month that the rain finishes. When he came, Chileya discouraged him and said, "The girl you want is not a good one. Many people do not like her because she is hopelessly lazy. She does not know how to prepare *nsima,* she is a useless woman. We want you to become engaged to Nele who is hardworking." But Jones Changolo, whose other name was Silanda, refused. The elders also discouraged him and said, "If you want a girl that is big in size you can choose Mpatame." Nevertheless, he objected strongly. They then said, "Well, you go ahead and marry her on your own but we do not like her." He replied, "Yes, that is all right, she is the one I want." These words were exchanged in the evening of the day he arrived from Mbereshi.

His father, Mufota, did not know anything about all this. That same evening, the whites, having heard that Jones had come, summoned Chileya and his relatives and asked them, "The young man has come. What is your stand? We want to hear from you in his presence." Silanda told the boy they sent, "Go and tell the whites that I shall come early tomorrow." The whites came and told me, "Your fiance will come early tomorrow, so wash your body well and dress properly." As I was dressing, Mama May came to see how I was doing and she gave me some oil to rub on my body. After a short while we saw the young man had arrived holding a lovely walking stick in his hand. He was very handsome. He waited outside. As she turned her head, Mama May saw him standing there. She ran to me and said, "Meli, hurry up! Your fiance is here." I went and greeted him and all my friends, too, greeted him. They whispered to each other saying, "What a tall handsome man, so dark — as dark as *lufungo* [a dark plumlike wild fruit]." Mama May led us into the house and called Robertson. They asked the young man if his intention to marry me was serious. He said, "Yes." He went home. The next day they came with *icumalui* and the ten sheep. He spent only two weeks at home and then went back to his job.

The Wedding

In the year 1902, the whites sent word to my man asking him to come back to wed me. Mama May particularly told him, "It would be a good idea for you to return and have the wedding, for I am going back to England. I want to marry off my 'daughter' before I leave." Silanda, not one to refuse, came at harvest time and the preparations got under way. Mama May told my uncle Kapempe and my father-in-law, Chileya, "I do not want this wedding to be organized by you. I shall do everything and I will not do it in a European way. I shall not even insist on going to church at all. I want to learn the Mambwe custom. I shall do everything properly; I shall buy the oil, perfume, and flour to anoint her during the wedding." She did everything and bought all the things required for any wedding. She even bought a black cloth. "But," she said, "I will not brew beer."

The wedding day came. Mama May invited many people, men and women, my relatives and my bridegroom's relatives. All came on the arranged day in the late afternoon when it was cooler. The women went into Robertson's room and began to dance to the *nsimba* [finger piano], while also playing *vingwengwe* [clay pots rubbed upside down against another object to produce a rhythmic sound]. They ululated. Yes, there was great rejoicing. I was hidden away in a dark corner and covered with cloth. After some time the women told Mama May, the bride's "mother," "Mother of the girl, why don't you come and take up the nsimba and let it be heard?" But she replied, "Fellow women, you must show me how." They forced her and she joined in the dance. When the people saw how she danced they went wild dancing, she got them to stop ululating and it became quieter. They danced on. The house was filled with excitement.

The bridegroom's party was sitting outside. He was ushered there. In his left hand he held a bow, arrow, and a spear and in his right hand, the tail of a zebra. A lot of youths had come and many people were beating drums and dancing *kaonje* [a type of dance]. Men would form a line on one side and women another line on the opposite side and then chose partners. They danced *kaonje* for only a short time and began to sing around the bride- groom. He raised the tail in his right hand and then lifted the left hand holding the bow and spear and then spread out both his hands to either side. Nearby a girl was carrying water in a clay pot resting inside a *civo* [basket]. The bridegroom dipped the tail in the water and then splashed it over people. The girls ululated. The youths then encircled the bridegroom and his best man, singing,

> *Siwinga Mwanche*
> *wazana twakwima inkolongo*
> *tusiule cisiu ciondo*
> *tusiule cisiu ciondo*

They continued dancing. The bridegroom and his best man out-danced everyone. The girl carrying the water put some of the water into her mouth and sprayed it on the faces of the bridegroom and the best man in order to make the oil on their skin shine.

While the bridegroom danced outside, I was inside being anointed with oils, perfumes, and talc. As they anointed me they also sang many wedding songs. One went:

Cilende ndulole . . .

Vino akauzo kaya onga!

After they had finished anointing me, the best man took *usule* [small objects equivalent to confetti placed on the bride's head] and patted the bridegroom on the face with it. Then they gave me *luwazi* [a cooking apron]. I took it and shyly bent my head. They then led me out of the house and sat me at the entrance. The bridegroom moved forward and lightly touched my head with the bow. People then shouted with joy; I was lifted shoulder high and taken to the gate near where Kawimbe school now stands.

While returning from the gate I held hands with the bridegroom and walked ceremoniously in short slow strides. During the procession, the bridegroom was brushing my bent head with the zebra tail, wiping off the *nkula* and *usule* as we walked. He dipped the tail into water and then brushed it over my hair, as if to clean my head. When we reached the house we stopped and I quickly went in. The bridegroom remained standing outside and they began to give him words of advice. After they had all spoken, Mama May, as the bride's "mother," came and took the bow, the arrow, and the fez hat from the bridegroom, then she entered the house and placed them on a shelf. Thereafter, the bridegroom and his party came in. When the wedding ended the whites advised my husband, "You are now married and it is a good thing, but our 'daughter' will stay with us. She will be yours when the new leaves come [September]. We want you to escort Mama May to Karonga [in Malawi] because she is going to England." Mama May gave my husband two shillings.

During the wedding, people feasted a lot because the whites had slaughtered two cows for the occasion. One cow was for the bridegroom's party while the other was for the bride's. In the evening the wedding moved over to the bridegroom's home. The next evening we were seated to receive more words of advice. The whites, including the bride's "mother," came to the village to witness the occasion. Early the next day they packed me a basket of mealie meal and I went back home.

When I reached the entrance I stood with the basket on my head, holding a walking stick in my hand. Mama May came out to welcome me, received the basket, and then gave me two shillings. From this day onward I never went back to my husband's home. Upon noticing this my husband wondered, "Hey, what kind of marriage is this where in the beginning they 'confiscate' your wife?"

The time for the journey to Karonga arrived. It was toward the end of the harvest time when we traveled to Karonga. We stayed there a whole month waiting for two white strangers, Stewart Wright and his wife. They finally came. Mama May told them, "Look after this girl and her husband. Do not give her to her husband until September." We finally went back home and I spent three weeks working for Mama Wright. Then they finally called my husband to come and take me away.

My Second Wedding

My father-in-law, Mutota, did not know about the wedding. Apparently he did not even know that I was engaged because most of the time my husband stayed with Sichikandawa, who wanted to totally isolate my husband from his other relatives. Thus all along, when the negotiations were going on, no one bothered to inform his father.

When Mutota heard that his son was married he became furious and said, "Just how can the Sichikandawa clan marry off my son without letting me, his father, know so that I could contribute a cow? They did not even tell me about the engagement

negotiations. All right, I shall also conduct a wedding, I, Simu-
kowe from Misansansa, *Kwakwe Kungwi Muntapona Nkuma*" [a
saying in self-praise].

Mutota began to prepare the wedding. He soaked a large
quantity of millet and made plenty of beer. Then they came to take
me for the second time. My father-in-law was at this time still at
Yanda. When he reached the gate they gave me a billy goat as a
token of welcome.

I was seated in the house. They gave me a piece of red cloth.
After anointing me, they gave me six *nsambo* [bracelets]. The
person who anointed me was my husband's stepmother, for his
real mother was dead. They allowed his stepmother to anoint me
because she was born into their family.

The next morning, my sister-in-law Namukale brought me
a small hoe from Lunda. It was very well decorated and beautiful.
When presenting me with her gift, she advised, "My sister-in-law,
look at me. In my family we are not many — we are only three,
with the youngest one seated over there. Even though they are
present at your wedding, we do not acknowledge the others." She
then handed me a tray full of millet with some bracelets on top,
ceremoniously inviting me to grind the millet. When I saw the
millet I said to myself, "Oh, dear me, how shall I grind all this
millet, a thing I have never done before in my life!. . . As if back
home at Kawimbe we grind millet." I took the bracelets and gave
them to Nyina Kangwa, asking her to grind the millet. When the
wedding came to an end we went back to Kawimbe, where we
found that a house had been built for us near the white people.

On moving into that house the whites gave us many household articles. Mama May and Mr. Purves had already packed the
things that were to be given to me. Dr. Morris gave us a lot of
paper, other writing materials, and medicines. The whites with
whom we came from Karonga gave us some plates and cups. Mr.
Ndelempa [Draper] said, "For my part, I am not giving you anything today, but I will help you with anything you may need from
time to time because Silanda has worked with us for a long time."

One day all the whites gathered to discuss the distribution of bridewealth my husband had paid to marry me. They then decided to give it all back to my husband. They told him to bring the rest that was still owed. They would then give back the money, the value of the ten sheep, and, in addition, a cow. He thus gave them twenty-five shillings. Then they gave him a small cow, which he gave the name *Acisi kwa mwene cili uku milimo ya Mambwe*. When interpreting this name he said it meant that white men did not care about wealth as the Mambwe do. And so we set up house. After one year we had our first child whom we named Elizabeth.

We Become Wealthy

As days went by, while we were still there, a *mzungu* [literally white person, but popularly anyone of Western culture] called Heman, a black, came from America, from the people they call Negroes. He stayed at Kawimbe only a short time before they sent him to Niamukolo, near the lake. One day he came from there to visit his friends, who welcomed him warmly at Kawimbe. I did not know he had come that day. I only heard the next day as I was to go out to the gardens to harvest millet. I then said to myself, "I shall come and greet him after work."

As we came from the gardens we met him just by the workshop. He stopped and saw me. I then greeted him, and he asked me, "Young girl, where are you coming from?" I replied, "Sir, I have come from the gardens." He said, "Why did you not come to greet me? Did you not know that I came yesterday?" I then replied, "Sir, work preoccupied my mind. In fact, I did learn that you had come only this morning as I picked up my basket to go harvesting millet. So I decided that we would meet when I came back." He then said, "Well, that is a fine young woman. I want you to visit me one day and afterward I shall come to see your baby."

When this man *[mzungu]* went back to his home, my husband bought a sheep and a goat as a gift. We started for Niamukolo, sleeping at Isoko and arriving the next day. However, while we were still in the wild bush on the slopes of mountains, the sheep broke its rope and ran away. My husband gave chase, but unsuccessfully, because there were plenty of stones. The sheep was never found. We reached our destination, found Bwana Heman, and greeted him. We told him how the sheep we were bringing had escaped into the hills. He thanked us for the goat. They accommodated us in David Musena's house. We spent five days and while there he served us with rice and fresh fish.

The days of our visit came to an end. The evening before our departure we told him, "Sir, tomorrow we are leaving." He agreed and told us, "Come and say goodbye to me in the morning." Early next day we went to bid him farewell. My husband was given a roll of calico drill cloth [merikani] and six shirts. The child was given little dresses and diapers. I was given a small roll of spotted cloth, fashionable for women, and a bunch of black beads [ntundukalu]. He gave us a tin of sugar, three boxes of soap, sugarcane, a bunch of bananas, and a bag of rice. He also gave us two people to help us carry the gifts. We left and he and his wife escorted us for a short distance and blessed us, saying, "May God be with you so that you have a safe journey to Kawimbe."

At this time our poverty ended. This man is the one who helped us very much because my husband then began to sell the cloth and other things he gave to us. Finally, we were running a little shop.

We Have More Children

Our first child, born in the year 1903, was indeed a very healthy child who did not fall ill very often. When she reached the age of two, however, she caught smallpox. This disease was very serious. The child suffered a lot and soon died. By the time she died the disease had blinded her.

In 1907 we had our second child, a boy. The midwife gave him the name of Satu. They used to praise him: *Mulanda Satuka ali yayili yatize yakwane uwamamba.* This praise arose because

Mr. Sichikandawa, my husband's uncle, often argued with his father over my husband. Both wanted to claim him. Each one would say, "He is our child," and the other one would say, "No, he belongs to us." That is why they gave the infant this name. It meant that they were giving a message to the father of the baby, to say in effect, "Poor man wake up, do not let these two people tie you down in servitude." They were really telling him to go back to his father.

After three months, we requested baptism of the child and he was given the name of Michael by Mr. Wright, who baptized him. Many people could not pronounce the name properly so he was given another name, Ernest. His spiritual name was Mfwambo. This child had many names indeed!

In the year 1910 we had another male child; this one was named Kela. He did not live long, only nine months. He died when he was able to crawl and laugh. In 1911 we had another baby girl, and she was named Lukoti, whose Christian name was Agnes. The last-born was named Henry.

How I Was Baptized

In the year 1910, all the missionaries gathered at Kawimbe. Missionaries of the Free Church of Scotland came from Mwenzo, Kondowe, Ekwendeni, and many other places in Nyasaland. Some church officials came from England. It was a very big meeting.

On Sunday there was a big religious festival and all Christians attended, but not I. When the communion ended Donald Siwale and Peter Sinkala from Mwenzo asked my husband why I was absent. He replied, "She is not yet baptized." They then came to me and asked me whether I would like to be baptized and I agreed. The person who baptized me was Mr. Robertson. When the white men from England were coming for the conference, Mama May told them, "When you get to Kawimbe, look for a girl named Meli and her husband, Jones Changolo." Thus, when they arrived, they were anxious to come to my home. Mr. Robertson came and said to me, "Today white visitors are coming to your home." I replied,

"But what are the dignified people going to eat in a poor man's home?" He replied, "They will eat whatever you will give them." I then replied, "Yes, a Mambwe saying goes, *'Umwenyi wakwe siche akalya tuno siche akalya'* [A guest eats what his host eats]." I borrowed plates from him. At midday they came. Both were men. They found that I had fried a chicken and boiled Irish potatoes, cooked pumpkins, beans, and prepared tea. They settled down and I served them the food. I thought they might refuse it, but I saw them eat willingly without any hesitation. They left in the afternoon. A few days later, they returned to England.

After a long time at Kawimbe we moved to Mfundula. When the whites saw us leave they were not happy and even took from us the girls they had given to us to help us with work.

The world war in 1914 forced us to move again. The Germans looted the little wealth we had and dug up the floors of the whole house in search of money. We moved to Kela. The boma [district officer] gave my husband the job of buying mealie meal for the forces. We stayed at Kela for a very short time and then the boma sent us to Chief Nsokolo's village where we lived until 1915. We left there and went on to Mwalu. At this place my husband distributed war supplies such as mealie meal and many other things to the military carriers. We were there only two months. At the end of the dry season (November) we came to Nchengwa where the missionaries had sought refuge. Here the boma told my husband to hunt for game to feed the soldiers. They paid him twelve shillings and sixpence whenever he killed a large animal, such as a bushbuck or an antelope.

In the year 1916 we returned to Kawimbe with the missionaries. This was a year of starvation everywhere around Musia's area where the Germans were. The boma told my husband to look for food to help people. He bought plenty of millet in Chief Chakonta's area and distributed it to all people who were suffering from famine.

My Husband Dies

In November 1918 we heard that the Germans were coming to Mbala. Many people came to witness the surrender of the white man. I and my husband went, too. When we were coming back my husband passed through Maswepa to collect the millet he had been buying for the boma. On the day that he returned, his relative Mbokosi came to talk with him. As they spoke, my husband said, "Brother, even though we are chatting like this I am a sick man. I feel pain in my back." It was Thursday, the 29th of January, 1919. That evening he became seriously ill and during the night I went to fetch medicine from Mama Ndelempa. Early the next day, the 30th, he was much worse and his elder brother, Cambala, came. He remained in that state on Friday, and on Saturday he came close to the point of death. When the sun was about to set, Ernest was in the yard outside making a toy bicycle from reeds without knowing that inside the house his father was on his deathbed. I drew him away and reprimanded him; he ran away and continued his toy-making. We suffered the whole night until, at cockcrow, he passed away. We started mourning. When I looked at the three children he had left me I was distraught, crying until there were no more tears to be shed.

In the morning of the first day of February, a Sunday, we sent word to the whites. They sent back a person with the message that he should not be buried until they came and prayed. Such crowds of people came to this funeral that one might think the entire population of Mambweland had come to mourn. We buried him. After we came back and the house had been cleaned, Inoki Nsokolo "boiled up" and said, "Jones was my debtor, I want all my money today." People who came to mourn him said, "Young man, have you lost your senses? The custom is to restrain yourself and not seize things abruptly. Be patient. Today we have only come to mourn." But the brute refused. He beat his walking stick on the ground so they let him have it.

Two weeks later the question of inheritance arose. All my late husband's relatives gathered and began the task of choosing a person to succeed my husband. The Sichikandawa family said, "Let us take it." They had even chosen Njoni [John] Kalyonga to be the heir. The Simusokwe family, however, objected strongly. There was a heated argument until the Sichikandawa family finally gave in.

The Simusokwe family chose Chimbala but he declined. Then Mbokosi stood up and declared, "I shall then succeed because I have the energy to go to all this [dead] man's debtors and collect all his money." I refused and said, "No, I cannot marry him because Mbokosi has a wife and I am a Christian and cannot therefore enter a polygamous marriage." On hearing this the people dispersed and the whole matter of inheritance ended there.

After a week, Mbokosi came back and told me he had divorced his wife. I did not believe it. A month passed. Then he came back and insisted that he had truly divorced his wife. After some time I gave in. He consummated the marriage and took me to his home.

When this man succeeded my husband, he took all the wealth left by my late husband and squandered it. With some of it he paid the fine in a case in which Silanda had been involved. He also sold all the cattle, together with other things. The children were not properly supported by this man and it pained me greatly. So in 1922 I left him and went back to Kawimbe to Mama Ndelempa, who gave me a domestic job.

In the year 1925, Harry Sichikandawa married me. This man said he was unmarried but he lied to me. When he took me with him to Kasama I found he had another woman from Bembaland, a Bisa of the Ngumbo clan. I stayed in the same house with this woman.

While I was still in Kasama, word came round that at the hospital they wanted some women to learn midwifery. I went and enrolled. We used to go into the villages and Kasama looking for pregnant women. In 1934, while I was working, my husband died. I returned to Kawimbe.

After returning I went to stay with my sons Ernest and Henry at Mulanda. There I found Ernest had had two children, Howard and Monica. Their sister Agnes was then in Nyasaland.

After a short stay my son-in-law came and took me to Nyasaland. In 1935, I came back and Mama Brooks at Kawimbe wanted me to help her look after schoolgirls. I went there and settled, not to teach but only to look after the schoolgirls.

The Days that Followed

As I did my job of looking after the schoolgirls I noticed that the white woman was very keen on working with me at all times. In 1936 a mishap occurred at Senga. Porrit's wife died. She was Mama May's daughter, whom I used to look after, the one I used to call "my sister" because her mother had cared for me as if I were her own child. Bwana Porrit found it hard to remain alone at Senga, for it was an isolated place. Therefore he came to Kawimbe and married Mama Brooks. The school was closed!

My job, too, ended and I went to Nyasaland. While there I received money from Mama Baker at Kawimbe asking me to go back to help her work in a home for orphans. I returned and we worked together looking after the children. This woman truly worked very hard in this cause. I did not work alone—for I had companions, Namuzoo, Causiku, Ndumoa, and many others. We all worked together very happily because Mama Baker was a good white woman, polite and cheerful.

In 1945 this woman went to help lepers at Kabalenge near Mbereshi. She then returned and worked among lepers at Kawimbe. Many people were upset about her departure because they liked her very much and trusted her. When she left, all of us midwives scattered to our villages like sheep without a shepherd. The hospital itself closed down. I remained looking after three orphans: Jenifa Chombo, Timu, and Chisambi.

While I looked after these children, the congregation chose me to become the preacher in villages surrounding Kawimbe, and in the same year ordained me as an elder of the church. Others chosen with me were Chisya Yambala, Bwana Adel, and Mama

Luxon, the lady in charge of the schools, who worked hard to develop primary education at Kawimbe. She was the one who started to send children to high schools at Munali and Chalimbana. Benjamin Simpungwe and David Namwezi were the first ones she sent. The day on which we were installed as elders was a great one because it was the first day on which we welcomed the leaders of the London Missionary Society. Many people from small congregations in villages came to witness what was going on. The missionary who officiated was Reverend K. D. Francis. People were overjoyed to see this new development.

Forever after I have praised God for rescuing me from great hardship.

PART II

History at the Turn: Essays in Contextualization

Note:

Undiluted personal narratives have a power of their own, not to be usurped by analysis. Yet in the interpretation of such texts, history claims a place beyond mere elucidation. The second part of this volume explores various avenues for moving between text and context and history as a larger synthesis. It follows the sequence of the chapters' composition, beginning with "Justice, Women, and the Social Order," a discussion that, on the spectrum from individual to collective, falls closer to collective, or broadly historical. It draws upon court cases and associated administrative records to construct a picture of context and to generalize about how women responded to new commercial, demographic, and juridical circumstances.

The title for Part II, "History at the Turn," gives emphasis to the fluidity and transitional nature of the colonial situation around 1900 and during the following decade. The chapters here give greater attention to authorship and interactions between the colonizers and the protege Africans who became closely identified with the "new era," the incoming values and the prescriptions about family and social relations they entailed.

SIX

Justice, Women, and the Social Order in Abercorn, Northeastern Rhodesia, 1897-1903*

African authorities on custom in the interwar years idealized a past when women were controlled. Yet anxiety about women did not prevail solely in the colonial period. Before accepting the dicta of elders about historical conditions, the evolution of the native court system under colonialism must be understood and the dynamics of earlier times retrieved. At the outset of colonial rule, the social order was under duress, responding to increased commercialization and concentration of wealth in the hands of local notables. Modifications of customs took place especially as inequalities became heightened and calculations of expendability entered many families and households where indebtedness loomed in a menacing way for men with very few material possessions or savings. Women and children were treated more and more as assets to be exchanged, appropriated, and deployed. I argue on the basis of evidence from Abercorn, the present Mbala in northern Zambia, that as economic and political circumstances changed, a shift of

---

*I am grateful to members of the History Seminar at the University of Zambia, Drs. Ian Phimister and Gervase Clarence-Smith in particular, for their incisive and imaginative comments on an earlier paper covering much of this material. A more personal sketch of Marshall is contained in my "'Tambalika': Perspectives on a Colonial Magistrate," *African Affairs* 85, no. 338 (1986).

practices pertaining to women took place. The first colonial magistrate presided in a neutral way as this adjustment took place. While he and his lieutenants discouraged manifest injustice, they did not seek to reform, let alone set, the rules for the struggle to control women.

The temporal setting for this analysis was a brief period of mushrooming and subsiding economic activity in Abercorn and the Tanganyika District of which it was the capital. The town was very much under the direct rule of the magistrate. The district was managed through a few European officials working with and gradually subsuming preexisting authorities, both African and European. As long as the early colonial investments called for a heterogeneous working population and created new and transitory communities, the magistrate was especially active in the judicial arena and strove to acquire a reputation for equitableness. In later times, when the administration became more routinized and the economy more stagnant, he expressed the opinion that the colonial courts had initially been too lenient toward women.[1] The evidence and processes discussed here, however, reflect the early colonial, seigneurial phase characterized by a combination of wealth seemingly controlled by the magistrate, personal rule, and localized allegiances.

The area of the Tanganyika District embraced the northwestern chiefships of the Bemba people, the bulk of the Lungu, and about half of the Mambwe. In the decades prior to 1894, the Bemba had used their military power to expand territorially and mount incursions into the Mambwe-Lungu areas. The most formidable personage in the north was Chief Mkoma of the Nyamwanga, whose capital lay beyond the Tanganyika District. Abercorn, at the southern tip of Lake Tanganyika, was settled as an unfortified administrative outpost in 1894. Although situated in the territory chartered to the British South Africa Company, it was in fact founded as an administrative offshoot of the Nyasaland Protectorate, which received a subsidy from Cecil Rhodes for this service.[2] Such a strategy followed the logic of commercial expansion, for in the decade before 1894 the routes westward from Lake Nyasa to the Abercorn region had been traversed with increasing frequency by Swahili and colonial trading enterprises. From Karonga at the northwest corner of the lake, a route to the southern tip of Lake Tanganyika had been regularized by the African Lakes Company (ALC), which entered treaty relations with the important chiefs to assure rights in land and the security of relay stations. The ALC did business with Africans and missionaries. The African trade was mediated mainly by regionally-based Swahili merchants who gave ivory in exchange for stocks of trade goods. Missionaries received similar trade goods, including cloth, beads, and metal wares, with which to pay workers and obtain produce. In addition, the missionaries counted on the ALC to transport themselves, their household belongings and provisions imported from Europe. The company therefore hired its own porters, retained provisioners, and maintained an African staff[3] (see map p. 5).

The resident aliens within the Abercorn magistrate's jurisdiction in the new Tanganyika District of Northeastern Rhodesia had become part and parcel of local political and economic life well before the coming of colonial officialdom. Whether missionaries or Swahili traders, they gathered around themselves a mixed population composing what may be called "polyethnic" communities, distinct from the neighboring older communities of some ethnic homogeneity. These communities, led by Christians and Muslims, contained persons drawn from assorted cultural backgrounds, some being of servile status, others clients, refugees, pawns, or retainers, and yet others transient or short-term sojourners. The most numerous element in polyethnic communities frequently derived from the vicinity, having consciously elected authority of outsiders, at least as long as the benefits of protection or economic opportunity outweighed the demands for religious or social conformity and the risk of being sold to strangers. Justice in polyethnic communities tended to be *ad hoc* and aimed at maintaining the kind of cohesion serving the purposes of the leaders. There was a tendency to turn a blind eye to popular methods resolving conflicts unless they posed a major ideological challenge (as to missionaries) or threatened the legitimacy of leadership.[4]

By contrast, the older ethnic communities of the Tanganyika District were led by chiefs with hereditary claims to rulership and a commitment to administer justice according to "custom" or with at least a show of ritual propriety. The chiefs' positions had been both enhanced and buffeted by the aggressive Bemba incursions of the late nineteenth century and by the increasingly well-armed merchants associated with the Swahili system. To assert that in 1894 the merchants were generally ascendant is not necessarily to imply overt hostilities between ethnic and polyethnic units. Many chiefs along the thoroughfares linking Lakes Nyasa, Tanganyika, and Mweru were engaged in a range of activities, mobilizing the resources of their territories, servicing caravans and contending with the disruptive Bemba, especially the "wild" Chief Ponde, whose raids became worse during the famines of the early 1890s.[5]

The political climate of the district in 1894 was affected by a general disarray brought on by a combination of regional difficulties, including interclan as well as intertribal conflict, strong elements of commercial calculation, famine, and social fluidity as people sought security. When H. C. Marshall, a former ivory hunter, planter, and junior officer in the Nyasaland service, began to pick up the threads of authority in 1893–1894 as the first colonial magistrate, he met very little opposition.[6] The two record books that form the core of evidence for the discussion of women and the social order in Abercorn from 1897 to 1903 were compiled during the high point in this official's career, after he had established fundamental relationships and principles for governing the district and before his domain was effectively subordinated to the overrule of the Northeastern Rhodesia administrator and judiciary.[7] It should be noted that from time to time deputies contributed to these records. W. R. Johnstone in particular maintained the tone Marshall had established and thus stabilized the reputation of the court as being independent of the personality of its occupant.

It was unusual for a magistrate and collector in a remote corner of the British Empire to proceed with Marshall's care for diplomacy and recordkeeping. He is not one of the famous "characters" of the early administration; colonial old-timers never spun yarns or contributed notes about him to the *Northern Rhodesia Journal*.[8] His memory, however, was preserved in and around Mbala, the former Abercorn, in the accounts of African elders whose tributes to him for peacemaking and reconstruction of Lungu life propelled me back to the archives with greater curiosity.[9]

In the following discussion, the court records are used in three different ways. The first section provides fuller background on the political economy being shaped by the magistrate-collector, the second takes up the alternative modes of judgment that had prevailed before, and the third considers women as actors in certain civil and criminal cases. The primary goal is to display the court records as sources and illustrations of social processes.

Social Configurations and Authority in the Tanganyika District

During the initial colonial decades, there was no issue more sensitive than control of women. As one evidence of wealth and power, chiefs had become surrounded by "wives," some married through the giving of bridewealth, others received from clients or appropriated, yet others forming a reserve to be distributed as favors or rewards. The bevies of women tended to develop their own strategies for amelioration, seeking sexual and social relations outside the royal monopoly and rebelling and running away in groups.[10] Control of a chief merchant's capital (actually a swollen household) was not easily maintained, given the creation of colonial economic units where employed single men were concentrated and the authority of chiefs was little regarded. This was especially true in times of acute famine and in periods of commercial uncertainty and loss of credit from Swahili traders.

At the turn of the century, the value of women as agricultural producers rose in proximity to the arteries of commerce around Abercorn, where there was a lively market for food. The demand was generated originally by transport personnel and workers in construction camps where steam vessels for Lake Tanganyika were built.[11] When women engaged in delivering and selling produce, circulation between the countryside and new settlements inevitably increased, with a concomitant rise in female awareness of social alternatives in the mushrooming camps, administrative centers, and commercial posts where women were few. The behavior of men in outlying communities confronted with this competitive situation ranged from protectiveness to jealousy and exploitation. Accusations of rape and adultery and counteraccusations of entrapment entered the magistrate's record book.

The Tanganyika District thus hummed with economic activity at the turn of the century. Although the Swahili trading system had been constricted by colonial regulation, it was given a fillip by improving prices for rubber gathered from wild vines.[12] Regional trade was systematized by Marshall, who appreciated and promoted the distribution of products with known exchange value, such as Tabwa salt and iron hoes. Older networks persisted even while new construction brought a number of workers from the Nyasaland area and absorbed lower strata of the Swahili social formation. The official reaction to such activity included both consternation at the extent of deforestation entailed by the citemene system of cultivation as production increased in the boom, and satisfaction that wages paid in kind had now to be in colored cloth and other consumer goods, not solely in white cloth as before.[13]

Prosperity, however, was precarious and transitory; the injection of external funds into the district subsided once the telegraph line and steamers were constructed, rubber vines destroyed, and salt from distant Uvinza became cheaper than that of nearby Tabwa. After 1901, taxation replaced commerce as the chief mode of extraction from the populace.[14] The seigneurial conduct of district officers eventually gave way both because of a weakening regional economy and because systematic administration became dictated from above. Meanwhile, the immediate impact of recession and colonial control was cushioned by a sturdy system of political alliances and steady moderation in the judicial sphere.

The judicial environment was much affected by prosperity and by Marshall's perceived need to be on good terms with the leaders of the diverse communities, ethnic and polyethnic, through whom labor and produce were to be obtained. Priority was given to chiefs, whose political status and command of people was, if anything, dignified by the magistrate. The ALC agent at the nearby post was told that tax gathering was neither to alter the former relationships nor to license Africans attached to the colonial rulers to exploit their own positions: "I never instruct natives to come to me or go to anyone else under threat of punishment as such an assertion must be traced to its origin. I must say that I have no *local* men just now working nor have I sent for any. To local chiefs I usually apply *personally* for workers and am much annoyed that your capitaos [overseers] have told you this lie."[15]

Marshall's laissez-faire attitude on social issues paralleled this sense of primary alliance with the chiefs and community leaders. The role of the colonial officials, he advised one of his juniors, was not to emancipate slaves: "You can protect runaway slaves, making a complete record of their cases, but you must neither directly nor indirectly induce such people to leave their respective villages. The inhabitants of the country are well aware that the administrative posts are for the administering of justice and any who have good 'cases' will readily enough bring their complaints to you."[16] Writing to the London Missionary Society missionary Robertson at Kawimbe with regard to a case of alleged adultery and the refusal of the husband to present his case in person: "Of course we cannot allow anyone to say he refused to come to Abercorn or to abide by the [any] decision given there. I am, therefore, sending to compel the attendance of the man Maliwanda. This is more especially necessary as you say he used force to extort payment. It appears his case must be a weak one to his thinking or he should be willing to come here, having nothing to lose, since you decided against him — and all to gain!" He added, "Speaking generally of *milandu* [disputes], I would say that any person being dissatisfied with arbitration or decisions on your part or on the part of any person, not an official, has a right to bring his or her case to the 'Boma.'"[17]

Confidence in the "justice" to be obtained through the magistrate was expressed by two chiefs in April and May 1901, from both of whom wives had run away. Chief Changala's wives allied themselves with men at the White Fathers' station, Kayambi, and Chief Ponde's wives took themselves to Kasama District to live with other men. Marshall wrote to the Father Superior requesting the return of the women or the "thorough" recompense of the chief. Insistence on rank and confidence in arbitration combined in a concluding instruction that "Failing an amicable and agreeable (to all parties) settlement — I desire you to send the women in question and the men to whom they are now married — to Abercorn — that I may settle the case."[18] A slightly different situation had prevailed in 1899, when two wives of Chief Chungu had run away to the magistrate's own village of Abercorn, claiming that they had been abused and virtually driven out. The chief requested only compensation equivalent to the bridewealth he had paid, whereupon Marshall allowed the women to remain with men of their choice on the condition that these men each pay five dotis of "good cloth" to Chungu.[19]

Several observations about these incidents are warranted. None of the chiefs contested the secession of the women, although they expected and received either the compensation they wanted or the return of the children. Such cases were treated extra-judicially, in a framework of political allegiance, and the magistrate left no doubt that he wanted these important men to be satisfied. Nevertheless, it is plain that chiefs no less than ordinary men were encountering difficulty and were unable to prevent women from gaining refuge in polyethnic, commercial, and colonial communities. Furthermore, the spiraling recession meant the passing of the old regime in which women were concentrated and redistributed by chief-merchants.[20] The magistrate used his combined juridical–political authority to moderate an indigenous practice whereby chiefs accepted female pawns in compensation for adultery when he learned that the innocent women pawned in this way were then passed from hand to hand in settlement of other obligations.[21] For a variety of reasons "good cloth" had become a universal medium of exchange while extra women, especially if they were disgruntled, had become a liability.

Indigenous Justice and Colonial Intervention

The retrieval of control by African men in certain spheres of mediation and domestic affairs resulted from the stabilization of conditions within a colonized political framework. More public matters and criminal cases of bodily harm and untimely death remained in the hands of the colonial authorities. Given the tendency for levels of conflict to escalate from the domestic to the public sphere, the separation of cases and competencies remained subtle. It is therefore appropriate to rummage further in the Abercorn records to understand better how older modes of justice and jurisprudence were regarded by all concerned. These are merely glimpses, but they pave the way for larger conclusions about the courses open to women and the role of the magistrate.

The incoming colonial authorities claimed immediately that murder cases belonged to their jurisdiction. Sovereignty was at stake, and chiefs in any degree of positive relationship with the colonial authorities quickly appreciated that no overt contest was possible. Marshall's courtesy in inquiring of Chief Mporokoso about the customary punishment for murderers received a deftly deferential reply. Such an offender, Mporokoso reported, would have been "heavily fined for spilling blood in the chief's town" in former times, but now judgment and sentencing were solely a matter for the colonial authorities.[22]

A more deeply entrenched judicial ritual, the poison ordeal, could not be subsumed so readily. As Marshall reported in 1900,

"The custom of *mwavi* drinking (the drinking of a poisonous concoction to determine guilt or otherwise) is so firmly believed in by all, that the heaviest sentences fail to absolutely stamp it out. Cases are undoubtedly fewer, but it will be many years before the custom is entirely abandoned."[23] This comment may have been promoted by a case originating in the Sumbu subdistrict earlier in 1900, which serves very well to display many features of the poison ordeal, including indications of awareness that it had been outlawed by the colonial authorities. Among the classic circumstances giving rise to a poison ordeal were suspicions of witchcraft or sorcery, where guilt of any sort was denied and clear-cut evidence was lacking.[24] The mwavi bark could be used in divinations, creating an atmosphere of mounting certainty that a particular person was an offender. Faced with this pressure and mobilization of public opinion, an accused person might demand the formal ordeal and hope to be exonerated.

In early 1900, one Chitembwa, who ultimately died from the ordeal, had become drunk and beat his wife, who died shortly after. The wife's mother believed him to be responsible and gave a chicken a mixture including *mwavi,* predicting that if it behaved in one way, a man had been the cause of the woman's death, if in another, it had been a woman. When the divination indicated a man, Chitembwa insisted on undergoing the ordeal: "Chitembwa took the *mwavi* in the early morning" and a male relative "tried by the recognized methods to get Chitembwa to vomit," but failed.[25]

The local chief sent all the surviving parties in this affair, including the mother-in-law, the brother, the doctor *(nganga)* who had supplied the *mwavi* and several others to the Sumbu subcollector, who referred them further to Abercorn. Because of the strength of evidence that the ordeal had been self-inflicted, all were judged to be accessories to the death and were punished according to their degree of responsibility. The nganga, admitting that he knew the ordeal to be illegal, was most severely punished.[26] The mother-in-law was second in blame, having invoked the authority of mwavi in the course of divination.

The correct procedure in precolonial times had required that the chief alone authorized a poison ordeal.[27] By 1900, in the Tanganyika District, however, chiefs carefully avoided implication in the persisting practice, although they could not deny involvement in other ways with witchcraft cases. Fwambo, the Mambwe chief, when he discovered a man near his compound depositing a suspicious substance, apprehended him and turned him over to his wives, who beat the trespasser and then forced him to swallow some of the substance, which proved to be lethal. When the case came to Marshall, it was heard out of court and Fwambo's explanations were accepted as adequate. As Fwambo explained it, the man had been given sanctuary in his territory after being driven from a neighboring jurisdiction for alleged witchcraft. In earlier times such a person might have received the same treatment, for the most likely alternative, the poison ordeal, tended to be used primarily in instances of conflict among peers. The incident at Fwambo's involved actors of great political inequality, for the trespasser had declined in status when he left a home community where he had kin who might have been enjoined to back up protests of innocence and gain recourse to the poison ordeal. Having fled, he became a refugee still clouded by an uncleared record and indebted to the chief for sanctuary. He was therefore handed over to the instant justice of the outraged women of Fwambo's household whose particular domain, the compound and gardens, had allegedly been violated.

The cases just discussed illustrate the ways in which women could be active in prosecuting and punishing alleged criminals. While there was doubtless room for manipulation, the poison ordeal was often appealed to by the weaker person or side in a conflict, as a ritual institution widely believed to be free of human arbitrariness. The poison ordeal was nevertheless a politically strategic matter, to be somehow identified with chiefship. Neither in the Tanganyika District nor in more firmly centralized polities nearby did chiefs have the strength to usurp the judicial function itself. They drew legitimacy from it, however, by their monopoly of the right of authorization and determination of the further penalties subsequent to the ordeals' settling of the metaphysical issue.

The records for Abercorn contain several reverberations of poison ordeals carried out among the Nyamwanga, whose rulers had developed the practice of sending agents to villages troubled by witchcraft, there to oblige a representative of every family to undergo the ordeal. This action effectively identified witches and cleansed the settlement. It would appear that the paramount chief also used the process of cleansing as a means of keeping domestic order in his own capital.[28] On several occasions, groups of women were reported to have fled Mkoma's place because of being subjected to the ordeal; such terror indicates both the great wealth and consequent concentration of "wives" around this powerful figure. The considerable degree to which Nyamwanga chiefs fused dynastic power with the popular belief system enhanced their ability to exercise social control at all levels.[29]

Although judicial actions in this nearby political culture were more integrated with secular authority than appears to have been the case within boundaries of the magistracy, it is necessary to reaffirm that the poison ordeal remained at root a popular institution. The White Fathers at Mambwe station had been alarmed to see it surfacing among the women of the community concentrated around them, and sought to purge the practice.[30] Again, it must be stressed that the resilience of the ordeal came from its being in part an escalated form of divination. It persisted because there were no alternative means of dealing with anxieties about witchcraft, which often arose in overcrowded, confined, defensive settlements or later on in more apparently normalized conditions.

Even though there are no known cases of women having been the focus of a formal, set ordeal with accusers and accused lined up as kin groups on either side of the individual appellant, there are grounds for speculation about the intimidation of individual women through a process of divination using the *mwavi* substance. A case at Kasama was brought in 1910 by a woman who complained to the colonial authorities after a certain man had accused her of witchcraft and carried out two kinds of divination by ordeal. The woman complained not so much against the man's private administration of a *mwavi* divination as against his refusal to accept its authority in establishing her innocence.[31] In the Tanganyika District, a man was reported to have attempted to force mwavi upon his mother-in-law, who had refused to hand over her very young daughter even though bridewealth had been paid.[32]

It is no accident that so few cases involving *mwavi* were actually recorded at the turn of the century in Abercorn. From the discussion of the economic and social situation prevailing at that time, it should be evident that there was a very open society and considerable circulation of people within the district. In some ways, the options of people under pressure of public opinion or domestic conflict to seek refuge and appeal to a "neutral" judgment, or to an agent superior to indigenous officials, had not changed. People were preoccupied with a number of visible reasons for changing fortunes. The argument can therefore be made that the poison ordeal as a means of judgment was not only suppressed but also in abeyance for other reasons, among them the presence of many outsiders in the district, the fluidity that made flight from an unhappy situation relatively easy and explainable, and, lastly, the accessibility of a benign magistracy.

The Magistrate's Court

Considering the civil and criminal cases recorded at Abercorn in this period as a universe in themselves, it is evident that women usually but not always figured as complainants in civil cases and as victims in criminal cases. The material bespeaks social fluidity not only in institutional shifts but also in terms of movement to urban communities full of opportunities and opportunism.

Varied motives emerge as to why women abandoned the countryside and were attracted to these centers of new activity. John, a man of Nondo on the Kalambo River, for example, complained that his wife had run away with a Tongo from the ALC's boatworks at Chipwa. The first husband admitted that they had tired of one another, so the Nyasalander was ordered to pay six dotis of cloth in order to keep her.[33] Another woman left a husband at Kawimbe to live with a man employed at the Kasakalawe steamer camp merely because he "clothed her better." The court was not sympathetic and ordered her back to Kawimbe.[34] To a woman who had been married as a slave wife in Kauta, a Swahili settlement, Kawimbe was attractive as a self-conscious center of liberation from slavery. She sought divorce from her Nyamwezi husband, who managed to save the marriage by agreeing to move with her to Kawimbe.[35]

Further evidence of the court's determination to keep families together arose when a wife separated from her husband, complaining that he had abused her mother. In settling the case, Marshall ordered a substantial compensation of eleven yards of cloth to the wife and four yards to the mother-in-law and warned that a recurrence would oblige the court to concede to her desire for divorce.[36]

Because the courts were required to discourage slavery as an economic system, assertion of rights over wages of female dependents was not accepted before the magistrate. Two cases brought out the existence of such circumstances. In one, the wife of a capitao in one company ran away with a capitao in another, complaining among other things that her husband had retained the wages she earned while working for a European. The husband, by way of mitigation, stated that she had been given to him by the chief or Jumbe of Kota Kota and was thus a slave rather than a free wife. According to norms prevailing in his earlier experience, she had to work on whatever terms he set.[37]

Inheritance of children provided men with a chance to sell the labor of their dependents, as became evident in the second case, one of contested custody. When it became known that a man had sent his deceased brother's child out to work on the missionary plantation in Niamkolo, the court ordered her to be returned to her mother.[38] In certain other cases, custody of children was also taken from men and given to women and exploitation of pawns was curtailed, especially when it became apparent that pawn holders were known to marry off the girls for bridewealth amounting to twice the value of the original debt.[39]

The civil court cases obviously tend to reflect and treat the social elements that were already on the move, as opposed to the more stabilized and localized households and productive units. Within this category of mobilized persons, the court supported male prerogatives but considered also the condition of women. It appears to have facilitated a flow from ethnic to polyethnic communities, from "slavery" to "freedom" and toward what seemed more permissive or at least initially less adverse conditions.

If in some sense equity was served by the civil proceedings, the maintenance of order was foremost in the criminal cases. Another set of attitudes toward women is exposed in these annals of violence. Rape, enticement, sexual exploitation, and harassment come to the fore. It should be noted that women were by no means always innocent parties, and even received corporal punishment upon conviction. Disorderly or aggressive behavior could occur in rural as well as urban surroundings. That some of the women left behind in their home villages were not entirely resigned to their sexual isolation was exemplified in the court record. An old woman in the Isoko Valley complained that after her son had been seduced by the wife of an absent ALC employee, the offended husband returned home and destroyed grain and pots belonging to the mother. The husband and youth each received ten lashes and the wayward wife four.[40]

The isolation of other women was exploited. In a case of sexual assault by a forest guard in an area declared to be a reserve for steamer fuel, a woman searching for domestic firewood was threatened with other punishment if she did not submit.[41] Similarly, men in caravans in colonial service were reported to force themselves upon women in back villages. Colonial employees did not invent such situations. For decades there had been a delicate balance between hospitality and imposition on the services of women along commercial arteries. Local men were known to oscillate between the role of outraged husbands and kin and that of promoters of casual sex if not prostitution. Nevertheless, the magistrate meted out especially severe punishments to his retainers when they were discovered to be exploiting their official connections, disturbing the peace, or otherwise besmirching the reputation of the government.[42]

In the construction camps and villages near Abercorn there were cases of indecent assault and beatings of women for refusing sexual advances. The offenders were often Nyasalanders, adjuncts of colonial occupation who until 1901 supplied a considerable proportion of the regularly employed labor.[43] Less violent friction between men and women was reflected in complaints of insults and other abuse by male domestic servants, whose distance from home, bachelor frustrations, and performance of tasks usually assigned to women or slaves may have led to special sensitivity. Caution is needed in analyzing the status and behavior of male domestic workers, especially as an element of rivalry may have prompted reports by fellow townsmen to the nearby colonial officials. Confining the discussion to the record itself, the evidence, of the actions of only a few, must be taken to be indicative, not representative.[44]

For a variety of reasons, the Abercorn magistrate at the turn of the century kept order most directly in that part of society characterized by polyethnicity and emerging stratification. The pace of change declined after 1901, when economic activity subsided. The number of Nyasalanders was further reduced by the protectorate government's prohibition of migrant labor beyond Nyasaland.[45] Kinship could then be reasserted as a dominant idiom of social accountability; marriage became primarily negotiated between lineages and disputes were adjudicated within and between communities, rather than by a colonial magistrate. The scene was now being set for neotraditionalism and ethnicity. African male elders continued to fear female volition and action.

Even before the regularization of local courts with their assessors and experts in custom, the moment of inheritance was a critical one for a whole sphere of male interests. As the Abercorn records indicate, the inheritance of widows was sometimes less important than the continuing control of their children.[46] That the magistrate occasionally awarded custody of a child to another female relative rather than to a male petitioner gives some evidence that while male rights were generally upheld, the courtholders demonstrably exercised independent judgment in estimating the welfare of a child.[47]

Conclusion

At the turn of the century, an ideological and practical shift in social relations was under way. The pawning and enslavement of women that had become part of an economic and social condition by 1893 was much diminished. In the ensuing decade, with the mediation of the magistrate, a certain number of pawns and slaves were redeemed by their kinsmen and the practice of meeting debts with the transfer of women declined; chief-merchant control of bevies of women and their ability to redistribute them was undermined economically and politically. Male authority of a decentralized sort was enhanced as the ideology governing the transfer of women became more entrenched under lineage elders through their control of marriage. Women's risks and opportunities were lowered and their affairs became more withdrawn from public adjudication and the public record.

The records for the Abercorn magistracy became less copious and meticulous in 1903, as a superior territorial judiciary began to make its presence felt. The judge of the High Court of Northeastern Rhodesia, L. P. Beaufort, had been appointed on June 22, 1901, but he made his first circuit to Abercorn only two years later. In early June 1903, his hearing of two cases of murder and one of embezzlement symbolized a loss of autonomy for the Abercorn magistrate.[48] Marshall remained the principal official in the Tanganyika District until 1910. While still a magistrate, he became more fully a colonial functionary, no longer a colonial seigneur with an internally integrated, semiautonomous realm.[49] Judge Beaufort, on the other hand, represented the ongoing possibility that a British official, when he had direct responsibility for judgment, could appreciate the multiple values that might rule the law. His opinion in favor of giving a mother custody of her child is appended as a postscript to this chapter.

The colonial situation as it matured in the years after 1903 was one of increasing monotony and peripheralization. The days of large caravans and raucous construction camps were past. The steamers that had been constructed at the south end of Lake Tanganyika no longer called there very frequently and commerce languished. Local men became more and more engaged in migrancy to distant places to the south or to the sisal estates of German East Africa. Local quiescence, I argue, provided an environment in which kinship ideology of control over women became more pervasive. Migrant male laborers demanded normalization of the rules that would govern their marriages when they returned with bridewealth. No doubt the marriage price and other conditions changed, but individual earnings signaled altogether different power considerations than had prevailed in the period before 1897.

The Abercorn records may be unusual in their intimacy, immediacy, and evidence of an epochal transition. Social processes are not invariably so well illustrated by court and court holders' records. Nevertheless, two overall conclusions are warranted: first, that court records ought to be sought out, and second, that like many other kinds of oral or documentary sources, they will not volunteer answers. Interpretation of the court records requires systematic attention to the historical and contemporary social, economic, and political contexts in which the disputants and the court itself were lodged.

Postscript

Very few cases from the realm of African family law reached the High Court of Northeastern Rhodesia, where civil cases usually concerned commercial and property relationships between colonial elements. The judgment reproduced here is also exceptional for its explicit sympathy for a mother, the respondent, who sought to retain custody of her child. In placing this case in context, it should be noted that the justice, L. P. Beaufort, had been appointed as the first incumbent when the High Court for Northeastern Rhodesia was established in 1902. His duties included reviewing cases in all the magistrates' courts, guiding them on the management of their jurisdictions, and hearing appeals.

In the case of Tongasi vs. Paulos, the domestic situation was not unusual. Both had been slaves of a common master to whom Paulos had paid bridewealth. Later, with the advent of colonial authorities, Paulos returned to his homeland in northern Nyasaland, married, took employment with a white farmer, and became a Christian. He subsequently returned to his former master's place, which lay in Northeastern Rhodesia, to claim his child by Tongasi. The dispute was settled by the local magistrate in favor of the mother and appealed by the father to the High Court. He had the backing of his employer, who persuaded the Dutch Reformed missionary, Pauw, to act as an advocate. Tongasi was represented by Mr. Tagart, a lawyer in Fort Jameson.

By 1910, when this judgment was rendered, Judge Beaufort was well experienced in a spectrum of judicial matters and possessed enough leisure and interest to indulge in jurisprudence. His successive consideration of English law, native law, and Christian principles displays a degree of intellectual playfulness. Beyond his manifest dislike of the judgmentalism of missionaries, there seems also to be a protective attitude toward an ill-used woman and her child, who belonged to the area of the court's jurisdiction, whereas the appellant was an "alien" Nyasalander.

Judgment in the High Court of Northeastern Rhodesia Rendered by L. P. Beaufort, dated January 5, 1910*

I reserved Judgement in this case on 25th November as I felt some doubt and difficulty — especially in the matter of Native Law or Custom, on which both Mr. Pauw and Mr. Tagart addressed the Court but on which neither of them offered any evidence. I have, however, made such enquiries as I could in the interval. The High Court has the Power under the High Court Procedure Regulations of deciding as to the custody of all children but in the case of native children it should have due regard to Native Law. Order-in-Council Sections 21(1) and (20) and Section 35.

By the Common Law of England a mother's rights were simply non-existent till recent times, when by Statute she was allowed to have the custody of her child up to 7 years, and later still up to 16 years, in cases of separation and Divorce. I emphasize separation or Divorce — for the English Law was founded on Matrimony; on the other hand, in case of intercourse of unmarried or irregularly married persons, it was the male procreator who was simply ignored: except in that he was made to support the child he had contributed to bring into the World. The only exception in favour of the Husband under the Statute relating to Divorce was when the wife had been guilty of misconduct.

Now judging this case by English Law, it has been proved that this woman has been guilty of misconduct of a sort, that is to say, that she did — when living separate from her husband Paulos — somewhat incontinently take another husband. But I am satisfied that this should not deprive her of any right she might otherwise have as I am quite satisfied by the evidence that he deliberately and of set purpose conduced by his own conduct to her so called

---

*High Court Civil Case Book. ZNA BSI.

misconduct: that he hoped to get rid of her, that he left her inadequately provided for, that he left her intending her to be tempted and to succumb, and that he entrapped her into what he now unctuously calls "Sin."

Again in English Law the Judge always had a wide discretion to be exercised on consideration of the moral or material advancement of the child. Here I have no means of deciding that either parent presents any great degree of either moral or material superiority over the other.

The conclusion I arrive at therefore is that, if English Law alone was considered, the question would be decided simply with a view to the child's welfare.

Now I am advised that by Native Law the children generally belong to the father, the real result of which is, that the father annexes any increment arising from them. This is natural. It follows from his views of the status of a wife — a cook, gardener, drudge, slave and concubine in one. But even natives presuppose that the husband and wife combine to be such — except in the case of formal and consensual separation. And when I suggested in conversation with natives the case of separation coming from one side only — a mere abandonment for no special reason except that a man or woman was tired of his or her partner — I was informed that a separation without adequate reason is absolutely unheard of, inconceivable. I consider that the facts of the case show such a wholly one-sided separation on the part of the man Paulos, that the ordinary presumption of the law and custom in favour of his rights is quite rebutted — that he has no right superior to that of the woman. By Native Law therefore I find that she is entitled to the custody.

Now, is this a decision of Native Law repugnant (in the words of Section 35 of the Order-in-Council) to natural justice or morality — to any Order-in-Council or to any Regulation? There is no Order-in-Council or Regulation dealing with it. What of natural justice and morality?

Here is an Atonga, from Nyasaland, with an Atonga woman

in Nyasaland as his senior wife, who comes to work here, and while here provides himself at some small expenditure — with a native woman of this country as drudge, cook and concubine. She bears the child as a result of such intercourse. He tires of her and — regardless of his obligations to support her — adopts such a course of conduct that she thinks she is free to ally herself with another protector, and then he claims the offspring. He abandons the woman in the name of religion and actually finds white men, of undoubtedly high religious and moral standard, to support his claim and to ask the approval of the court to conduct at once heartless, sensual and selfish on the grounds that it is done with a good motive, as a necessary preliminary to becoming a Christian. He is an industrious respectable native: he is still sufficiently pagan to be allowed much latitude, he is not sufficiently Christianized to be too rigidly judged. He must become Christian at any cost — though a grave wrong is done to one or more unoffending women. The fact that he gets rid of the woman he is tired of, and obtains a child he will someday make money from, is a mere accident. I reprobate most strongly the idea that the first step in Christianity is to do an act cruel, selfish, and immoral: that is wholly contrary to my ideas of Our Lord's teaching. I know I am at issue here with not only the Dutch Reformed Church, but with the Universities Mission of the Church of England and very likely with other missionaries from David Livingstone downwards.

But our Great Teacher taught that one should do unto others as we would be done by. And I follow that rather than the teaching of modern divinity — that a man cannot be at once a Christian and a bigamist. The status of the woman, her rights and claims, are already sufficiently lightly esteemed among natives without invoking Christianity to give it the further blow of holding that the salvation of one man is to be procured at the price of cruelty to several women. I find morality and justice approve the decision founded on Native Law. If natives come here from other countries and form alliances with natives of this country, it is done either with a view of abandoning the woman when tired of her — in which case the man will meet with no sympathy here; or it is done with a view to settling in this country, in or near the wife's village, and making themselves a permanent home there. The alliance of Paulos with the woman was of the former sort, and I order the child to be handed over to its lawful mother by the father, who has dealt unfairly with her by native custom and has no claim by English Law.

Notes

1 H. C. Marshall, "Notes on the Bemba" (1910), in the Marshall Papers, National Museum, Livingstone, Zambia. See also M. Chanock, "Neo-traditionalism and the Customary Law in Malawi," *African Law Studies* 16 (1978), 80, and "Making Customary Law," in *African Women and the Law,* eds. M. J. Hay and M. Wright (Boston, 1982).

2 While the political administration of Northeastern Rhodesia was taken directly in hand in 1895 by the British South Africa Company and thereafter became more and more autonomous from the British Central African Protectorate (Nyasaland), the judicial hierarchy continued to be subject to the judicial oversight of the governor of Nyasaland.

3 M. Wright and P. H. Lary, "Swahili Settlements in Northern Zambia and Malawi," *IJAHS* 4, no. 3 (1971), 564.

4 The White Fathers at their newly founded Mambwe station discovered and introduced sanctions against the appeal to the poison ordeal. Mambwe Diary, 18 October 1891, APB.

5 See Mama Meli' story, p. 91 ff. above for an African account; see also A. D. Roberts, *History of the Bemba* (Madison, 1973), 246 ff.

6 Roberts provides a photograph of Marshall and the Abercorn constabulary, 1893, opposite page 223 in *History of the Bemba.*

7 The principal sources cited here are the two letter books, Zambian National Archives (hereafter ZNA) vol. 1 (BSI 145), covering the period 11 May to 8 June 1899 and vol. 2 (BSI 146) 24 September

1900 to 1 October 1903. The court record book (BSI 144) runs from 20 February 1897 to 13 January 1903 and contains 127 numbered cases and added notes on arbitration. On the title page of the court book Marshall noted: "Besides imprisonment recorded, many minor cases have been summarily dealt with and in many cases of disputes I have acted as arbitrator."

8 Dr. Blair Watson, the magistrate-collector of Mweru District, 1893–1903, figures more prominently in this genre. See "Robert (Bobo) Young Relates his Exploits," *Northern Rhodesia Journal* 2, no. 2 (1953): 65-71 and I. M. Graham, "A Quarrel at Lake Mweru, 1896–1897," *Northern Rhodesia Journal* 4 (1959–1961), 552.

9 I am especially indebted to Moses Sikazwe, court president at Mbala in 1972, for generously sharing his knowledge.

10 An early report is contained in the White Fathers' *Chronique trimestrielle* 59 (1893). The incident took place near the Mambwe mission about the end of November 1892.

11 Marshall to Native Commissioner, Mporokoso, 4 March 1901. ZNA: BSI 146.

12 Report upon the Rubber Industry, 31 December 1900. ZNA: BSI 146.

13 General report for the year ending 30 September 1900. ZNA: BSI 146.

14 Marshall to Native Commissioner, Kalungwizi, 19 December 1902. ZNA: BSI 146.

15 Marshall to ALC Agent, Kitua, 11 April 1901. ZNA: BSI 146.

16 Marshall to Grier, 1 March 1900. ZNA: BSI 146.

17 Marshall to Robertson, 5 September 1901. See also Johnstone to P.W. Jones, Niamkolo, 15 August 1899. ZNA: BSI 146.

18 Marshall to Father Superior, Kayambi, 17 April 1901, and Marshall to [Magistrate], Kasama, 7 May 1901. ZNA: BSI 146.

19 Case 40, 1 December 1899. ZNA: BSI 144.

20 This economic leveling of chiefs and the attendant revaluing of women merits further research.

21 Note, 18 June 1902. ZNA: BSI 144.

22 Case 60, 24 June 1900, with note of letter from Johnstone at Mporokoso to Marshall, 1 August 1900. ZNA: BSI 144.

23 General report for the year ending 30 September 1900. ZNA: BSI 146.

24 A range of empirical and analytical literature has been surveyed in the process of arriving at the generalizations offered here. The background work is contained in M. Wright, "The Poison Ordeal: An Historical Essay," a paper presented at the University of California at Los Angeles, 1973. Marshall also took the line that the mwavi ordeal was a mechanism of appeal not only in cases of alleged witchcraft. Marshall to Robertson (Kawimbe), 5 September 1901. ZNA: BSI 146.

25 Case 54, 5 April 1900. ZNA: BSI 144.

26 Case 54, 4 April 1900. ZNA: BSI 144.

27 Note, 12 November 1900. ZNA: BSI 144.

28 Donald Siwale, interview, 19 February 1972. See also J. A. Chisholm, "Notes on the Manners and Customs of the Winamwanga and Wiwa," *Journal of the Royal African Society* 9, no. 36 (1911).

29 Evidence heard, 16 July 1900. ZNA BSI 92. For Marshall's attitude toward Mkoma, see his letter to Neu Langenburg District governor (German East Africa), 27 August 1906. ZNA: BSI.

30 White Fathers, Mambwe Diary, 19 October 1891. APB.

31 "The defendant. . . accused the plaintiff of being a witch because his betrothed wife became sick and died. He prepared Mwavi and compelled her to go with him to the place where he had got it ready and she said: — 'If I have killed your wife let it boil over towards the West.' The water boiled over towards the East and thus established her innocence. Not being satisfied he went out to apply the 'hunting test.' He returned having killed a female Mpombo which again established her innocence. The plaintiff was angry at the defendant having treated her as a witch and applying two tests to her. . ." Case 15, 1910. ZNA: KDH 1.

32 Case 51, 9 March 1900. ZNA: BSI 144.

33 Case 34, 28 August 1899. ZNA: BSI 144.

34 Case 69, 17 October 1900. ZNA: BSI 144.

35 Case 37, 29 November 1899. ZNA: BSI 144.

36 Case 71, 15 November 1900. ZNA: BSI 144.

37 Case 84, 17 February 1901. ZNA: BSI 144.

38 Case 96, 4 February 1902. ZNA: BSI 144.

39 Unnumbered, 9 April 1900. ZNA: BSI 144.

40 Case 59, 17 May 1900. ZNA: BSI 144.

41 Case 72, 16 November 1900. ZNA: BSI 144.

42 Evidence from Sumbu is particularly strong on this situation. Cases 6 May 1902, 2 June 1902, and 10 July 1902. Sumbu Case Book. ZNA: BSI 151.

43 For assault on a woman, a policeman received five years' imprisonment and fifteen lashes monthly for the first year. Case 29, 26 July 1901. ZNA: BSI 144.

44 Case 57, 28 April 1900, Case 58, 29 April 1900, Case 104, 17 April 1902. ZNA: BSI 144.

45 Marshall to Native Commissioner, Mporokoso, 11 February 1901. ZNA: BSI 146.

46 Case 39, 3 December 1899, and Note, 1 November 1902. ZNA: BSI 144.

47 Case 70, 30 October 1900. ZNA: BSI 144.

48 High Court Record Book f4/2. ZNA: BSI 146.

49 Marshall's attitude toward the people of the district remained consistent within the limits of his power, as was evident during his 1906 visit to Kayambi mission. Before arriving there, he had already excused certain communities in the vicinity from their annual tax because famine prevailed.

SEVEN

Bwanikwa: Consciousness and Protest Among Slave Women in Central Africa, 1886–1911

This study necessarily begins with a survey of missionary, administrative, and African male interactions and ideologies, but its premise is that we can reconstruct the experience of slave women only by seeking out the most direct and immediate evidence possible for the actions and words of women themselves. Only in that way can we hope to get nearer to the consciousness of African women and to their perception of "slave" and "free" status.[1] Hence I draw heavily on the autobiography of one particular woman, Bwanikwa, and also upon the testimony given by women in early colonial court cases. These statements make it clear that whatever white and black men may have thought about the leniency of female "domestic" servitude, women felt themselves to be slaves in the fullest sense and did everything they could to emancipate themselves.

Clarification of two theoretical assumptions, however, is in order. The first concerns lineage as a focus of history. The second has to do with the classification of the social environment and the merits of recognizing precolonial quasi-urbanism. Elsewhere I have argued that in East Central Africa it was colonialism that raised lineage to dominance as a staple of local politics. The commercial conditions of the late nineteenth century gave power to chiefs and merchants whose wealth allowed them to control unrelated people.[2] Slave women usually belonged as property to a man, although they were occasionally assigned to serve and were

151

sometimes effectively owned by other women. Kinship was an important part of the repertoire of male strategies, but women, given a vigorous trade in which slaves were valuable commodities, were assets of a new order and were no longer exchanged merely in marriage. The women who became pawns or slaves had no recourse to kin and were not lineage-controlled. From the point of view of production and exchange relations, the difference is that between a sphere of influence achieved by merchant capital on the one hand and colonial merchant/industrial capital on the other. The latter restructured the lineage and ethnic community that the former had destructured. The commercial milieu of the late nineteenth century in Central Africa spawned quasi-urban conditions at places where large fluctuating populations were fed, housed, and otherwise serviced. The society of such communities may be called polyethnic and heterogeneous. In some ways they anticipated modern towns, not least in requiring individual agility in forming and reforming relationships.[3] Slavery in such circumstances, then, was a feature of a relatively "open" society.

Western Images of Female Status

"Add slavery to polygamy, and reduce a woman to the status of a slave, then you have the sum of human degradation, the lowest creature on God's earth—a slave woman."[4] With these aggressive words in a missionary pamphlet published in 1916, Dugald Campbell appealed to British women to join in the work of Christianizing Central Africa. He counted upon the circle of mission subscribers for support, even though humanitarian and antislavery sentiment was generally diminished in colonial and metropolitan circles in general. His genuine alliance with Christian women of the Luapula-Katanga region of northern Rhodesia and Zaire had placed him well to put forward their case. The figure around whom he built his appeal, Bwanikwa, is also the focus of the present paper, which looks into the changing historical circumstances of unfree women in the period from 1880 to 1911. The time was one of commercial transformation interrupted by colonial intervention with its institution of courts and specific mandates to abolish slavery on the one hand, and its concurrent measures of economic reorientation on the other. Myriad cross-currents of ideology, economic reconstruction, and social control complicate the critical exercise of extracting material about women's slavery and consciousness, but only by such an effort can we enlarge the compass of social history in treating this important transitional period.

For Western observers and activists in matrilineal Central Africa in the early colonial period, there were important social conditions and institutions seemingly more deeply rooted than slavery that required correction. Missionaries and officials represented different interests, however, and consequently diverged in their visions of a desirable social order. The officials by 1911 had struck alliances with male chiefs and elders. H. C. Marshall, the magistrate of the Tanganyika District, concluded that the colonial courts had been too favorable to women and the "excessive liberties" of Bemba women should be curbed. He reported further:

> Quite recently Chief Mporokoso, after touring his villages, told me that the women of the country were growing out of hand, and that the results were becoming apparent in a decrease in the birth-rate.

> The character of the Wemba Woman must be borne in mind. . . . Always notably independent—always more or less of a shrew—prone to unfaithfulness—she is now taking advantage of two central facts; firstly that the laws of the country are in her favour, and secondly that, with the present unprecedented influx of wealth, the taking of a lover is an easy and a profitable pastime.[5]

Junior wives in matrilineal societies, Marshall saw, had few structural sanctions preventing their marital separation, for ritual obligations were performed by the senior wife, and the bridewealth at stake for the junior wives was very slight. Through a delegation of judicial authority to local African authorities, Marshall hoped to stabilize polygamous families and diminish anxiety on the part of husbands and elders. Local courts indeed became the instrument for imposing norms and customs in the interests of senior males, and with their effective monopoly of law at the family level, complaints about female slavery and exploitation ceased to be a matter of judicial record.[6]

Central to the missionary ideal of social order was the monogamous, patriarchal family. An editorial in the Plymouth Brethren's journal underscored the distance between such a notion of family and the prevailing matrilineal conditions:

> In Central Africa, socialism, polygamy, and the law of "mother right" deprives the father of all authority over his own children, and places them under the control of their mother's oldest brother, living probably in some other part of the country. All this makes it difficult. . . to apply New Testament injunctions to "fathers," "mothers," "husbands," "wives," "parents," and "children" in the family. Until there is some semblance of family life produced as a result of gospel teaching, it is out of the question to rush in to the third or church circle.[7]

African society, too, had its ideals. The first missionary in Garenganze, F. S. Arnot, reported the popular conviction that slavery was impermanent, dissolving by the third or fourth generation as full kinship rights were resumed.[8] Indeed, women could be more quickly absorbed because of a persistent ambiguity as to their status and functions. Performing typical female roles alongside free but nevertheless dependent women of a household, their servitude was less explicitly coerced than that of male slaves. The contemporary Dutch scholar of slavery, H. J. Nieboer, made a universal statement about the origins of slavery that carried considerable truth in the Central African situation. When there are no laborers in the modern sense of proletarians, he wrote, and "a man wants others to perform the necessary drudgery for him, and cannot impose it upon his wife, or wives, or other female dependents. . . he must compel other men to serve him; and this compulsion will often assume the form of slavery."[9] A slave, by this definition, was a male forced to do the labor that women would otherwise do. The practical distinction between the rights of slaves and of free women was so comparatively small that almost all definitions have presumed that slaves were male.[10]

To the official mind of the times, as represented by H. C. Marshall, "actual slavery"—hard, menial labor and the lack of inheritance rights—was a condition of men, on the whole, while domestic slavery of "people of the harem," mostly women, was not onerous.[11] By 1911, the older mode of control by chiefs over bevies of women was disintegrating and everyone knew that purchase of slaves had been effectively terminated; the anti-slavery chapter of colonial intervention was officially closed. Domestic slaves and servile women became less visible in all parts of the colonial record as World War I neared. Even though women were prominent parishioners, specific references to them as persons faded in the narratives and ethnographies produced by missionaries in the interwar period, and earlier material reprocessed at this time became more and more static.[12]

While norms and ideologies must be appraised continually, it is not promises of emancipation or reincorporation that are at issue, but rather the actuality of conditions obtaining for the first- and second-generation slaves—female slaves for the purpose of this discussion—within a particular time frame. For the generation in the decades before 1911, it can be shown that women were slaves in a genuine sense, and conscious of their status. Furthermore, they acted wittingly to emancipate themselves.

Bwanikwa's Life

Bwanikwa lived between the early 1870s and the late 1920s in the present-day Shaba of Zaire and Luapula Province of Zambia. Her autobiography was narrated in a Luba dialect and translated into English by Campbell, who arrived in Katanga in 1892 as a missionary of the Plymouth Brethren and met Bwanikwa for the first time about 1895. After 1898, as an adherent, temporary employee, and self-supporting church and community activist, she was an intimate of the Campbell family. The text of the autobiography, published as an appendix to Campbell's book, *Blazing Trails in Bantuland,* covers only the time of her enslavement, about two-thirds of Bwanikwa's life. To retrieve something of her later years, it is necessary to draw upon statements mediated by the missionary.

For our purposes, the autobiography has been segmented to allow for a commentary upon the several phases of time, place, and circumstance that mark it.[13] The initial phase occurred in Garenganze, an African state ruled by Msiri (Msidi in some accounts) until his death in December 1891. An intermediate phase, of the greatest insecurity for Bwanikwa, coincided with the establishment of control by the Congo Free State in the 1890s. During the last phase, after the turn of the century, she moved across the Luapula River with the missionaries to Northeastern Rhodesia. In the course of these three phases, Bwanikwa underwent a process of absorption into a household as a slave concubine; then became an uprooted person being subject to sale, making escapes, and seeking protection at heavy cost; and finally succeeded in establishing for herself a strong position within a Christian community. Successive political environments shaped her options, as did changing socioeconomic conditions, but in interpreting her story we must take special care also to consider age-specific aspects of status within the female life cycle of pre-adolescence, fertility, and postfertility.

Garenganze

The story has often been told of how Msiri came as a Nyamwezi trader to Katanga, established relations with the Sanga chiefs, dominated the salt and copper source areas, and superseded the Kazembes as the overlord of an area from the Lualaba in the west to the Luapula in the east.[14] In 1886, he was at the peak of his career, having made Garenganze in general and Bunkeya in particular a hub of commerce. The Nyamwezi element in the ruling group were known as Yeke. While Msiri attracted to him a number of Yeke who served various functions in the state, he also had to contend with unincorporated Nyamwezi-Swahili settlements on his domain's periphery, which had the capacity to obstruct the flow of traffic. Similarly, disturbances by the Luvale or Lunda to the west could block caravans. The Bihean group among the Ovimbundu were reliable commercial allies at the time of Arnot's journeys, and he and other missionaries reported in detail on their approaches from the Angolan coast.[15] The most active frontier of Garenganze lay in the north, where the Luba were continuously raided, tested, and treated as a source of slaves.

Administratively, Garenganze was a tribute-gathering state with personal representatives of the ruler residing in various districts. These representatives were male and female relatives or wives, women who had usually been married as a result of diplomatic exchange with a lesser ruler. The Yeke and Swahili were patrilineal in most respects, although some strata of the Nyamwezi practiced modified matrilineal succession. In super-imposing his rule over the matrilineal groups in Garenganze, Msiri drew legitimacy by taking noble wives. To a certain extent, these women were hostages who could become powerful functionaries if they proved their loyalty and effectiveness. Msiri enlarged his circle of power by using not only kinship and marriage but also investiture. Chiefs of indigenous communities sought and paid well for gradual promotions as officers of the state.[16]

Economically, the state rested upon tribute in food gathered after the harvest; monopolies of ivory, copper, and salt; and private enterprise in slave trading.[17] Warriors sent to the frontiers on punitive expeditions were allowed to retain their captives and sell them at will. By extension, all slave owners in Garenganze had the right to buy and sell slaves without regulation. Ivory, on the other hand, was subject to the most rigorous control through a system of surveillance over its movements, from the departure of a hunting party through every step of delivery and marketing.[18] Msiri monopolized all ivory, in contrast to the one-tusk royalty generally expected by Central African rulers.

The capital of Garenganze, Bunkeya, lay in a large basin plain over which were spread many discrete settlements. According to estimates by an early Belgian administrator, there were forty-two villages with a total population of some 25,000 people.[19] Msiri's principal wives presided over large communities composed in part of female slaves assigned them by the ruler, who retained ultimate ownership. These women formed the backbone of the agricultural labor force. During the critical periods of the agricultural cycle, the labor force was augmented by teams of men whom Msiri and his principal lieutenants personally supervised.[20] Bunkeya's over-riding function was to generate and store surpluses of food to see its fluctuating population through the long dry season and to provision caravans.

Demographically, Bunkeya was like a port town with its own farms forming a peri-urban complex. The stable resident population was overwhelmingly female. Arnot complained about both the extent of polygamy and the ease of divorce.[21] The frequent comings and goings of caravans and military expeditions offered opportunities to rearrange sexual partnerships. Amidst this free-wheeling social environment, Msiri held an open court in which anyone could state his or her case. Arnot observed that large numbers of women attended the court and constituted most of the throng on major public occasions. He also drew attention to the unusual tenor of the judicial system: "The rights and privileges given to women. . . form one of the remarkable features of Msidi's government. Women are allowed to attend the courts, and to have a voice equally with the men, and Msidi succeeds pretty well in dispensing equal justice."[22]

Because slaves were not a focus of state appropriation, they could be treated with a degree of dispassionate justice and pater-nalism by Msiri. The case of a young slave girl who ran away from her mistress after a severe beating, then traveled more than six miles by night in order to throw herself on the mercy of the ruler may be exceptional. Still, it demonstrates how Msiri could accept a refugee and arrange to place her under more benevolent custody, simultaneously reinforcing his relationship with a client, the girl's new guardian, who in this instance proved to be Arnot himself.[23]

The heyday of Garenganze encompassed both Bwanikwa's enslavement as a small girl and her life as a young woman in the Yeke community. Her narrative is as follows:

I, Bwanikwa, was born on the banks of the Dindie, a small river in Lubaland. Our part of the country was thickly populated, and our principal chief was Goi-Mani. My father's name was Kankolwe. My mother was called Mikomba. I was one of a family of five. Our only brother had died; four girls remained, of whom I was the second oldest.

My father had a dozen wives. His head-wife was the daughter of chief Katumba. She was an important woman. At the time I refer to, the head-wife had just died. According to Luban custom [my father] was mulcted for death dues. He was ordered to pay three slaves, as compensation for his wife's death, and to ensure inheritance by the dead wife's sister. They did not produce a sister to take the dead woman's place till the death has been paid for to the relatives. Three slaves were demanded, and my father could only raise two.

One of his four daughters had to be handed over to make a third, and I was chosen. I was the second oldest, as I said, and my father loved me. When he handed me over to my master, he said to him as we parted: "Be kind to my little daughter; do not sell her to anyone else, and I will come and redeem her." As my father was unable to redeem me, I was left in slavery.

My father did not come to redeem me, and my master sold me to some of Msidi's people who were out man-hunting. I was sold for a packet of gun-powder, worth two shillings and sixpence, and was taken to Chifuntwe's village in the Balomotwa country. At that time I was small, unable to walk.

It appears that my master had, at this time, offended the principal chief, and was ordered to pay up several slaves. Amongst those slaves given to pay for my master's crimes, I was handed over. Thus I was sold again. The chief to whom I was given in payment of a fine, handed me to one of his warriors as wife, saying, "Take her as your wife, she's young." After a while he said "She's only a young girl, and I don't want her." He sold me to a man named Mukoka for a gun. Mukoka bought me, with another woman and child, intending to sell us later to the Biheans. He took me as his wife. I bore him a child which only lived three days. His other wives were kind to me. Though he sold many other slaves to Biheans, he never sold me, nor did he threaten to do so.[24]

Congo Free State, 1890-1899

Msiri was killed on December 28, 1891, by an officer of the Congo Free State (CFS) forces. Bunkeya was immediately abandoned by virtually all its inhabitants, including Bwanikwa, and became a place of military encampment. The depredations of the CFS soldiery together with the sudden removal of the dominant political figure and protector, Msiri, called into question the durability of Garenganze and social relations as they had prevailed. The moment of "conquest" must be seen in perspective, however, for the period of deterioration did not begin in December 1891. Over the preceding two years, there had been a crisis in Bunkeya, the milieu being affected by Msiri's illnesses, irregularities in supply of arms and powder, visits by rival agents of the British South Africa Company and the Congo Free State, and rebellion by tributary Sanga leaders whose alliance had been a cornerstone of the Garenganze "empire."

An increasingly irascible Msiri suspected his principal Sanga wife of disloyalty as early as 1888.[25] Charges against her and her son were then dropped as an act of grace, but in 1889 she was executed for complicity in the death of Msiri's important governor who had controlled the western approaches to the state. The Sanga took this act as a cause of war. They began to harass Msiri with guerrilla tactics, burning granaries and houses in night attacks. An atmosphere of insecurity prevailed throughout Bunkeya, but Msiri endured the incursions quietly, until fresh supplies of powder could be secured.[26]

Many other factors damaged the integrity of Garenganze at

this time. The single word that best describes Bunkeya in 1890, 1891, and 1892 is hunger. Food production, distribution, and storage failed for a variety of reasons. Msiri was no longer healthy or secure enough to lead his men into the fields, reserves were destroyed by Sanga actions, and postharvest tribute was hardly forthcoming. Insecurity and withdrawal of labor from cultivation in the Bunkeya valley were paralleled by a shortage of rain. During the long dry seasons of 1890 and 1891, the situation was desperate, and the foulness of what little water was available drove away the missionaries as well as large numbers of the inhabitants. New settlements were made in more mountainous, defensible areas and in well-watered river valleys. Msiri himself contemplated moving, but delayed in order to show that he would not "run away" under Sanga pressure.[27]

The CFS representatives had established an outpost on the Lufoi River, to the east of Bunkeya, in 1890. The missionaries chose a station site nearby in order to enjoy the umbrella of civilization it supposedly extended. Then, after the death of Msiri and the final dispersal from Bunkeya, many people sought refuge with the missionaries. The Free State presence, meanwhile, did not ease matters. Famine affected the colonial forces as it did other people. A new tributary system was difficult to install given such depleted reserves and political anarchy. In 1893, locusts further damaged the crops and prospects for a speedy reconstruction. The missionaries began to distance themselves from the CFS authorities and were physically estranged from 1894 to 1896, during which time they abandoned Lufoi and moved eastward to set up a new network of stations,[28] gathering large followings of people dislocated from the shattered Bunkeya complex. Perhaps the most extreme example of this phenomenon was Luanza. Luanza (known at first as Chipongo), on the west side of Lake Mweru, was in a zone that had been peripheral to Msiri's state. As Campbell described it,

Luanza... developed into a hiding place for the riff-raff of Katanga. The flotsam and jetsam of Msidi's old, and now extinct, kingdom drifted in, and a new start was made. Murderers, too, made it a city of refuge; Arabs, fleeing for their lives from the avenging Belgians, halted, or hid in Luanza's rabbit warrens; and slavers, escaping from State prisons where they were undergoing terms of imprisonment for their misdeeds, headed for Luanza.[29]

As Campbell's account suggests, the Congo Free State engaged in campaigns against the old trading elements, both Swahili and Ovimbundu. They had also to contend with ongoing Sanga resistance and a major rebellion by their own soldiery.

After a two-year absence, the missionaries returned to the Lufira Valley in central Garenganze, where Msiri's successor was beginning to reestablish a capital. They were given a large public reception by the Yeke and a warm welcome by the Belgians.[30] The fertile Lufira Valley was under extensive cultivation, and the stage was being set for a restoration of the Yeke dynasty as rulers of a dependent African state. Political rewards for supplying auxiliaries were reaped after a number of actions, but never so fully as when the Sanga offered overt resistance and were finally defeated by a combined CFS-Yeke force in 1899.[31]

So it was that the Garenganze oligarchy retrieved a position of importance and became administratively integrated into the unfolding colonial regime in Katanga. The missionaries, soon after the restoration was complete, developed a nostalgia for the old days: the past slavings and excesses of the Muslims and Biheans, who had been the major armed aliens in the region, paled in comparison to the CFS's cruel exercise of its monopolies of rubber and ivory as well as its military license.[32]

That a settled civil administration in the Congo Free State did not exist in Katanga at the turn of the century is confirmed by the memoirs of Verdick, the principal official. Antislavery quickly vanished from the rhetoric and practice of the regime once its commercial rivals had been defeated. Much exchanging of slaves went on in Katanga without official concern except when the peace was disturbed, as for example by quarrels over the price of a slave woman, which could prompt the administrator to lock up a whole party of Biheans.[33] The colonial courts to the east of the Luapula River and Lake Mweru, in Northeastern Rhodesia, by contrast, did slowly become places of appeal by slaves. But before 1899, when Kazembe capitulated, the Kalungwishi-Luapula area was also one of minimal colonial control. Much escaped the attention of officials at all times, and certainly the collector at Kalungwishi, newly appointed in 1893, was not able to concern himself with every skirmish in the commercial and social sphere, especially when transient Congo natives were concerned.[34] His messengers and police might exploit the threat of his intervention in order to obtain a bribe, but a woman without a male advocate or economic resources would have found it virtually impossible to be noticed judicially.

Bwanikwa's life from 1892 to 1898 reflected the many uncertainties and efforts at reconstruction that marked the initial colonial years both to the west and east of the Luapula River and Lake Mweru:

> I lived with Mukoka till Msidi's death and the break up of his power by the Europeans. At this some of us slaves saw our chance, and fled. We scattered. Men, tired of Msidi's despotic rule, would take some or other woman slave, and both would head north, south, east, or west, in search of freedom and a new start in life. When possible, each headed for the old homestead.
>
> A well-known elephant hunter and fellow-slave in the same village, whose name was Kabongo, took me, and we ran off east. Our old master set out in search of a new home and village site. We crossed the Luapula River to Kazembe's to try and begin life anew. Chief Kazembe cast his eyes upon me, and asked Kabongo to give me to him for a wife. Kabongo refused. We left Kazembe's capital, came back west, and settled in Sakungami village. We lived and cultivated there for two years. Some slaves heard of our old master having built at the Luisi River, and suggested our returning together.

My husband refused at first, but afterwards agreed to join the party.

When Chief Mukoka saw me come back, he said, "My wife's come back." On hearing this, Kabongo was angry, and said, "No, I won't let you take her from me; she's my wife." Thus the altercation grew, and they almost came to blows.

Kabongo had killed a bull elephant, and intended to give the tusks to the chief. However, owing to Mukoka taking me from him, he hid his ivory in the forest, and threatened to kill some of Mukoka's people in revenge. Mukoka was afraid of Kabongo's threats, and sold me to a band of West Coast slavers who had just turned up. Said he, "If I'm not going to have her, neither shall he." He sold me to the Biheans, and I started, a slave bound for the West Coast. Immediately I left, Mukoka caught Kabongo and killed him.

On the road west I took refuge with Inansala, Msidi's sister, who hid me in one of her houses. Shortly after, she was caught and eaten by a lion. On account of her death I was afraid, came out of hiding, and traveled to the mission station. At this time I had never heard the Gospel, and was very ignorant.

I met a man named Wafwilwa, who, seeing me alone, asked me to be his wife. I refused at first, but he persisted, and would not leave me. I had need of a protector, so I finally gave in and became his wife. We lived near to the mission at Lufoi. Wafwilwa, with two others, was sent to build a mission house on Lake Mweru. We women accompanied them there. On arrival he was sent to the Government Post Office with mission letters, and Wafwilwa insisted on my going with him. His reason for my going soon appeared.

On arrival at Kalunguisi, in British territory, he sold me secretly to some Arabs for calico. I overheard whispered conversation among the Arab traders. Said one of them, "She's very pretty" *[Mzuri sana]*. I became suspicious, and said to them "Who is pretty?" "Oh," they said, "we're just talking." Then I heard someone say, "She's the slave they're buying." I became afraid and began to cry. Shortly afterwards the Arabs came to me and said, "You're our slave now. Go into the house and sleep; it's night." Then I knew I had been sold again. I refused to enter the house, but my refusals were met by force.

I was pushed inside the house, and a woman kept guard over me. Wooden bars were put across the doors to prevent my escape. The woman was soon fast asleep, while I kept awake. I got up in the middle of the night, removed the bars, and, getting out, ran to the soldiers' headquarters in the government location. I hid there. In the morning the Arabs, finding their had slave escaped, went to Wafwilwa and made him disgorge his ill-gotten gains.

The soldiers threatened to report the matter to the magistrate, but Wafwilwa paid them up, and begged them to say nothing. They then handed me back to him; we recrossed the lake and rejoined our friends. Mishi-Mishi was then a Christian, and on hearing my story was angry with Wafwilwa. I refused to live longer with him.

Mr. Campbell then came from the West Coast, via Lufoi. A man in his caravan named Kawimbe, nephew of Chief Mwemmena, asked me to be his wife. I married him. Wafwilwa, seeing this, sent in his account for my keep while I was with him, and Kawimbe paid him a gun. Thus I was enslaved for the tenth and last time.[35]

Luapula, Northeastern Rhodesia, 1899-1911

Johnston Falls, where Campbell and his entourage moved in 1899, was a typical colonial outpost with its own dependent community of police, messengers, and traders. The spot had a natural advantage, being one of the main ferrying points on the Luapula and a center of fishing and fish trading. People from the plateau came with hoes, axes, beads, cloth, and food to exchange.[36] Johnston Falls did not continue to develop as a major center, however, for it was malarial. The administration regrouped on the plateau at Fort Rosebery (Mansa) and launched a campaign against sleeping sickness in 1908 that forced most people to move from the tsetse fly-infested valley. The circulation of population between the Belgian and British territories took on new dimensions, however, reflecting different modes and levels of tax collection, the lack of forced resettlement on the Belgian banks of the river, and the opening of the Katanga copper mines for which labor recruits were sought in Northeastern Rhodesia. The flow of labor expanded primarily because the local economy of resettled people was weak and the officials left no doubts as to the alternatives. Those who did not enter the wage labor market, preferably working in Rhodesia, were threatened with three months on a chain gang.[37] The inducements of high wages offered artisans in Elisabethville, the mushrooming capital of Katanga, very nearly stripped the Mbereshi mission of its industrial personnel.[38]

The high point of the Johnston Falls mission station may have been the spontaneous movement of conversion that took place in 1905. For the Plymouth Brethren, the "end of sterile years" came at the same time at Luanza, Johnston Falls, and Koni.[39] Campbell had called on the chiefs and headmen shortly before the wave hit Johnston Falls to complain that their people were unreceptive. The first break then came when an important *nganga* (medicine man) rose in church to declare his conversion. A group of seven came forward the next Sunday, and "a few Sundays after there were eleven more, and I got frightened and stopped them. I was afraid that the thing would become popular and they did not understand the step they were taking."[40] The backbone of the new movement, it emerged, was not chiefs and headmen but older women. In the homely term of the Scots, it was "grannies," the advisers to young girls and women, who became the foremost evangelists. Their female converts often resettled in the mission community at Johnston Falls.[41] There are hints that revival also occurred in the secret societies as seats of spiritual opposition, and it was alleged that families broke up because of the increasing militancy of societies demanding that their members all be initiated.[42] For a variety of reasons that deserve more research, widows and isolated women became the preponderant element in the early Christian church.

A narrative of Bwanikwa's life as a Christian at Johnston Falls must be compiled from Campbell's writings. It will be recalled that when she returned to Luanza from Kalungwishi, Bwanikwa had turned for protection to one of Msiri's former functionaries, a convert then in mission employment. Campbell recalled her at this time as "still a slave to her ninth master, and wearing the sad expression so often seen in Bantu women of middle age," but regularly attending services.[43] She probably came into the possession of Kawimbe, Campbell's servant, shortly before they moved back to the Lufira Valley to be near Msiri II. Part of the celebration of the missionary's return had been the presentation of girls by the leading Yeke; four from Msiri II and two from each of his principal officials. Other people were deposited in the "freed slave home" after the Belgian captain Verdick defeated the "Arabs" and dispersed the Swahili commercial settlements. Still more were ransomed from traders by the missionary himself. To all of these, Bwanikwa was an exception—she had joined voluntarily.[44]

The relationship of Bwanikwa with her husband was good, except that "at times he would taunt her with the gun he had paid for her."[45] Her conversion following a serious illness was publicly celebrated by baptism before she left Katanga for Johnston Falls. It is uncertain, however, how long she worked for wages in the missionary household. She became especially close to Campbell's wife: "She is my wife's right hand and true helper, yea, more, a real companion and sister."[46] At Johnston Falls, she embarked on more independent activities:

> She did not so much as hint that she would like our help. She set to work. She was a potter, and in her spare time she dug clay, and moulded and baked cooking pots and water jars. These she sold or bartered for something else, which she sold again, taking care of the profits. She cultivated and planted, and disposed of the produce. She kept fowls, and sold eggs and chickens. She bought breeding goats, and tended them, and traded the surplus, with the result that in course of time she had gathered together sufficient money to buy an elephant gun. She bought it at Nkomba's village, on the Luapula, and adding an expensive shawl which she had bought as interest, she went to her husband, paid her debt, and redeemed herself.

Kawimbe "received her on the new footing of a free woman and his wife."[47] "The neighbors knew, and in the villages along the Luapula River, near Johnston Falls, the people found out."

> We, too, saw the difference in their relationship. As a free woman, side by side, he and she went off to their fields together. They ate

together at home, an unusual thing among Africans. They sat and chatted together on the veranda of their house, and speaking of each other to outsiders there was the tone of deference and respect formerly lacking. About this time her husband made a profession of conversion. . . . [48]

Bwanikwa satisfied missionary standards as a model for other women, being "diligent in business" and providing "a godly example" of domestic duty.[49] She became known as a doctor, treating women in particular, and in 1905 she led other women evangelists on extended visits to villages, "at her own expense."[50] During the last years of her life, she returned to Luba country, where she once again lived within a Christian community.[51]

Slave Women and Colonial Courts
Cases concerning alleged slavery of women far outnumbered cases of male slaves in the courts of Northeastern Rhodesia. A full analysis of these court records requires a consideration of all the cases and detailed knowledge of the history of the boma community and its administrative hinterland. I have endeavored in the preceding chapter to study Mbala (formerly Abercorn) in this way.[52] Here the cases have been drawn almost exclusively from the Kalungwishi (Mweru-Luapula) District Office, a choice that was made because Kalungwishi appears in Bwanikwa's narrative and was one of the two bomas that dealt with cases in the Luapula area at the turn of the century. Had she gone to a colonial court, it would have been either to Kalungwishi or to Fort Rosebery. Although I concentrate on Kalungwishi here, a reading of court records from Abercorn, Kasama, Luwingu, Fort Rosebery, and other neighboring administrative centers confirms that the disputes heard at Kalungwishi were not unusual.[53]

Kalungwishi had become a rather quieter, less pugnacious place by the turn of the century than it was when Bwanikwa first encountered it in the early 1890s. Kazembe had capitulated, and the more settled early colonial situation redefined official functions. These included tax collection, enforcement of sleeping sickness regulations, enumerating labor, keeping an eye on the Congo border, and presiding over a small commercial and salaried nucleus in Kalungwishi itself. Court was held as cases arose.

Consciousness and Protest

The very existence of missionary patrons with antislavery convictions and the capacity to grant refuge affected women's consciousness. Bwanikwa's success not only in ransoming herself and becoming a free woman but also in approximating equality with her husband and her patron's wife was doubtless unusual. When did her ambition to be free and equal become fully crystallized? Campbell remarked that "a new hope seemed to arise . . . when she had reached a haven and found among the missionaries friends in whom she could trust and to whom slavery was abhorrent."[54] The opportunity that the colonial courts offered for the conduct of disputes contributed, too, to a more focused consciousness and gave new scope for manipulation.

Before turning to the conditions protested by slave women, let us consider how the ambiguities shrouding female status could be stripped away. As Arnot and other sources attest, absorption phrased in familial terms was well understood as a means of social control preferable to active coercion of slaves. The real status of a dependent woman remained murky, and women resisted adverse clarification. Reluctance to give way psychologically to slave status is evident from the testimony of a woman named Mwawa:

> On my mother's death I lived in Lubwebwe's village and for some reason or other (I was too young then to know) he [Lubwebwe] gave a doctor some things in connection with a *milando* [dispute]. When my sister Chishala gave birth to a child and this child grew up Lubwebwe married her. I thought this was funny. He says he is an uncle of mine and yet he marries his grand-niece. After a long time he eventually told us we were his slaves. This child who had married Lubwebwe had a child and it was burnt one night when lying asleep.

Lubwebwe was not at home at the time but when he returned, he found the child very sick: the wounds were not healed and the child eventually died. Lubwebwe then accused us, his slaves, of killing the child and told us not to bury the child till we had given him goods. We had nothing to give him but gave him a string of beads. Then he allowed us to bury the child. . . . I began to think about it and came to the conclusion that Lubwebwe was not my uncle at all, that I and my sisters were slaves only. So we looked for some of our male relatives to set us free. Then my son came to visit us and I told him about it. That day Lubwebwe beat me and told me next day he was going to take me to Mushoba to sell me as a slave.[55]

The legal distinction between free and slave was very often driven home when damages requiring compensation were assessed. In Garenganze, the life of a free person was compensated by the payment of slaves, the life of a slave by payment of goods.[56] Slaves conscious of their status knew what had been paid for them, and Bwanikwa is representative in giving precise detail about her initial sale "for a packet of gun-powder." The usual payment for slaves was a mixture of petty commodities reflecting the near-currencies prevailing in their localities.[57] Overt sale and the handing over of trade goods set a seal on slave status that could only be legally broken on the slaves' part by ransom.

The strategies of a female caught in slavery included many extralegal measures. As a recapitulation of Bwanikwa's actions will show, these strategies ran a gamut from accommodation, to strategic alliances, to escape. The first time she broke with a master, during the dispersal from Bunkeya, she allied herself with a fellow slave who was nevertheless an important man. Reentry into an organized community was difficult in the disturbed conditions, and Kazembe wanted a high price (Bwanikwa herself) for taking in the refugees. Refusing that option, they were obliged to retreat to Mukoka—the very ex-husband, master, village head from whom they had separated. Bwanikwa was more isolated in the subsequent sequence; she ran away from the Biheans, invoked the protection of Msiri's sister, a remnant leader of the Garenganze state, and finally returned independently to the center of Garenganze, to Lufoi and the missionaries. There she could not sustain a nonslave status. At Kalungwishi she again ran away from alien traders. Once back at Luanza, she successfully appealed to a convert with authority in the African community who was a former lieutenant of Msiri. But it was only after she became attached to a very powerful patron, Campbell, that the social base for her final self-ransom was established.

The quest for legal emancipation through the payment of ransom outside the colonial courts sometimes met with frustration and led to appeal there, as Nasila's 1907 testimony before the Mweru-Luapula court indicates:

> I was the wife of Kazembe Kanyumbo and he said I was a slave. I took beads, value £1 and gave them to Kazembe, who released me. Kazembe Kanyumb died and Kazembe Kambwali took over his wives and sent me back to my mother. He then took me and I lived with Kazembe Kambwali. I agreed to this and lived in his huts. Now he has taken me and given me to his capitao Sakaliata. I refused as I was not a slave and I took some beads and calico and gave them to Sakaliata. Sakaliata refused to release me.[58]

Colonial men also failed to understand the intense desire of women to perform a formal act of self-emancipation. An insistent woman caused embarrassment to J. E. Stephenson after he left the service of the British South Africa Company and became a settler. The complainant was a former nursemaid whom a chief had given to one of Stephenson's wives and who later married his cook. After the cook's death, she demanded the right to ransom herself, and when Stephenson refused, saying she was not a slave, she appealed to the district officer. As Stephenson wrote:

> Technically in her own eyes she was still Chisimongana's "slave" though she had had no job and had been doing exactly as she liked for several years previously, ever since she had married the cook.

However not a bit of it — she was, she insisted, a slave, as Shaiwira
had presented her as such to Chisimongana...and she insisted
she must pay her mistress £2 in order properly to purchase her
freedom.[59]

In popular perception, there was an additional definition of
freedom. Women wanted to be reunited with their kinsmen or
close friends, often in a cultural homeland. The missionaries were
chagrined that their ideas of freedom were not acceptable to the
women who lived with them as liberated slaves; they ruefully
admitted that such women felt themselves slaves still, so long as
they had not returned home to their relatives.[60] Such reunions
did eventually flourish, especially after colonial pacification curtailed slave trade and promoted lineage calculations. But once
again, caution is advised in balancing the ideal against the real
exercise of options. Six freed girls had once been delivered by CFS
officials to Campbell for fostering. By World War I, three were
"Christian mothers" — that is, absorbed into a new community:
one had returned to long lost relatives; one had been lost track of;
and one was a prostitute in Elisabethville.[61]

In resolving the status of slave wives, the courts often took the
step beyond facilitating ransom, of calling for bridewealth payments in order to legitimize the marriage and secure the rights of
husbands against resurgent lineage claims.[62] Husbands, however,
had to give up rights of ownership. One witnesss before the
Mweru Luapula court, Mumba, stated: "I was taken from my
village and made a slave long ago. . . . I was taken to CFS. There
Simba's men caught me and took me to Kilwa Island [in Lake
Mweru]. Simba gave me in marriage to another slave of his,
Muziowandevu, who is still living with me."[63] Muziowandevu
claimed that Mumba was not a slave and agreed to pay bridewealth to her rediscovered relatives to retain her as a wife.

Consciousness of slave status did not necessarily lead to actions
aimed at ending it. A dependent enjoying relatively favorable
conditions and without a relative to bring a case remained quiet.

Those who arrived in court, on the other hand, sought relief from one of two sorts of situations: being subject to two masters, or being threatened with sale and/or physical abuse.

Aggravation in a slave woman's life often arose from having multiple masters. This condition sometimes surfaced belatedly. A chief or headman giving a woman to a client as a wife often retained certain property rights in her, as the woman well knew. Chondwa complained: "I am a slave of Musesya. Long ago I was given to Musesya by Chiwanampembe of Belgian Territory. Musesya gave me as a wife to Chiembere, a . . . native of his village, and I bore him one child. I am still Musesya's slave and want my release."[64] The cases already cited show that a particularly dangerous moment for a slave woman came when her owner died and his property was claimed by his heirs. Rights of owners prevailed, on the whole, over rights of husbands. Another common variant of competitive demands by two masters was persisting demands upon the labor power of women even though they had been allowed to marry. The owners in these cases were often older women who could not cope with agricultural and domestic work previously performed by the slave. Men with other domestic resources tended to give slaves away as they would a daughter, and the older women's hesitancy in finalizing the transfer caused resentment. Kandegi pointed up this situation by claiming that her owner had been paid bridewealth, but then hung on: "I am Lukwesa's slave. She refuses to allow me to marry and threatens to kill me."[65]

Physical abuse and threat of sale were both means of intimidating slaves. Bwanikwa looked back nostalgically to the days of her life in Garenganze when Mukoka "never sold me, nor did he threaten to do so." As the early colonial period became characterized by contrasting civil conditions in the Congo Free State and Northeastern Rhodesia, the threat of being taken to the Congo Free State was perceived to be a threat of sale and served to propel women into court. The behavior of Kawimbe in becoming impatient and fearing for his investment in Bwanikwa, however, bespeaks a rather different situation. Given her strong position within the Christian community, his harassment served rather as a goad to accelerate her self-ransom than as a plausible threat of sale.

The rapidly changing economic conditions and terms of trade in the Luapula districts after the turn of the century encouraged new modes of litigation as kin reclaimed their lost relatives, wives sought to have their marriages legitimized, and heirs tried to realize something from their legacies by demanding full compensation and quibbling over the exact sum involved. Although the colonial courts were mandated to effect emancipation, they consistently ordered compensation, and thus encouraged owners to give a full account of the price paid for the slave. Ransom thus became a way of liquidating assets in slaves even though slave trade had been abolished. The permutations of interests served by the colonial courts are too many to allow for any simple statement about their biases in such cases. Suffice it to say that they both conveyed a formal freedom that women sought and upheld the rights of owners of property.

Conclusion

Bwanikwa and others in her generation of slave women were demonstrably persons of ambition and courage, of willingness to assume normal family responsibilities and to fulfill conventional female roles. In plantation economies, emancipation was often followed by vagrancy laws and other regulations aiming to reattach "free" men to their former workplaces. In Central Africa, where slavery fitted into expanded domestic community relations of production, the reflex of the colonial authorities was to promote social control through marriage, preferably with strong principles of male dominance.

The social and economic conditions that had framed enslavement were marked by manipulation of indebtedness and calls for compensation. Women who were assets paid to meet such demands never questioned this transfer; even those who achieved freedom insisted upon sealing it by liquidating the debt. Women did protest against coercion, intimidation, and exploitation, especially when such problems arose from the necessity to work for two masters. Variables of women's life cycle and pervasive social institutions such as matrilinearity require careful attention if the dynamics of slavery are to be fully rendered. The research agenda is complex, and includes determining how general were the upward mobility and lessened sense of exploitation that were the happy lot of some slave women in Central Africa. Other women chose alternative avenues of emancipation. Attention must be given to their choices and the reasons for them — that is, to downward mobility, intensified disposability, and actions of women to moderate the ensuing conditions of slavery and exploitation.

Notes

1 "Family, Community and Women" sought to balance the preoccupation with the slave experience of "Women in Peril" as first published.

2 P.-P. Rey, "The Lineage Mode of Production," *Critique of Anthropology,* no. 3 (1975), urges closer historical examination. M. Douglas, "Matriliny and Pawnship in Central Africa," *Africa* 34 (1964), made an important statement about the social reflexes that encouraged pawnship but attempted to isolate pawnship from slavery. I. Kopytoff's idealization of benevolent kinship incorporation is articulated in "Indigenous African Slavery: Commentary One," *Historical Reflections,* no. 6 (1979). For reservations, see F. Cooper, "Indigenous Slavery: Commentary Two," *Historical Reflections,* no. 6 (1979).

3 Historians of modern copper-mining towns consistently ignore precolonial urbanism and set up highly misleading dualism. See, for example, B. Fetter, *The Creation of Elisabethville* (Stanford, 1976), 9.

4 D. Campbell, *Ten Times a Slave but Freed at Last: The Thrilling Story of Bwanikwa, A Central African Heroine* (Glasgow, 1916), 12.

5   Marshall, Notes on Slavery, 1910. Marshall Papers, National Museum, Livingstone.

6   M. Chanock, "Making Customary Law: Men, Women and Courts in Colonial Northern Rhodesia," in *African Women and the Law,* eds. M. J. Hay and M. Wright (Boston, 1982), documents the regularization of local courts and the attendant consequences.

7   *Echoes of Service* (1897: 282–83). This missionary journal contains many detailed reports from the Plymouth Brethren as well as editorials on social policy. Peter H. Lary has generously shared his research notes from this source concerning the Luapula District.

8   F. S. Arnot, *Garenganze: Or, Seven Years' Pioneer Mission Work in Central Africa* (London, 1889), 242.

9   H. J. Nieboer, *Slavery as an Industrial System: Ethnological Researches,* 2nd ed. (The Hague, 1910), 419.

10 The excellent short definition by M. I. Finley, "Slavery," *Encyclopedia of the Social Sciences,* vol. 14 (New York, 1968), and the recent article by Orlando Patterson (1979) both imply that the slave is male.

11 Marshall, Notes on Slavery, 1910, Marshall Papers. J.E. Stephenson, Marshall's contemporary, made a distinction between "he-slaves," who were apt to be inveterate wrong-doers, and "she-slaves," who were pawns or hostages. See Stephenson, *Chirupula's Tale* (London, 1937), 65. See also *Chirupula's Quarterly Review,* HM ST 1/3, NA 2 (1950:2), ZNA.

12 Some analogous problems of official, missionary, and African consensus history are treated by T. Q. Reefe, "Traditions of Genesis and the Luba Diaspora," *History in Africa,* No. 4 (1977).

13 The autobiography is appended to D. Campbell, *Blazing Trails in Bantuland* (London, 1934). For a statement about its composition and translation, see *Blazing Trails,* 202.

14 The received dynastic tradition is contained in the work of a retired administrator, A. Verbeken, *Msiri, roi du Garenganze* (Brussels, 1956). D. Campbell, *In the Heart of Bantuland* (New York, 1969), chap. 25 also treats it, but in a summary way.

15 Arnot, *Garenganze,* 234. Arnot also published selected letters and diaries of colleagues, see F. S. Arnot, *Bihe and Garenganze* (London, 1893).

16 Arnot, *Garenganze,* 234. D. Crawford, *Thinking Black* (New York, 1912), 191.

17 E. Verdick, *Les premiers jours au Katange (1880–1903)* (Brussels, 1952), 43.

18 Arnot, *Garenganze,* 234.

19 Verdick, *Les premiers jours,* 32.

20 Arnot, *Garenganze,* 170, 174.

21 *Ibid.,* 194.

22 *Ibid.,* 241.

23 *Ibid.,* 245.

24 Campbell, *Blazing Trails,* 210–11.

25 Arnot, *Garenganze,* 225.

26 Arnot, *Bihe and Garenganze,* 68.

27 *Ibid.*

28 Campbell, *Blazing Trails,* 70–71.

29 *Ibid.,* 82.

30 *Ibid.,* 95.

31 Verdick, *Les premiers jours;* Verbeken, *Msiri, roi du Garenganze;* Campbell, *Blazing Trails,* 101.

32 Campbell, *Blazing Trails,* 191.

33 *Ibid.,* 76. For Bihean countermeasures, see *Echoes of Service,* 252.

34 Dan Crawford came from the Congo Free State to Northern Rhodesia in 1893 and met the officer in charge at Kalungwishi, an isolated youth quite baffled by Africa, "a miniature edition of Great Britain in breeches, the death sentence in his power." "There he is, day by day, looking into our wild unknown Interior, two big business-looking revolvers ever lying on his table, and full of forebodings," Crawford, 406. See also Tapson, "Note," *Northern Rhodesia Journal* 2, no. 5 (1955): 89–90.

35 Campbell, *Blazing Trails,* 211–13.

36 *Ibid.,* 114.

37 R. S. Wright to LMS Secretary, December 8, 1908, Central Africa Correspondence, Box 15. C. W. M.

38 B. R. Turner to Hawkins, 30 August 1912, Correspondence, Box 15. C. W. M.

39 Crawford, *Thinking Black,* 473.

40 Campbell, *Blazing Trails,* 180.

41 *Ibid.,* 183.

42 *Ibid.,* 160; Crawford, 234–35.

43 Campbell, *Blazing Trails,* 83.

44 *Ibid.,* 45.

45 Campbell, *Ten Times a Slave, 20.*

46 *Ibid.,* 28.

47 *Ibid.,* 24.

48 *Ibid.,* 25–26.

49 *Ibid.,* 28–29.

50 *Ibid.,* 28.

51 Campbell, *Blazing Trails,* 183.

52 See also M. Wright, "'Tambalika', Perspectives on a Colonial Magistrate," *African Affairs* 85, no. 338 (1986).

53 There are several dozen pertinent cases in the Kalungwishi Native Court Record Book (KTL, ZNA). Case books for the surrounding districts contain more than 120 such cases, concentrated mainly in the years 1898–1906.

54 Campbell, *Ten Times a Slave,* 24.

55 KTL Civil 11, 1908. ZNA.

56 Arnot, *Garenganze,* 242.

57 Examples of payments in the late nineteenth century: eight hoes and two rolls of tobacco; fifteen pieces of calico and one load of salt; three hoes and two locally woven cloths; eight hoes, one load of salt, and four yards of calico. KTL. ZNA.

58 KSL AAA, 1908. ZNA.

59 Stephenson, *Chirupula's Tale,* 246. Lewanika in 1906 had accepted a fixed rate of two pounds for compensation/ransom in the Barotseland Protectorate, and it prevailed in Northwestern Rhodesia. No equivalent regulation was made in Northeastern Rhodesia.

60 Crawford, 219.

61 Campbell, *Ten Times a Slave,* 21.

62 KTl Civil 63, 1906. ZNA.

63 KTL Civil 14, 1904. ZNA.

64 KTL Civil 27, 1904. ZNA.

65 ZNA, KTL Civil 6, 1900.

EIGHT

Tatu Mulondyelwa Recollected: Memoirs as Sources for a History of Women at the Turn of the Twentieth Century

The story of Tatu Mulondyelwa contained in "Tatu, The Kidnapped Mbemba Child" is as much a testimony about the life and consciousness of the narrator, Elise Kootz-Kretschmer, her missionary "foster mother," as it is about Tatu, the observed.[1] Nevertheless, it will be argued that Tatu in several respects personifies the last generation of enslaved girl children. Kootz-Kretschmer's emotion-laden memoir extends only to 1916, when the German missionaries were detained as enemies by the Allies, in her case the Belgians, whose war-time occupation extended eastward to Tabora.[2] Kootz-Kretschmer was never able to return to Utengule, the mission station near the present-day town of Mbeya in southwestern Tanzania where she knew Tatu. The account, therefore, is silent about the later years, leaving us with questions about Tatu's final choices and constraints as a mature married woman, mother, or grandmother. What it captures, on the other hand, is a vivid picture of early colonial society and the varied niches within which an uprooted young person might be socialized.

The tension of alternatives is palpable in Kootz-Kretschmer's rendering. That women at the turn of the century had, and exercised, choices in locating themselves socially is well documented elsewhere in this volume. Here we have the opportunity to explore a set of alternatives peculiar to German East Africa, where the colonial regime built an alliance with Swahili-speaking agents and stressed the prestige of military service. Christian mission stations were thus not uncontested as foci for the implantation of values and aspirations for Africans aiming to succeed within the new political order.

Kootz-Kretschmer's account of Tatu is of a recollected relationship, not an independent personal narrative in the way that most of the Utengule texts are.[3] The combination of ethnographic awareness, missionary elaboration and nostalgia in the narrative presents formidable challenges in the evaluation of text and context, and has led to a handling of Tatu's life in a way different from that of others presented in this volume. Here we contend with the unequivocal authorship of a foreigner, who in the guise of an interlocutor sometimes underscores her own incongruence in African society and at other times assures her readers that Christianity and traditional values could be harmonized so long as the intrinsic discipline of family and kinship remained intact.[4] In addition to being a memoir, therefore, the pamphlet served as a Christian morality play, the evil and dangerous elements being dramatized by references to the permissive character of Swahili society.

In 1898, the famous explorer-ethnographer Oskar Baumann made a distinction between "scientific" and "anecdotal" presentations of African life.[5] For his final rendering of African society, he chose to be anecdotal, contributing to the genre of narrative by those we call intimate outsiders. Like Baumann, Kootz-Kretschmer figured in the dual roles of ethnographer and teller of tales. Her evolution in the scientific direction seems to have been a gradual one, perhaps beginning from contact with Friedrich Fuelleborn in 1898 and 1899, developing with a team research effort carried out in association with several leading churchmen, encouraged by Mission Director Paul Hennig, and finally coming under the academic patronage of Professor Carl Meinhof.[6] Parallel to the composition of her memoir of Tatu, Kootz-Kretschmer was immersed in the translation of first-person accounts by

African members of the Utengule community. This inevitably inflected her reconstruction of Tatu's life, especially with respect to her parental home, of which she had no recollection. The story of Chisi, among the "Women in Peril" narratives and first published in *Die Safwa,* exemplifies the kind of material that contributed to the invention of Tatu's origins.[7]

Within the genre of intimate outsiders, a distinction must certainly be made between men and women. The insights provided by men were frequently based on their physical intimacy with African women. Baumann's delight in and fascination with women is indicated not only by his narrative choices, but also in the photographs he took that serve as illustrations in his posthumously published book. Also belonging to the male wing of this genre was the important military officer and administrator Ernst Nigmann, who figures in the discussion below of relations in colonial-dependent military communities. More tangential but useful perspectives are provided by two other intimate male outsiders, the lascivious Italian traveler Marius Fortie and Chirupula Stephenson, the polygynous, eccentric ex-British official.[8] The diaries of Magdalene von Prince amplify the view of an early colonial military-administrative center, Iringa, and serve to underscore the difference that an observer's sex could make in the observation of women.

An important point of contrast between Baumann and Kootz-Kretschmer concerns their relative commitment to a radical view of change. Baumann by the last years of the nineteenth century had become highly critical of the arbitrary and cruel treatment that slave women received at the hands of their Arab masters. He began to portray matters from the point of view of the affected women, without ideological animus against Islam but with a clear sense of the vulnerability of concubines.[9] Kootz-Kretschmer, as will become apparent, took a triumphalist position about how liberation was to be achieved in a "new era" of Christianity, especially where it superseded Muslim-commercial culture.

In reality, the Swahili language and other elements of the

commercial system that had spread before the coming of the missionaries or the German occupation, proved too useful to the colonial state to be set aside or readily supplanted. Collaboration with Muslims was a hallmark of the early colonial state, nowhere more strikingly displayed than in the colonial army, the Schutztruppe, the world of Nigmann.

During the early colonial period that terminated with the Maji Maji War of 1905–1906, the soldiers belonging to the Schutztruppe had both expeditionary functions and local responsibilities as the police in districts under military administration. The expeditionary aspect was identified with the traditions laid down by Hermann von Wissmann, an experienced explorer who was given command of the imperial forces mobilized to contend with the Bushiri Rising of 1889. The caravan was a mobile community acting as an entity in order to cultivate hosts and provisioners and avoid costly hostility as well as assembling an armed force that could tip the balance in local rivalries or contests.

The women attached to caravans and expeditionary forces were more numerous than much of the literature on the nineteenth century transport system has allowed.[10] Their presence and functions varied according to the ownership and leadership of the caravan/expedition. In some cases they were taken along with the intention of establishing outposts on a new or uncertain frontier of Swahili trade, in others they were slaves newly acquired in the locality of an established base where they became absorbed into a relatively stable domestic situation.[11]

After 1906, as military administration was succeeded by civil, the role of the Schutztruppe in the executive and judicial operations of the colonial state was reduced. The importance of the reorganization and separation should not be exaggerated, however, for the askari, the uniformed and armed enforcer, remained an instrument of the colonial state. Police shared the same training and culture as the Schutztruppe.

The text of the memoir follows. Readers are invited to go through it once as a simple story. Certain footnotes have been supplied to give explanations and indicate literature that will not be treated in the ensuing commentary. Four topics, presenting background and problems of interpretation and contextualization, are addressed in the commentary. These are broadly chronological in terms of Tatu's life, beginning with her alleged Bemba origins and the nature of the Bemba identity as it may have affected the processes of incorporation of slaves and ex-slaves among the Safwa, the people indigenous to the Utengule area. The Swahili-Muslim-askari society as an alternative to early colonial formation is then considered, followed by the emergence of a missionary-led community at Utengule as a focal point of contradictions between intervention, local definitions, and ethnic reconstruction after the turn of the century. Finally, Tatu's options are considered in light of features of female decision making and autonomy as revealed by the narratives both by African members of the Utengule community and by outside observers.

Tatu, the Kidnapped Mbemba Child
by Frau Missionar E. Kootz[12]

Kidnapped by Arabs

It was the morning of a beautiful but hot day, of which there are many in the interior of Africa, where the sun shines to the joy of the natives and often to the sorrow of the Europeans who live there. As it grew light outside, the sleeping village gradually awoke. After breakfast, the men shouldered their hoes and axes and went to their work in the fields. The women bound their youngest securely to their backs in sheepskins, set baskets on their heads, took up the gourd flasks filled with *ulesi*[13] gruel for the children on their backs, and followed their husbands. The older girls went along. Were they not able to use the hoe, then they minded the youngest, whom the mother had laid on a carrying skin while she worked. The older youths drove the livestock to pasture, and so the village, in which only a few old people, unable to work, and the younger children remained, became quiet. The boys shaped cows out of clay while the girls bound ears of maize to their backs and played dolls. The village lay there calmly in the morning sunlight. Only the chickens scratched around the huts, and the doves cooed and flew in and out of the dovecote. If only it would stay like this! But the enemy was even then drawing nigh, soft-footed. Arabs stole in looking for "goods." Not only did they take food and whatever else struck their fancy, they also reached out their greedy hands toward the helpless old people and the unprotected children. And as quickly as they had come, they disappeared with their booty. When the parents returned from the fields, they faced a ransacked and destroyed village. Or had they been warned by the rising smoke as the raiders set fire to the village and had rushed back? Or had the raiders surprised them at work in the fields and struck down the men and fettered the women? Tatu could not tell us. She only remembered that they were playing in the village when the Arabs arrived! She never saw her mother or father again. She did not even know the land from which she was kidnapped. Homeless, orphaned, unprotected, and without help, she and the other children were made to wander the narrow paths into the distance. Or were they driven through pathless wilderness when the raiders thought it necessary? The wails of the children went unnoticed and their cries for their mothers ceased at the threats of the strangers, whose possessions they now were.

In the evening they halted under the open sky. The tired children fell asleep, lulled by the warmth of fires lit to keep wild animals away. Did Tatu dream of her home? How often did she perhaps awaken and call for her mother? This night was so very different from the other nights of her life. She had spent her nights pressed closely to her mother and rolled up in the same mat as she. Had she been older, she would have considered running back and searching for her mother. Some captives tried, but only a few succeeded in escaping.

The march continued the next morning. Little brown feet plodded the narrow pathways. How often did the driver threaten the children with a spear, when they were too tired to go any farther? Perhaps he even took one up on his back and carried him for a bit now and then. Had he actually killed the child with his spear, he would have done himself out of his expected profit.

Because of the suffering of the trip, the little slaves had almost forgotten their homeland during the long way to Lake Nyasa. The obtuseness of their race helped them to do this and by the time they had reached their preliminary destination, the home of the Arab chief, Tatu felt safe and was contented. Tatu was well situated at the camp of Mlozi, the great Arab. She had food to eat and she grew along with the other slave children, so that she would later command a good price as useful "goods." However, it was to come out otherwise. God had other plans for little Tatu.

The Arab chief lived with his entourage in the English territory, near Karonga on the northern end of Lake Nyasa. It had taken the English a great deal of effort before they took control of the land belonging to this captain of the raiders. His life came to a violent end. He was hanged.[14] His camp was blown up and his people fled with their slaves across into German territory, where they were permitted to settle by the Songwe, the big river that flows into the Nyasa. "And what did the Arabs do there?" I asked Tatu. "They cultivated rice," was the reply, for there is swampland at the banks of the Songwe as is necessary for growing rice.

With the Bibis in the Askari Village

Tatu was sold from one owner to another several more times, until finally she ended up in Langenburg, the German military station, and later the Bezirksamt, the seat of civil government. There Tatu was no longer a slave child. The Bezirksamtmann[15] was now her master, but not in the same manner as Mlozi, who could do with her as he wished. This new master, in contrast, cared for the dark-brown child who had been entrusted to his protection. Here there was no raid and no death screams of the fallen. And Tatu would not be sold again. She was free.

The many little houses and huts that one saw standing in Langenburg had been built for the black soldiers needed by the Bezirksamtmann to rule the large area and keep order. Baron von Eltz set up the station close by the shore of the Nyasa. His soldiers were colored creatures, mostly able soldiers from the Sudan, some of whom, like the Bezirksamtmann himself, had already served the German nation under the renowned Major Hermann von Wissmann.[16] The colonial officers gradually accepted sons of the country into their troop, trained them, and then retained them for many years. It was not, therefore, a service with which one could be finished in a short time. He who joined up as an askari knew he was bound for a protracted period of time and consequently brought along his wife if he had one. And it was good this way, for then the man was well cared for. The wife cooked his food and when he returned from his duties he did not have to stand first at the wooden mortar and let the pestle fall onto the hard kernels of maize, or kneel by the grinding stone to grind the *ulesi* into flour. That was woman's work.

And when the askari was ordered to war by the officials, his wife accompanied him in the baggage train, carrying the child on her back, the sleeping mat, water container, cooking pot, and stirring spoon on her head.[17] Thus the askari could lead a family life in spite of his military service and was, therefore, not so easily tempted to live a dissolute life. For all of this, however, he needed a home, and for the length of his service this was for him the village built up around the local government office. Each askari received his own hut for himself and his family, and such an askari village, with its many rows of huts, could look very attractive, for under the direction of the Germans, order and cleanliness were given their due place in the village.

Now the Bwana Kubwa, the colonial master, was well able to keep order in the village, for he had the power to punish and could, when necessary with the help of punishment, educate disorderly people to that which they might not have achieved on their own. But his power did not reach into the huts. If a bad woman had entered the hut and quarreling and insubordination ruled within the mud-smeared walls, then the askari, the lord of the hut, had to fend for himself. If he was a native and his wife also a daughter of the country, it was the most easily dealt with. More often than not, however, the wife of the askaris originated from the distant coast and had earlier come into the interior of the country with the troops and now led a life of licentiousness.

In the language of the people of the coast, Bibi is the name for woman. Perhaps the Bibi's first husband had beaten her for some reason or other and she ran away from him and was quickly taken by another into his hut. Her relatives were far far away. There was no father and no brother nearby from whom the deserted husband could reclaim the brideprice. There was also no one there who could have demanded from the second husband the customary price for which the family would normally relinquish their daughter. If the Bibi was not happy in the second hut, then perhaps she ran to the third. No one showed her the correct path and no one cautioned her to live a virtuous life. But there was also no one to stand by and protect her when evil befell her and when she was unjustly treated, for she had long since lost any connection with her family. It was in this manner that many askari females became women who no longer allowed themselves to be led by the good moral values such as prevail also among heathens. Instead they did only that which they desired at the moment and what their evil hearts suggested.

Our Tatu came as a foster child into such an askari hut and to such a soldier's wife. She was perhaps nine years old and she was happy to have a home and to belong somewhere. The Bezirksamt-mann could do no more for the slave child than to pay for her keep; her upbringing was entrusted to her black foster parents.

This first foster mother was no good example for the brown child; she was one of the flock of fallen women. She hated her husband and made his life miserable. Tatu came next into another hut as a foster child and then into yet another, for the foster parents also lodged complaints against Tatu, who was often disobedient and unruly.

The Arsonist
And then misfortune arrived. Tatu was sitting at the hearth one day in the hut of the third or fourth foster mother. The foster mother was conversing with another askari woman who had come for a visit. They did not, however, have a knitted-stocking in their hands, onto which they could cast stitches and make the needles fly! Instead they held a gourd bottle, half filled with water, into which a tube was stuck. That was their tobacco pipe. And when they sucked at the tube with their lips, the tobacco burned so prettily, the water in the bottle bubbled, the tobacco smoke filled their lungs and gave them pleasure. Then they felt good and they gossiped even more with each other. And when the women's tobacco pipe no longer burned well, she got up to light it again. She went in front of the door of the hut,

plucked a few straws of grass from the roof, held them in the hearthfire, and blew on the embers. But in the same instant that the grass burned brightly, a gust of wind blew in through the open door, the flame leapt up to the low, dry ceiling and a second later the hut was on fire. The two women fled, but Tatu stood in front of the burning hut and watched how the fire, with the help of the wind that blew from the lake, made quick work of the hollow bamboo and grass building.[18]

Soon the entire settlement stood around her. They asked one another, "Who started the fire?" And soon the Bezirksamtmann was also there and asked gravely and severely, "Who set fire to the hut?" A harsh punishment threatened the culprit, for there had recently been several such fires in the soldiers' village. The Bezirk-samtmann had to take greater precautions in order to put an end to this negligence or spite. Who was now guilty of this fire? Nobody had done it. The two women had flown and remained hidden and Tatu, whom they had found next to the burning hut, stood with a clear conscience in front of the angry Baron and said, "No, it was not I." Poor child! How do you hope to prove this? Appearance is all against you and you have so often angered the one who pays your keep through the complaints that your foster parents have brought forward.

A rigorous investigation was held in order to discover the culprit. Suspicion remained on Tatu, despite her insistence that she was innocent. And as even that same askari woman was called as witness, whose burning bunch of grass had set fire to the hut instead of the pipe, Tatu could only lower her eyes, eyes that had until then looked about for help. No help came to the poor girl from that woman. The woman only testified that Tatu had been the one and she herself had seen how the girl had set fire to the hut.

Baron von Eltz, the one who had built up Langenburg, had already been resting peacefully for several years, buried under the sandy beach of Lake Nyasa. Tatu's judge was his successor. He had found the freed slaves as charges of the colonial government and despite the efforts he took with them, they caused him so much trouble. In addition to that, the insubordination among the very varied inhabitants of his soldiers' village had grown ever greater. He had to become stricter and now a girl, whom he meant well, stood before him accused of arson. Arson carried the sentence of chains. So Tatu had to be chained! Thus read the judgment. Poor judge! Poor girl! Did the lines etch themselves into her brow then, the ones I often observed later, when I had to call her to account for some reason or other, and that quickly disappeared as soon as they saw evidence of love?

When she had served the sentence of chains and was free again, she wanted to take her further fate into her own hands. She let herself be persuaded by an askari to follow him out of the country. Perhaps it was she who convinced the askari to take her along. The colonial lord of Langenburg had thought it necesssary to punish Tatu, but that still did not remove her from his care. He learned quickly enough that the girl had disappeared from the settlement. The pursuing messengers found them on Lake Nyasa. The steamer had to relinquish the refugee and the askari made his journey alone.

Tatu Finds Foster Parents

From that point on the Bezirksamtmann determined that the girl must leave the place where no one was able to trouble themselves over her upbringing. He pondered: She was now about thirteen or fourteen years old. This time they had been lucky enough to get her back. She would soon try again to go her own unprotected way. Therefore, she should be taken away from the restless military station, far away from the place that could never become the slave child's home. One of the missionary stations that had grown up in the country must and would take Tatu to rear, as they had taken in other freed slaves. It would be preferable to send her to the station the very farthest from the site of her previous existence — to Utengule in Safwaland, on the other side of the mountains. Following these considerations, the request came to us, whether we would take in this child who was supposed to be the epitome of all bad things. It went without saying that we were ready to do this, but I was very anxious about the task, for I knew the sort of problems the missionaries in Rungwe had with the freed slaves. And we were getting a girl who at such a tender age had set a fire and run off with an askari.

The same messenger who had brought the request immediately took our affirmative answer back with him into the Konde country to Langenburg. And from then on we awaited the arrival of the unfamiliar child. At first in vain. Month after month passed without hearing anything else about the girl. We even began to think that the Bezirksamtmann had thought it better to marry the foster child to an askari, or to send her to one of the stations in Kondeland. My uneasiness at the huge task that her upbringing would entail for us had long since given way to worries closer at hand. We began to forget the girl.

And then suddenly she was there! In May of 1900 a certain Herr von G. journeyed through our area and also visited our station at Utengule. When we heard that he came from Langenburg, we brought the conversation around to the slave child and the request of the Bezirksamtmann. Herr von G. then said, "Oh, yes. So it is. The girl came along with my caravan, but she is still very tired from the march. When she has rested, I will send her to you." So it was only out of concern for her safety that the Bezirksamtmann had not sent the child earlier. He wanted her to make the five-day march from Langenburg, later called Alt-Langenburg, to Utengule only with a safe escort. And such a safe escort had only now made itself available.

In the afternoon the child arrived, she who had spent her childhood homeless and orphaned. We asked ourselves if she were likely to find a home at the missionary station, where longing for a distant place and an unrestrained life could overcome her. Bathed and with a fresh cloth wrap draped over her and tightly knotted under her arms, but without any other piece of luggage or possession, she stood in front of our house. She looked at me calmly with her big, dark eyes as I greeted her, and unafraid and without hesitation she returned my greeting with a handshake. But her otherwise even-featured and even engaging face had a reserved look. I could not communicate with her, for she spoke a language strange to me. But I still wanted to show her that she was welcome. I went and fetched some bananas, and when I returned, she was already kneeling beside our fifteen-month-old foster son, who was lying on a mat. She played with him and I was amazed at how the child joyously reached out his arms toward her. Then she took the bananas from me, but before she ate some herself, she placed a piece in the mouth of the small white child. In the shortest time they were friends. The small child let her take him onto her lap and played with her. Her previously severe features softened, her eyes sparkled, and her mouth laughed so that one could see her white teeth sparkling. I breathed a sigh of relief and my heart was lightened. That was supposed to be a criminal and she had won the love of the smallest in the house so quickly?

She was a child of the Bemba tribe. This she told me later. The homeland of the Bemba lies southeast of Lake Tanganyika. It was there that she was kidnapped. And she was called Tatu. Tatu means three; simply three, nothing more. A number, then, a name that one of her earlier owners had given her. How might her mother have called her? Surely not three or four! No, when she was born her father gave her a special name, based on some experience her parents had had at the time. Perhaps she was called Fig, but that did mean something: Her parents liked to eat figs, or the father was eating one just as the birth of a daughter was announced. Or he named her Child of Hunger because she was born in the time of scarcity, when her parents sometimes suffered from hunger. Or he named her Medicine Horn because of the horn that the witchdoctor had hung in the mother's hut a year before the child's birth. Or he named the child just Traitor. But how can one name one's own, newly born child Traitor? How unkind and how meaningless! Yes, to us white people, to us foreigners! The native who has a child called Traitor knows immediately what it signifies and what sorrow lies hidden behind this word used as a name. He knows that the first born brothers and sisters of this child all died and the father wants to say with this name: You are only deceiving us with your coming, you will not stay with us. Just as the others left, so will you leave. Who can prevent it? Even Tatu will not always remain Three. She will choose a new name for herself. And which one will please her?[19]

A Good Soul

A new era had dawned over the land that had been plagued by the kidnapping of slaves. And Tatu had already become thoroughly acquainted with this new era from the one side. Had anyone earlier heard of or ever known freed slaves? Unconditionally free? They were dragged to the coast and brought to far away places. Sometimes the march lasted many, many months, sometimes even years, depending on whether the slave dealer spent more or less time on the

expedition. But all the kidnapped people were uprooted, their home-
lands faded behind them, and the future was not theirs to determine.
And if they were captured so young, like Tatu, they did not even
have a memory that could accompany them. "We were playing when
the Arabs came!" That was all that Tatu remembered about "then."
She had forgotten the sounds of her native tongue, also the name of
her mother. Where was her home? Later on she had learned that she
was a child of the Bemba tribe. But after her capture she was only
"at home" where she was fed. Thus first at Karonga on Lake Nyasa,
then near the Songwe River, next as a freed slave child at the German
military station, and now at a place where the new era, spreading
over the country, drew the line most sharply against the old era: on
a mission station. Here Tatu was supposed to be a child again and
learn to forget slavery. Here she was also to be shown that man is
only really free when he loosens himself from the chains in which
sin has bound us poor creatures. Tatu as well could only become a
truly free human being when she surrendered herself to Jesus.

First of all she was given a small hut near our house in which to
live, a sleeping mat and a cooking pot and flour in order to cook
herself meals. During the day she came to our house, cared for the
foster child, played with him and learned the lessons at school and
learned writing, reading, and Bible stories. My husband was pleased
with the quick-witted, talented child. At that time we already
had some Nyika youths at the station who had become Christians
and others were under instruction. Tatu asked for this special kind
of lesson.

What a beautiful life it was after the pressure that had lain on her
since early childhood! Her daily nourishment was given to her
lovingly, she had simple work and the small white child was attached
to her, the brown Bemba girl, as if she were his own big sister. She
herself was considered the child of the white people by the other
inhabitants of the station, whose language she had soon learned.
No one could call after her any more, "You! Slave!" No one could
threaten her any longer, You are going to be chained! as her black
foster mothers had occasionally done. For at a mission station there
is no sentence of chains. Now the wounds that had been beaten into
her child's soul throughout the years of slavery could heal.

Tatu also attended a baptism. This experience made such an

impression on her that she soon after came and asked to be baptized like the others. She also wanted to belong to Jesus. Thus she was taken into the next group of candidates for baptism. How eagerly she learned! She amazed my husband time and time again by her exceptional mental capacity and with her correct answers. When none of the black pupils knew how to answer the question, Tatu always helped when needed and soon became the mainstay of her teacher.

And just as she was during that time often the only one among the flock of baptismal pupils who could answer the questions that were asked, there soon came a day when she was the only one not to leave her "parents" when a tidal wave broke over the mission of Utengule and threatened to destroy the budding work. My husband had often had to struggle against laziness among the workers and if he admonished the individuals, they became insolent and with evil words they aired the discontent that had arisen among them. For this reason my husband wanted to discharge the ringleader and paid him off. But then pure revolt broke loose. All the workers gave notice, demanded their pay, and wanted to leave the station. But before they did this, they wanted to burn down their huts.

What was this? The mission station at Utengule had been standing for six years. It had developed into a small Christian community and more and more people asked for the lessons that would enable them to be accepted into this same community. And now this collapse! Where did it come from and did they all really want to leave us? The entire village that had gradually grown up around our living quarters was excited and in a state of unrest. All the quieter was it at our house: We stood completely alone. The courtyard and veranda, where there was usually such rich and often loud life, were empty. The cook from the kitchen, the helper in the workshop, the handiman from the construction site had all disappeared. Only one black face looked so trustingly up at us, as before: It was Tatu. In addition to her usual work, she now took over other chores, but her mere presence was a comfort to us in these dark hours. With her and the small, brown playmate of our foster child, who had also remained and probably did not know what was happening around him, we ended the day and waited for the storm to pass. And it did. The instigators of the strike, in which the young Christians had also become involved, were discovered and the others who had only let themselves be deluded, returned to order. The prime mover in the whole quarrel, the main issue of which was whether one was obliged to obey the missionary as one was the government official, fared very badly the following night. He was probably stung on the foot by a poisonous animal, or was it an unknown tropical disease? And he came limping to my husband in the morning, asked him for an audience and said, "Look at my thickly swollen foot! I wanted to leave Utengule early this morning, but God has punished me, and I cannot leave!" In a few days peace had been restored to the station and the days passed in the old way, filled with their rich work. But since that day Tatu was twice as much our child.

During that time she had grown up and one day one of our Christians, Msisili, who served my husband in the carpentry shop as hired help, came and asked for the hand of our foster daughter. We were very happy about this, but he was to wait a little longer, until she had grown older. I told her, "Tatu, someone asked for your hand in marriage." At first she was very surprised, but then her happiness showed. "Do you know Msisili?" I asked her. She could not remember him at first. When he passed in front of our house a little while later, I pointed him out to her. They must have become friends quickly, for when shortly thereafter he left Utengule to learn cabinet-making in our main station, Rungwe, he left her the harvest of the field he had planted and that meant a great deal. Then she would come proudly bearing a basketful of maize or *batata*,[20] and also with pumpkins from "her" field. When the suitor came to visit from Rungwe, she was permitted daily to cook his porridge. How carefully she always did this! The portion could not be big enough or prettily enough arranged. Again and again she would shape the stiff mass on the heaping plate and spread it smooth. And, beaming, she would then walk into the village to his hut with the porridge on her head and the bowl of vegetables in her hand.

A New Name
A bright ray of love and a feeling of security now lay over Tatu's life. The sad childhood with its fright and need was past and a life of freedom and peace lay before her. Did Tatu have peace in her heart? It did not always seem to be so. The fight of light with the dark

strength of sin also had to be fought within Tatu. Truly she was a dear nanny for our small white foster son and he loved her greatly. Truly she had grown dearer to me during the dark days of the strike in our village. Time and time again she was the most attentive of the flock of candidates in the baptismal class. She grew in knowledge, so that we asked ourselves at times, "From where does this child get her intelligence?" But when she was then called upon to show by her actions that she understood the way of life expected of a Christian, her eagerness waned. The typical faults of her race, carelessness and laziness, were often grounds for complaint. Also with respect to habits of cleanliness and truthfulness, her training presented many difficulties. How often have I sighed and lost patience with her.

Then the day of the baptism neared and the question of whether or not Tatu was ready to be baptized troubled us. But also the other question, whether we had the right to refuse, because of her faults, a child of the mission with such a grasp of Christian teaching who had asked for baptism. My husband finally decided to baptize Tatu after all. She was not quite a Christian but did want to become one.

She had already begun to make her baptismal gown in the sewing room. Until now, like the other girls in the village, she had only wrapped a cloth around herself and bound it tightly under her arms. For the baptism she wanted a dress that came down to her ankles, with a belt that gathered it in at the waist. This was, however, too ambitious a task for her unskilled fingers. She did not progress with her sewing and I had to help her. A beaded headband also went with the Christian women's attire. This manner of decorating oneself is an ancient custom of the Safwa people. What joy it brought to our women and girls that they were allowed to keep this adornment in this new era that had taken from them so many of the customs of their forefathers. When I helped the candidates put on their new Christian clothes before the ceremony, and I asked the girls and women to see their beaded headbands, I did not ask in vain. In answer they stretched out their hands and showed me their jewelry and their eyes sought mine and I always saw a deep joy shining in them. In Tatu as well.

At the test that the candidates for baptism had to take in front of the attentive congregation, Tatu answered the questions best. What else could one expect with her knowledge? And as a new name, she chose for baptism the name Mulondyelwa. The old era when she was a slave and was only Three, nothing more, should now fade away. The new era into which she had entered brought her a new name, Mulondyelwa: "Someone Is Leading Me!" Thus she wanted to be called. She was someone's possession still! But this new master, to whom she belonged of her own free will, did not drive her in front of him, often through the trackless wilderness, but rather guided her forward on her way through life.

Mulondyelwa did not always loyally follow her new master. Often she stopped, so that he had to call her back to him. Once she even strayed completely from the correct path and lost herself in the darkness. She did not always willingly do the work assigned to her. Often she neglected it completely and needed to be punished. Once she was even found in her hut not wholly sober. She had learned to drink beer from the askari women as a young girl and it had become her greatest temptation in life. Her master, however, to whom Mulondyelwa had entrusted herself, did not let her fall, but rather raised her up again and led her farther. At his next stay in Utengule, Msisili, the suitor of our dark foster child, approached my husband and told him he would not take Mulondyelwa to wife, but rather that he had asked for the hand of a Safwa girl from his home in the mountains. We were sad about this, for we would gladly have seen her become the wife of this industrious man. But we understood his desire not to wait any longer, as would have been necessary because of the girl's young age.

Mulondyelwa accepted without complaint that Msisili, of whom she had clearly been so proud, had given her up. Once again I often saw the sharp lines over her eyes and the lips firmly pressed together. Poor child! Soon another suitor presented himself, one of our herdsmen, but he was still so young and still a heathen. At the home of his father he would have had to wait and work for many a year before he could think about taking a wife into his hut. But the white people, the Europeans, were quite different from the Safwa. Ndisa, for so he was called, would have had to work four to five years or more for a Safwa girl and bring his father-in-law many goats, hoes and clothes. As a result he would become a sensible husband who knew how to value his dearly "bought" wife. Mulondyelwa, the "child" of the missionaries, he could have for free; not a single year's work and not one goat was required! Why should he not take her, even if she had once been the betrothed of another man? Year after year had passed. We had left Utengule and journeyed to Germany to gather strength. When in 1906 we again resumed our work at our station, Mulondyelwa was already Ndisa's wife and he himself was no longer called Ndisa, "Stick," but rather Mwitwa, "The One Who Is Called." He had also taken instruction and become baptized.

Conclusion

We want to accompany our Mulondyelwa up to this point in time and now take leave of her. Her life had its start in darkest Africa. Her small feet were made to wander a long way on stony pathways and along these paths drew sharp, pointed thorns: thorns of hot, burning pain, but also thorns of sin, that tore into the conscience of this girl. But then the new era lighted her life, the one that had dawned in the countries here in the eastern part of Africa. A bright ray of light fell along the path of Mulondyelwa's life. Love for her God became her goal through her wanderings with their sin and need. Utengule became her earthly home. Utengule means place of peace. As a child of God she had come to know peace. I sometimes saw peace shining from her dark eyes that could light up so brightly with happiness. But I also saw the tortured expression that her features bore when she had lost that peace again, through some injustice. Here, where we leave her, the actual struggle for the crown, the victor's laurels, begins for the young woman. Will she call out again and again for the help that is leading her, even when she hesitates in her course? Mulondyelwa! Across the lands and seas that separate us now, I call to you, my brown foster daughter! Do not forget what He did for you. Do not forget why you are called Mulondyelwa.

Commentary

The wrench of captivity and removal to distant places plays an important role in the rhetoric of this text. In these remaining pages, the issues of identity are explored in several dimensions, the implications of Tatu's "Bemba" origins, the askari subculture from which she was removed, and finally the turn-of-the-century early colonial world of Safwa women into which she was expected to become domesticated.

A "Bemba" by Origin?

Kootz-Kretschmer indicates many features of Tatu's alienation: her ignorance of the names of those in her intimate family, no recollection of her village or its location, loss of mother tongue, and so on. In some undisclosed way, "later" she found that she was Bemba. Among the possible reasons for assuming this identity is the fact that the preponderance of her fellow-slaves liberated in the mid-1890s spoke dialects similar to Bemba. Also, a number of politically distinct groups have become known collectively as the "Bemba-speaking peoples." And then, too, the fearsomeness of Bemba warriors and their impact on regional affairs in northeast Zambia in the later nineteenth century did not go not unresisted:[21] some of the enslavements resulted from countermeasures against the Bemba. Nevertheless, Bemba expansion had the effect of superimposing a political hegemony, and this tendency to blot out local distinctions was academically and politically reinforced in the naming process of twentieth-century colonial ethnography.[22]

Of thirty-six freed slaves on the list compiled in March 1895, shortly before the dispersal of Mlozi's followers, nine were certainly from groups of this language cluster — five being Bemba, one Bisa, one Tabwa, and two Chishinga. The nine Senga may have had similar origins, since there were Swahili strongpoints in that area.[23] All thirty-six claimed a specific political-ethnic origin, but without a fuller narrative, it is impossible to get at subtleties of status or prior acculturation. A very common language of the slaves, other than the Kiswahili of their owners, would have been a dialect that could be labeled "Bemba" for lack of a known place or political personage with whom to associate and identify. The prevalence of slavery within Bemba society itself must also be noted. The missionary ethnographer Father Louis Etienne reported that the death of a woman in childbirth in precolonial times was often attributed to adultery on the part of the husband, the punishment for which entailed the delivery of at least one female to the clan of the deceased. Such a person or persons could be disposed of as a slave.[24]

Among the Safwa, who lived beyond the peripheries of Bemba aggression, the "enemies" in the form of predatory raiders in the late nineteenth century were first and foremost the Ngoni. Then came the Sangu, who occupied their country and more systematically subjugated them. Before the advent of the Sangu, probably in the later 1860s, an incident occurred that laid the foundations of increased wealth and power for several prominent Safwa leaders. A caravan of coastmen had joined forces with a band of Ngoni intent on raiding a Safwa village.[25] After this action, the Ngoni departed and the coastmen proceeded deeper into Usafwa. A stronger chief called on others to join him in liberating the Safwa women and children who had been taken captive. In defeating the coastmen and restoring the captives taken in their own area, the Safwa chiefs obtained a considerable quantity of ivory and a number of slave women who had been purchased from the Bemba. These became known locally as the "Bemba women." According to one narrator whose father had participated in the operation:

> The Bemba women were very, very many in our country and even today [1912?] there are some here who were lifted from the "Rungwana." The others have all since died. [Chief] Zambi took various of them as wives and had by them very many children. The families that spring from the Bemba women are numerous here in Usafwa.[26]

These Bemba women were famous for their high fertility, but they also remained slaves, disposable if the chiefs began to think that they would be troublemakers.[27] By the first decade of the twentieth century, however, those who had succeeded as wives were honored mothers and forebears.

Tatu, it is reasonable to infer, qualified for the imprecise identity of "Bemba" current at Utengule—that is, a female from the
area of Bemba raids who had become the property of coastmen
and was ultimately absorbed into Safwa society. By seeing such
elements for the construction of an identity, we are no nearer to
knowing positively where Tatu was actually born, only that as
she was called upon to develop a plausible label for an essentially
irretrievable phase of her life, "Bemba" served.

The Askari Subculture

The historical trajectory of colonialism in east and central Africa
was broadly the same regardless of the particular imperial power
responsible from day to day. The regimes went from military to
economic strategies, relying in the first instances upon rather
personal rule by isolated officers. Later they installed a more
bureaucratic form of government with formal, increasingly ho-
mogeneous structures of local government. As colonialism moved
from its early, more personal manifestation of authority toward
systematic hierarchies, the nature of paternalism changed. White
district officials were subordinated to the center, the colonial army
was reformed and separated from the police, and as will become
evident in the subsequent discussion of Usafwa, patriarchal authority had to be strengthened or even invented in order to extend
the chain of command to the village level. The concern of the
present section is with the world from which Tatu was extricated,
that of the askari subculture as an appendage of the nascent
colonial state.

Kootz-Kretschmer casts the *bibis* as unscrupulous camp followers, much as moralizing Westerners have viewed women in
permissive urban conditions. As a Christian missionary, she was
also bound to see Islam as part of an antipathetic cultural package.
While the Sudanese and many of the locally recruited askaris
were Muslim, they were by no means all strictly observant, as the
account of Nigmann's bugler in the later discussion will exemplify.
Contingents of the same "Turkiyya" Sudanese were to be found

in the 1890s in Uganda, where they had been living as a garrison of the Equatoria Province stranded by the Mahdi's control of the middle Nile. Lugard employed them in the conquest of western Uganda and a number became absorbed into the society. "Nubian gin" became a regular part of the alcoholic repertoire and has achieved fame as the locally produced commercial Konyagi of the present. The Muslim female urban culture of Kampala continues to provide an alternative to isolation and anomie.[28]

Women members of askari-expeditionary society of necessity operated within the social formation and norms of their contexts. Drawing upon the open premises of urban culture, these structures were fluid and the Germans did everything they could to routinize the domestic life of their soldiers. A circular by the governor in 1903, addressing the question of how women and dependents could be legitimately attached to askaris, had asserted vigorously that "polygyny and possession of slaves is strictly prohibited to Muslim as well as to heathen askaris."[29] After the Catholic bishops in 1912 complained that captive women were held as slaves by members of the Schutztruppe, a survey of all companies resulted in a largely negative finding. In a few instances, women were discovered to be irregularly married and these were given their choice of whether or not to remain with the soldier, who was obliged to contract a formal marriage, sealed by bridewealth.[30]

The Sudanese corps in the colonial army of German East Africa was initially recruited in 1889 by Hermann von Wissmann after he was commissioned to reorganize the military forces challenged by the Bushiri Rising. German imperialism had been given a bad start under the charter granted to the German East Africa Company. Faced with intense opposition precisely at the point of entry on the coast and its immediate hinterland, he turned to Egypt and signed on six companies of Sudanese, each of one hundred men, who had become unemployed following the success of the Mahdist state in expelling the "Turks."[31] He also brought in one company of "Zulus," actually Nguni of the Gaza state in southern Mozambique, but it was the Sudanese who proved to be the ideal colonial soldiers, being experienced, effective, and willing to stay on for long terms of service and even retire in the country. In due course, rather than remaining in their own companies, they became dispersed, serving as the under-officers and trainers of local recruits. Every inducement was provided to retain them and when they were beyond active army service, they were assigned to police units. Pay, housing and retirement benefits for regular soldiers of the Schutztruppe were systematized after the Maji Maji War of 1905–1906. These progressive terms of service were general to all soldiers and contributed to their extreme loyalty. The desirability of retaining the Sudanese, it may be argued, played an important part in institutionalizing the privileges of the soldiery.[32]

At the conclusion of the Bushiri war, Hermann von Wissmann led an expedition to accomplish the effective occupation of southwestern Tanzania, operating with an imperial commission but funded by the German Anti-Slavery Society. He supplemented the existing Schutztruppe by recruiting Sudanese once again in Egypt and also signed on an assortment of others, including Somalis and Swahilis.[33] Access was by way of the Zambezi and Shire rivers and Lake Nyasa, where a German steamer was assembled and established a regular service. Until after the turn of the century, this route remained the easiest and most reliable one for colonial purposes. Baron von Eltz and a residual force, counted as police rather than army, were left behind in Langenburg at the end of 1893 to build a regional administration.

Langenburg in 1894 has been described as an enclave built upon a triangular spit formed by a river delta behind which was a sheltered anchorage. The central boma, offices and fort combined, was of logs with a double-storied tower carrying small cannon. The garrison consisted of four Europeans and eighty irregular troops, "drilled and officered by Soudanese. Most of these irregulars are drawn from the Atonga, and the local tribes inhabiting the country around the North-End of Lake Nyasa. They look smart and soldier-like in their khaki b[l]ouses and red fezzes." The brickworks used the fine local clays and construction of brick buildings was underway, the gardens were abundant and there were fifty head of cattle and quantities of goats, sheep, pigs, chickens and ducks. "The houses of the soldiers are situated in line on both sides of the parade ground, and beyond are the workers' houses, and bricksheds."[34]

This idyllic picture drawn by a British visitor did not anticipate the Nyakyusa Rising of 1897, early in Tatu's residence in Langenburg. The Nyakyusa resistance grew from popular animosity, above all against forced labor for construction of the district headquarters. A large number of princes, rulers of autonomous areas but revering common dynastic founders, banded together to withstand punitive expeditions.[35] The Bezirksamtmann of the time was Captain von Elpons, nicknamed Hamusini for the number of strokes he imposed in physical punishments.[36] It is undetermined whether von Elpons was one of those imperial men of action who courted a military confrontation in order to achieve hegemony by outright conquest rather than by infiltration and diplomacy, or if he simply wanted to build by forced labor for lack of centrally provided funds. In any event, he made it clear that he would tolerate no resistance. Parallel examples of the ruthless district colonial boss were to be found in British as well as in German times, but in provoking a rebellion amid a people who had missionaries as their allies, the Bezirksamtmann shortened his time in the district and hastened the institution of reforms. In 1900, the headquarters moved to the Nyakyusa uplands. The ranks of police included locally recruited men, one complaint having been the inability of the police to communicate in Kinyakyusa rather than Kiswahili.[37] In 1905, the police strength for the Langenburg District stood at 2 white subofficers, 9 "colored" subofficers, and 115 askaris.[38]

For a somewhat interior view of the officers and soldiers of the time, we turn to Ernst Nigmann, who presents himself as the image of benevolent paternalistic colonial service in the military mode. He was among the officers seconded from the German army to serve in German East Africa. In contrast to Elise Kootz-Kretschmer, whose overseas work was a likelihood from her birth into the Moravian community and whose destination could well have been any of a number of non-German-controlled parts of the world, Nigmann represents the deployment of personnel from national service in Europe to national service in the empire. In his own estimation, there was no better situation than that of Bezirkschef: "For a creative, active man, there was hardly a more ideal position than that of a military district Chef: stimulating, autonomous, multi-farious, at once instructive and rich in success."[39]

His history of the Schutztruppe gave special credit to the officers of the German army who contributed to the scientific knowledge of the colony.[40] Among the works of ethnography was his own impressive study of the people of the Iringa District, *Die Wahehe.* With his long residence and wide-ranging responsibility in Iringa, it is not surprising that his volume of humorous recollections contains valuable anecdotes of life in the community surrounding the commandant there.[41] Before drawing upon these recollections, however, background on Iringa is called for, since it was by no means identical with Langenburg, the scene of Tatu's transitory attachment to askari society.

Iringa was founded as a colonial stronghold in the second half of 1896, when German expeditionary forces under Captain von Prince occupied the center of Hehe country and forced Chief Mkwawa out of his capital. The conquest of the Hehe required two years, during which Iringa was a garrison town with numbers amplified by auxiliaries, allies, and refugees, swelling to much greater size than the frontier outpost at Langenburg.[42] Among the social consequences of protracted warfare, according to von Prince's wife, Magdalene, was a depressed condition afflicting older women. The ratio of sexes was lopsided in Iringa, with the shortage of young men arising from war casualties, compounded by the numbers of additional women brought in as captives. Young women fared relatively well and wore new cloth while old women had almost nothing to put on. A rule seemed to apply:

"The older and uglier, so much crueler the work and meaner the pay." The Iringa population contained another category, "mamas," or campfollowers, who looked after the poorer, effectively single men of the station town. The commandant considered such women to be promiscuous and the focus of disorder, persons whom he would ideally have repatriated to the coast.[43]

Magdalene von Prince's published diary most fully reflects the circle formed by the recognized wives of professional soldiers, officers, and underofficers. In late October 1896, she noted, "Now the women began to come to air their problems. Each day I have six to eight of them, who also expect refreshments."[44] Magdalene saw herself as a patroness, not a judge. She also identified her own circumstances with those of "my ladies."

> My Sudanese women are in many respects my fellows in destiny: they also are strangers here, having left their homeland in order to follow their husbands to an unknown country. At the moment they too are grass widows, for the Sudanese are our best askaris, and are taken along on every expedition.[45]

Still childless herself, she remarked on the pride with which the relatively few Sudanese women who had children displayed them. For most, "as a consequence of the stress and burdens of the journeys on which they had to accompany their husbands," she wrote, "their children died at the tenderest of ages."[46] Regular askaris generally had male servants, generically called "boys," who lightened the domestic load of wives. Lacking their own children, they may have welcomed the services of apprentice girls as well. The girls who came to be under Magdalene's wing as orphans were taught to sew and launder, but she found it difficult to find an askari's wife, including those of local recruits, who was willing to act as a servant.[47]

When the Sudanese wives assembled at the commandant's house in March 1897 to celebrate the Eid at the end of Ramadan, they were served sweets and coffee. The wife of the ranking

Sudanese officer, the Effendi, accepted a glass of wine. In commenting on this event in her diary, Magdalene underscored the uniformity of the tobes, predominantly white and yellow in color, and of the display of silver jewelry. Rank was reflected in the quality of the cloth, from fine to coarse, and in physical appearance ranging from the finely chiseled features of the Effendi's wife at one extreme to, at the other, the round, amiable faces of the temporary wives of lesser soldiers. Such qualities were not to be confused with goodness or badness, she hastened to add.[48]

Nigmann's tales of Iringa are those of a commandant with no German family in evidence. The cares of the wives and of other women, as well as of the askaris, were occasionally brought to him. Of the two tales illustrating his views of himself as drawn into women's lives, the first presents an instance in which his patriarchal authority and benevolence were put to the test by the petition of a protégée of the administration that her marriage be arranged. Nigmann states that Johari had come to Iringa as a foundling, a child of about nine when she was found in an uninhabited place by askaris sent out to police an intervillage conflict. After returning to Iringa, they gave her to someone in the military community to be cared for. She subsequently appeared at one of the commandant's regular court days, an attractive and mature woman who took the public occasion to propose that as she was a dependent of the administration and he its local head, Nigmann ought to see to her marriage. Nigmann agreed. Turning to his corporal for advice as to which of the government's servants needed a wife, he ascertained that the askari Saidi, a member of the military band, had recently lost his wife. While Saidi was being fetched, Nigmann publicly inquired whether Johari had any property, and upon hearing her predictable statement that she was poor, gave her an authorization to select two cows from the official herd to have as her own. Saidi appeared and readily agreed to the marriage. He was admonished to have many children, for in Nigmann's view the population was not growing as quickly as it should and "we need people to occupy the land, guard the cattle and be Askaris."[49]

This entire sequence was performed wittingly by all parties, who also knew that the public was being drawn into the process. Nigmann, indeed, made it clear that the quality of justice meted out by the Bezirkschefs was an important means of extending the influence of the colonial rulers.[50] On the other hand, not all hearings were held in public. Within the community, a more confidential role of counseling was performed. Askaris came with personal problems, and patriarchal responsibilities extended also to the wives, who turned to the commander of a company to deal with sensitive matters.[51]

Another of Nigmann's tales had to do with an older Sudanese and his difficult wife. A certain Bibi Faida appeared one day at Nigmann's office in her finest garb to complain about her husband, in Nigmann's terms a splendid bugler and a fearless soldier with whom he had been shoulder to shoulder in engagements during the Maji Maji War. But Abdu was an inveterate drunkard who often had his pay docked because he spent so much time in prison. Upon being asked what she expected Nigmann to do about this situation, Faida finally said that Nigmann could execute Abdu. Nigmann protested that his superiors at the capital would not approve, to which she replied that once he explained that he was getting Abdu out of the way in order to marry her, certainly they would be satisfied. Not wishing to offend her, the commandant said that he had three wives in Germany to whom he had to remit his salary and until one of them died, he could not afford to marry her, so she ought to stay with Abdu.[52]

Beyond the humor of this situation, there are indications of a cultural accommodation within the personalized and interdependent world of askaris and their officers. The situation of the raconteur, uprooted from the scene of his authority by Germany's loss of the war and its colonies, and separated also by the evolution toward less personalized command, no doubt led to idealization and must be taken into account as shaping this tale. Nigmann's official reports, however, suggest that the milieu was loaded with intimacies as well as inequalities. To carry the interpretation of

Nigmann's account beyond the available evidence is hazardous, but worth the venture if it will open new avenues of consideration and investigation. His choice of three as the number of wives to be supported in Germany, for example, indicates that he may have had one with him, perhaps a Muslim mistress. Such relationships were quite public in Iringa at the time and figured in Nigmann's reports in 1908 and 1909, when Muslim brotherhoods were regrouping and bringing their women back to more exclusive association. The occasion for innovation and greater control was a millennial message calling for ritual purity in the face of the imminent day of judgment. For the first time, women joined the congregations at prayer in the mosque and danced at Muslim funerals.[53]

Nigmann first got wind of the movement when a German reported that his mistress-housekeeper had announced that she must leave him in order to comply with these teachings. Turning to his trusted Muslim underofficer, Nigmann received reassurances that no proper Muslim would want women in the mosque, and that the movement was not so much antiwhite as simply denominational, just another example of missionaries preaching that their adherents should not marry beyond their particular church.[54] It subsequently became apparent, when there was a general resignation of Muslim male domestic servants in Iringa, that the movement had broader implications.[55] By then, however, the Germans had decided that the phenomenon was not politically threatening and they allowed it to subside without reacting. The loyalty of the Schutztruppe, sealed by the Maji Maji campaigns, respect for Islam of the orthodox variety, and enhanced privilege, remained secure.

To develop a fuller account of women and ex-slaves in the askari subculture will not be easy because of the changes already under way in the years before 1914, with the segregation of the Schutztruppe as an army in camps away from the district headquarters. The campaigns of World War I kept the forces continually on the move and led those who survived to be dispersed.

Still retrievable, however, are family traditions that celebrate the era of early colonial askari communities. In association with a fuller search of the contemporary literature generated by Africans, intimate outsiders, and others, these traditions will enrich not only an interpretation of the memoir of Tatu but also that of social history of the colonial and postcolonial state in formation.

Authority in Usafwa: Limited Patriarchy and the Unresolved Colonial Situation

Turning to Utengule and Safwa society, we find another context that colonial and missionary authorities sought to stabilize. To understand the nature of its instability is to venture into the complexities of a popular culture that supported no political centralization on the part of its own leadership. The chiefs were little more than exalted headmen able to accumulate greater followings and resources in the circumstances of commercial opportunity and alliances that existed in the late nineteenth century. Also at this time, the Safwa experienced the occupation of the more centralized and militarized Sangu. The Sangu era saw the development of a pattern of collaboration and resistance that the Germans encountered and sought to manipulate. The Sangu paramount chiefs dominated the immediate vicinity of Utengule, their capital in exile, and posted representatives in more distant areas, sometimes at the request of the Safwa who feared encroachments by other aggressive African societies wishing to control a corridor of trade.[56] The Sangu also dealt with conflicts arising from disputes among the Safwa themselves. The Safwa resented Sangu hegemony but later exhibited the same inability to resolve the divisiveness within their own ranks under German colonialism.

In 1899, the Sangu were restored to their country to the east of Mbeya and the Safwa were "liberated" with a ceremony recognizing the symbol of resistance, Chief Mwaryego, as their senior. He established himself near Utengule, not far from the place evacuated by the Sangu chief and his entourage. The chief's mansion and compound were ceremoniously put to the fire by von Elpons, who expected the Safwa to be grateful and obedient. The paramountcy of the Safwa chief Mwaryego proved, however, to be ineffective. By 1901 and 1902 his capacity to maintain order was so demonstrably feeble that a new German Bezirksamtmann, very committed to civil rule, declared that Usafwa had dissolved into anarchy and that brigandage was common. Not even the remaining Sangu subchief, once a figure of great respect, was able to exert influence.[57] The Utengule mission was in many ways an outpost of German colonialism. The reputation of Johannes Kootz, the missionary in charge, vacillated over a wide spectrum. In the first years, on the doorstep of the Sangu capital, he was disparaged by the paramount chief as a "woman" not worth listening to because of his pacifist stand. A boycott of the missionaries ordered by the Sangu ruler had been totally effective in cutting off supplies of Safwa labor and provisions; the holdup was outlasted only by means of relief caravans from mission stations in Nyakyusa country.[58] As the missionaries began to learn the Nyiha–Safwa dialects, they gained a reputation for being on the side of the subjugated. Rumor had it that Kootz was writing constantly to Langenburg to plead for them and was thus responsible for their formal liberation and the removal of the Sangu.[59] Much as Elise Kootz–Kretschmer later disavowed the perception and attendant reputation, it was true that the missionaries were connected, even if not in their own eyes, to a political arm of the German colonial regime.[60]

The gathering of a Christian community at Utengule resulted in the later 1890s from the recruitment of Nyiha laborers from outside the sphere of Sangu power, followed at the turn of the century by an immigration of headmen with their villagers to occupy the lands made available by the displacement of the Sangu.[61] The headmen of these settlements exercised their own authority, but could not prevent members from removing themselves to the mission, where the missionary had jurisdiction. Typically, new residents were male, often having been introduced to the Utengule mission as migrant workers earning money by employment for a month at a time. One such former worker told of his interview when he returned as a would-be settler requesting land on which to cultivate and build a home. He followed the usual steps in requesting land from a headman, choosing a man from the community to sponsor him, and then being questioned closely on the circumstances of his leaving his old place. Ruxindixo-Benyanga began with a simple statement: "I wish to move to Utengule," to which Mutengovuraro (Kootz) replied, "From whence?" "From Songwe, Marema's place." Asked, "Have you possibly committed an offense in your home community on account of which you have fled?" he answered, "No, I have not offended at home. I simply want to move here." Then Kootz said, "That is well, move here then."[62] Kootz had several ways of checking on Ruxindixo, for Marema's senior wife and son had become Christians and the chief himself had discarded his second wife in anticipation of becoming a Christian.[63]

Attendance at religious instruction, which was daily announced by the ringing of the bell, was only recommended, not required as a condition of land occupancy. It was nevertheless a matter of clientage for workers and settlers to attend instruction, and young men thus predominated in the classes. For older women, on the other hand, community was established by attendance at Sunday services, where, in 1900, Kootz complained of a preponderance of Safwa women. For older women in particular, perhaps partly owing to Kootz's yet imperfect command of Kisafwa, it was sometimes only after years of attendance that Christian ideas began to make sense.[64] The painfully slow progress made by the virtuous and constant older women had not prepared the missionaries for Tatu's quickness, and they were subject to qualms that her conversion might be facile.

The event that riveted the relationship of Kootz-Kretschmer and Tatu, the strike and threatened exodus of late 1900, occurred just at the beginning of the German officials' project for indirect rule through Safwa chiefs, when they were preoccupied with the building of "New Langenburg." The majority of striking workers were not Safwa, but rather Nyiha who had formed the backbone of the community and were also the nucleus of resident adherents. Utengule itself was at the time in the throes of major construction, with the missionary's home and the church going up, and brickworks and carpentry shops in full swing. In contrast to the colonial administration, which from time to time requisitioned labor as tribute or in lieu of taxes, the missions paid for contracted labor in construction and for herding and other tasks. The strike of 1900 seems to have been precipitated by a number of factors, including Kootz's efforts to gain greater productivity through work discipline. Parallel to this speed-up, Kootz had called upon adherents to contribute their labor on Sundays when the regular workers were off, and to carry loads for the missionaries "on rare and very special occasions."[65] Kootz fired the leading dissident and discovered that, in solidarity, all the workers and residents turned against him and threatened to leave. The old Sangu slur from the early days, that as a pacifist he was only a "woman," was used to diminish his authority.[66] Kootz-Kretschmer cites a variant that made explicit the difference between the missionary and the Bezirksamtmann, who had to be obeyed (i.e., could commandeer labor). The difference between the Bezirksamtmann and local headmen and compound seniors was of the same order, for they too regularly experienced secessions or threats of secession when they were deemed to be tyrannical. Safwa independency typically surfaced in April, a month named Rejaxa or rebellion, because the ripening crops made it possible for exploited dependents to renegotiate their attachments.[67] The awe enjoyed by the colonial authorities was itself something that had to be renewed with shows of force, more regular inspection, and withdrawal of recognition from Mwaryego. The unruly Safwa were not yet ready for Indirect Rule.

After the strike, the missionaries decided to court the Safwa and played up nuances in their ethnic differences from the Nyiha. Especially after returning from leave in Germany in 1906, Kootz-

Kretschmer became an ever more enthusiastic student of local culture. As the community matured, African leaders joined her in the remarkable project of recording the narratives of first-generation Christians. The new context of colonialism saw the incorporation of Safwa men into subcontinental patterns of migrant labor, including circulation to the gold mines of Southern Rhodesia as early as 1906.[68] The Utengule texts, however, remained mostly local in their preoccupations and still very engaged with the eventful times of the late nineteenth century and the conflicts played out during the transition to the colonial era.

Female Choices and Female Autonomy

The women of the Utengule Christian community whose narratives are available moved there, for the most part, to be with their sons and to look after grandchildren. Brothers came to join brothers. In general, it would seem that in the years of Tatu's adolescence, marriageable girls were scarce and most marriages entailed finding partners in non-Christian villages. What gave a Safwa character to the community was precisely the mother-son bond. Indeed, the basic social and economic unit of the culture was the "house," comprising a woman and her own offspring.[69] Mothers supported their sons while they engaged in brideservice, and sons and daughters of the same mother could expect to inherit access to land and even some belongings through her. Kootz-Kretschmer was aware of this passage of property through women but made little of it, commenting that when she liked her husband, a woman handed her inheritance or acquired land over to him.[70] Much as she favored male authority, she had to grant the regularity with which houses seceded and young dependent males escaped the control of senior men presiding over large compounds. She also acknowledged that husbands were obliged to work on the fields assigned by their lineage to the wives, and had no right to control the harvest.[71] Thus, when Tatu was proprietary toward the produce coming from the garden her fiance had hoed and left to her, it was by no means abnormal.

It is unclear whether a suitor engaged in brideservice served only the house—essentially his mother-in-law's unit of production—or could also be engaged on the separate fields a man established, using only dependent male labor, in case he wanted to have a harvest to invest in trade or prestige activities.[72] The elaborate customs of avoidance between father-in-law and son-in-law prior to the birth of the first child suggest that the suitor's work was for the house, not the father. Whatever the usual lines of obligation, Kootz-Kretschmer underscores how lucky was the youth, such as Tatu's husband, who did not have to provide brideservice and a ritually prescribed succession of gifts.

A fundamental condition in Safwa society was the right of girls to refuse a man up to the last minute before moving to his family's compound, even though he had performed years of brideservice and made the required gifts. In view of this permissiveness toward girls, it is understandable that Chisi's master had refused to make her available for marriage in the conventional way, as the chief had recommended, for he knew that by simply making her his own slave wife, he obtained much greater security than was enjoyed by the fathers or the suitors of free women.[73] The other relatively riskless way of marrying was to choose a widow or separated woman, which might be accomplished either with a smaller investment or simply by agreement with an autonomous woman. The route of simple agreement seems to have been that which prevailed between Chisi and her second, rather shadowy, husband, and it best fits Tatu's arrangement with the herdsman who took her on, in a sense, as an abandoned wife.[74]

The manner adopted in female narratives about marriage tends to diminish the element of agreement. Chisi, for example, says of her second husband only that "he took me." The convention, maintained by pretense when necessary, was that a girl did not know a suitor before he approached her parents or guardians. The authority and responsibility for the contract lay with the elders. Men took the initiative, even though women subsequently made choices, participating in rearrangements even while preserving the appearance that others were in charge. Conventionally, there were three modes of initiating a Safwa marriage. The first was by making a contract with parents, usually with the assent of the girl, followed by brideservice. Given that the agreement of a preadolescent girl was not binding, it was probably safer to attempt one of the other two means, elopement or abduction, to be followed by brideservice and the presentation of small livestock, cloth, and hoes.[75] Women who were offered several of these options at the same time by different men might elope, leaving the recognized suitor, who then lost the value of services given, even if he was able to retrieve the gifts. Needless to say, such goings-on frequently resulted in quarrels and feuds among men.

The narrative of Murotwa-Ntamata contains evidence of a host of disputes in which women precipitated conflicts, ranging from a senior man's futile protest against marriages that were technically endogamous and thus illegitimate, to the elopement of a girl to whom another had been engaged through brideservice, to the marriage of a widow to a man unrelated to her deceased husband and thus not a legitimate successor.

Murotwa himself was an interloper:

In July 1902, I discussed [marriage] with Havenberi Ndjerije secretly because she already belonged to someone else. And when we had agreed, we ran away to Manganya and stayed there two days. On the third day my brother...came and said "Nypya! I'm in trouble [literally I am afire] in the village through your fault in running away with the girl."[76]

Reprisals had already been taken by the time the brother returned with the girl to engage in negotiations. The parents were divided, the mother favoring Murotwa and her husband feeling bound by his contract with the man who had done brideservice. In this case, the girl's biological father was able to intervene and tip the balance in favor of Murotwa, whom he offered the alternatives of bride-wealth or brideservice. Murotwa, now in wage employment, could not afford to move to the father's distant compound for several years, so he gave the small stock, cloth and other required presentations and then delivered a "niece" as a pawn until he was able to raise enough money for the cow required as bridewealth.

From the standpoint of women and feminists, a key question raised by Murotwa's compromise is about how the "niece" came to be available for delivery as a pawn. Grandmother Narwimba conveys an affected person's observations in her account of the struggle against the definition of her children and grandchildren as part of a disposable fund available to the chief. At Utengule, she joined a community that had a similar capacity to identify with victims. Msatulwa, the established leader in 1908, recounts how he had earlier, when still a slave, fended off the proposal of a passerby to buy his "sister," a girl who happened to be sitting with him. The passage is not explicit, but Msatulwa suggests that a proper offer for a girl would be secured by wealth provided by a father — that is, through customary marriage making, not payment of commercial cloth made in Europe, stocked locally by the African Lakes Company, and increasingly, at the turn of the century, associated with Europeans like the Greek whom Msatulwa mentions, who were engaged in rubber trade using many African agents.[77] Msatulwa's position after the turn of the century was enhanced by various services as an interpreter for the district authorities when they were called in to cool local turmoil.[78] Narwimba's account can be used in a complementary way to supply a vantage point of one entangled in the side effects of "self-help" violence at the popular level when she describes how a boy child totally unrelated to the disputants became a hostage in a conflict that finally required the intervention of askaris and the German Bezirksamtmann.[79]

Conclusion

Tatu's story has a special quality owing to her recognized intellectual brilliance and her overt disinterest in the menial tasks of either a domestic servant or an ordinary Safwa woman. It makes no claim to be an autobiography and is weak as biography in being so much the product of Kootz-Kretschmer's consciousness. On the other hand, the contribution of an intimate outsider's observation of her resistance may expose more about her temperament and unwillingness to conform than would a more autobiographical narrative. The first-person accounts of older ex-slave women tend to recount their tribulations but eventual happiness. Here we see only a troubled and obstreperous young woman, not yet a mother. The reconstruction of contexts may permit us to expand on the modes of socialization that surrounded and attempted to claim her. Historical inquiry cannot, however, reveal how and why, by 1915, she had surrendered to them only in part.

Notes

1 *"Tatu, das geraubte Muvembakind"* (Herrnhut, 1927), translated by Katya Skow, July 1988. The missionary spirit of this pamphlet is indicated by its attribution to "Frau Missionar E. Kootz," rather than as in her ethnographic work, published concurrently, Elise Kootz-Kretschmer.

2 Kootz-Kretschmer was underway on a return to Germany in 1916 when she was detained. As she describes her repatriation through the Belgian Congo, her most prized baggage was what we call the Utengule texts, which were searched seven times by customs officials and reviewed three times by censors. This wealth of oral evidence recorded between 1906 and 1916 was published between 1926 and 1931 in the three volumes collectively titled *Die Safwa, ein ostafrikanischer Volkstamm, in seinem Leben und Denken* (Berlin, 1926–29). The first and second contain her translations into German with notes and commentary and the third publishes some but not all of the vernacular originals, a number of which did not survive the war (*Die Safwa,* vol. 1, 9).

3 The evidence from others in Utengule will be used in the commentary below, especially the section on the situation of ex-slaves and other women after the turn of the century.

4 Shula Marks in *Not Either an Experimental Doll* (London, 1987) confronts the problem of colonial, African elite and African aspirant figures interacting with one another in a thwarted relationship. Her presentation of this triangle is aided by a more balanced set of documents, correspondence generated by each of the women. For questions of authorship, see M. Wright, "Autobiographies, histoires de vie et biographies de femmes africaines en tant que textes militants," *Cahiers d'études africaines* 38, no. 108 (1988).

5 O. Baumann, *Afrikanische Skizzen* (Berlin, 1900). The ethnographic work most proximate in every way to the composition of these tales was O. Baumann, *Der Sansibar-Archipel,* 2 vols. (Dencker and Humblot, Leipzig, 1897).

6 *Die Safwa,* vol. 1, 10. See Friedrich Fuelleborn, *Das Deutsche Njassa und Ruwumagebiet: Land und Leute* (Berlin, 1906).

7 *Die Safwa,* vol. 2, 321–31.

8 Nigmann, like Baumann and Kootz-Kretschmer, wrote in several modes. See his *Die Wahehe* (Berlin, 1908), *Geschichte der Kaiserlichen Schutztruppe fuer Deutsch-Ostafrika* (Berlin, 1911), and *Schwarze Schwaenke* (Berlin, 1923). Chirupula Stephenson wrote a candid autobiography and also as an old man after World War II turned out his own small newsletter containing ethnographic tidbits, commentary on culture and changing times, and advocacy. For a discussion of his life and literary legacy, see M. Wright, "Chirupula Stephenson and Copperbelt History," *African Social Research,* no. 14 (1972). M. Fortie is known only for his autobiography, *Black and Beautiful: A Life in Safari Land* (Indianapolis, 1938), the first section of which covers the years 1901–1909.

9 Baumann himself pointed out the chapter on "Salama" as his most considered conclusion about what slave-concubine women endured (*Afrikanische Skizzen,* 2, 55–69). Conditions and policies in both British and German East Africa were reviewed "scientifically" in F. Weidner, *Die Haussklaverei in Ostafrika* (Jena, 1915).

10 Details of women's roles and women's loads among Swahili regional traders are given in J. E. Stephenson, "Muhammedan Early Days in

the Copperbelt of Northern Rhodesia," National Archives of Zambia, Occasional Paper 1.

11 M. Wright and P. Lary, "Swahili Settlements in Northern Zambia and Malawi," *IJAHS* 4, no. 3 (1971).

12 Katya Skow, the translator of this memoir, has reflected on the experience as follows: "I found it easier to capture the contradictions of the author's attitudes toward African culture than to re-create her childish manner of address. I was left confused about whether her audience was intended to be a youthful German-reading one or Tatu herself."

13 *Ulezi* is millet, the staple grain used throughout the region for the thin porridge given to children, the stiff porridge of the main family meal, and the brewing of beer, a vital feature of reciprocating work arrangements.

14 There are many accounts of the "Arab wars" in northern Nyasaland (Malawi). The literature published before 1970 is cited in M. Wright and P. Lary. For a subsequent discussion of local history in the Karonga District at that time, see O. J. M. Kalinga, "The Karonga War: Commercial Rivalry and Politics of Survival," *JAH* 21, no. 2 (1980).

15 A Bezirksamtmann was the civil commissioner in charge of a large district, about the size of the modern political regions of Tanzania.

16 The Sudanese component of the askari-military community is discussed below.

17 In the time of Swahili caravans, important male members brought along "junior wives" who attended to their needs. Other women carried assigned commercial loads, usually beads. See Stephenson, "Muhammedan Early Days," 8–9.

18 Fire: For households dependent upon open fires, the risk of burns and damage to highly flammable dwellings constituted a subject of public concern and private discipline. In the narrative of Mama Meli, an incident of her carelessness around a fire precipitated one of her sales (Meli, p. 98). The contrast between free and unfree and male and female ways of reckoning liability in cases of arson and accidental fire is indicated in the early colonial court records of Northeastern Rhodesia. In the usual way of settling for damages in late nineteenth-century east-central Africa, a man had to pay compensation. The court at Abercorn in June and July 1902 heard the case

of one Kalemirwa, a Bemba, whose sister had figured in an elaborate chain of events precipitated by a fire that got out of control. "One Sichuwalkika accidentally burnt the village of Kafola when drying fish. From Chief Changala this man obtained the girl Mukuka to settle his case with Tonga-Mwenya who had paid a gun on his account to [the headman of] Kafola." When the court inquired further as to how the girl had come to be used in this way, it ascertained that a well-born youth had been convicted of adultery with one of Chief Changala's wives and had delivered the girl Mukuka as compensation to the chief. How he had commandeered the girl as an asset is not reported (ZNA BSI 147). Women having no claims to property, like slave women cut off from male relatives who might settle a case for them, had to take punishment of a more directly physical sort. Girls and young women in general needed to be vigilant about fire and slaves might rightly fear that they could be made scapegoats, bearing the consequences of others' inadvertence.

19 As indicated, names were often changed. A provisional name at birth frequently reflected the kinds of circumstances the author notes. When the child survived infancy, it received another name and might at maturity choose his or her own name. These personal names were in addition to ancestral or family names. The Moravian practice of choosing baptismal names with a pietistic reference extended this tradition of naming.

20 *Batata* locally meant sweet potatoes.

21 The introduction to Meli's story contains elements of a family history shaped by Bemba overrule (see p. 93). For a comprehensive discussion of Bemba expansion, see A. D. Roberts, *History of the Bemba* (Madison, 1973).

22 W. H. Whiteley, *The Bemba and Related Peoples of Northern Rhodesia* (London, 1951). Among "Bemba-speakers" in 1933 were the Bisa, Aushi, Unga, Kamwendi, Mukulu, Ngumba, Chishinga, Tabwa, Shila, Bwile, Twa, and Bemba proper. The Bemba then numbered 114,274 and the Bisa 41,591. The rest collectively made up the other 50 percent counted in this linguistic group.

23 Nauhaus to Committee, 7 March 1895. Berlin Mission 4.1.8b, Bd. 1; Wright and Lary, 561 ff.

24 L. Etienne, "A Study of the Babemba and the Neighbouring Tribes" (Kasama, n.d., mimeographed), 8. The distortion of punishments by

commercial relations and indebtedness in the late nineteenth century must be recalled. Matrilineal societies and high-status families of deceased women combined to increase the exactions and subsequent risks for women given as compensation. See Bwanikwa's account of her own origins in slavery, p. 159.

25 E. Kootz-Kretschmer, "Abriss einer Landesgeschichte von Usafwa in Ostafrika," *Koloniale Rundschau* (reprint, 1929), 8–9.

26 *Die Safwa,* vol. 2, 170.

27 *Die Safwa,* vol. 2, 215.

28 D. H. Johnson, "The Structure of a Legacy: Military Slavery in Northeast Africa," *Ethnohistory* 36, no. 1 (1989), 72–88. See I. Smith, *The Emin Pasha Relief Expedition* (Oxford, 1972), 260–61, and M. Bartlett, *The King's African Rifles: A Study in the Military History of East and Central Africa, 1890*–1945 (Aldershot, Gale and Polden, 1956), 50–57. The persisting vigor of Muslim female urban culture is indicated by Christine Obbo's paragraphs on Nubianization in *African Women: Their Struggle for Economic Independence* (London, 1980), 108–10.

29 Governor von Goetzen, Circular, 3 July 1903, TNA G9/7. By 1903 the colonial forces were composed of an amalgam of men, increasingly of East African origins. To the small numbers of Swahili belonging to the original Wissmanntruppe had been added the Manyema and then the Nyamwezi: ethnic groups that had been closely associated in the late nineteenth century with the precolonial caravan trade. The annual reports of the German East Africa Protectorate contain details of this composition and reflect changes.

30 TNA, G9/4.

31 Nigmann, *Geschichte,* 2–4. See also C. von Perbandt, *et al., Hermann von Wissmann: Deutschlands Groesster Afrikaner: sein Leben und Wirken unter Benutzung des Nachlasses* (Berlin, 1906).

32 Nigmann, *Geschichte,* 125.

33 C. von Perbandt, et al.

34 BCAG 1, 12, 26 September 1894. For photographs of Langenburg in 1899, see F. Fuelleborn, *Das Deutsche Njassa und Ruwuma-Gebeit: Atlas* (Berlin, 1906).

35 M. Wright, "Nyakyusa Cults and Politics" in *The Historical Study of African Religions,* eds. T. O. Ranger and I. N. Kimambo (London, 1972), 168.

36 See for example Murotwa's narrative, *Die Safwa,* vol. 2, 303. Ruthless German commandeering is described by Fortie, 29–30.
37 M. Wright, *German Missions in Tanganyika: Moravians and Lutherans in the Southern Highlands, 1891–1941* (Oxford, 1971), 63–64.
38 Nigmann, *Geschichte,* 167. The "New Langenburg" station is the present-day district political center called Tukuyu. A company of Schutztruppe was eventually, in the years just before World War I, garrisoned at Masoko, some kilometers downhill.
39 Nigmann, *Geschichte,* 77.
40 *Ibid.,* 79ff.
41 Nigmann served in Iringa between 1900 and 1908.
42 See A. Redmayne, "Mkwawa and the Hehe Wars," *JAH* 9, no. 3 (1968), 409–436.
43 M. von Prince, *Eine Deutsche Frau im Innern Deutsch-Ostafrikas* (Berlin, 1903), 61, 79.
44 *Ibid.,* 98.
45 *Ibid.,* 78.
46 *Ibid.,* 79.
47 *Ibid.,* 45, 201.
48 *Ibid.,* 78–79.
49 Nigmann, *Schwarze Schwaenke,* 142.
50 Nigmann, *Geschichte,* 78–79.
51 Nigmann, *Schwarze Schwaenke,* 162.
52 *Ibid.,* 164.
53 See J. Iliffe, *German Colonial Rule in Tanganyika* (Cambridge, 1970), 190, 195. See also B. G. Martin, "Muslim Politics and Resistance to Colonial Rule," *JAH* 10, no. 3 (1969).
54 Nigmann report, 10 September 1908, TNA G9/4b.
55 Nigmann report, 11 February 1909, TNA G9/4b.
56 *Die Safwa,* vol. 2, 273.
57 Fuelleborn, 491. See also Kootz-Kretschmer, "Abriss," 28–29.
58 Wright, *German Missions,* 67–68.
59 *Die Safwa,* vol. 2, 184.
60 *Die Safwa,* vol. 2, 193, 225. See also Periodical Accounts (PA).
61 *Die Safwa,* vol. 2, 227.
62 *Die Safwa,* vol. 2, 184.
63 PA 5, 49 (1902), 14. The trickle of people from Marema's is also indicated by Chisi's narrative, p. 89.

64 PA 5, 37 (1900), 260–61.
65 PA 5, 49 (1902), 14.
66 *Die Safwa,* vol. 2, 228.
67 *Die Safwa,* vol. 1, 159.
68 PA, 6 (1907), 570.
69 A. Harwood, *Witchcraft, Sorcery and Social Categories among the Safwa* (London, 1970), 23.
70 *Die Safwa,* vol. 1, 62. See also Harwood, 23.
71 *Die Safwa,* vol. 1, 164.
72 *Die Safwa,* vol. 1, 164.
73 See p. 85 for Chisi.
74 See p. 88 for Chisi and p. 197 for Tatu.
75 *Die Safwa,* vol. 1, 55. See also the story of Chisi, p. 89.
76 *Die Safwa,* vol. 2, 203.
77 See p. 70.
78 *Die Safwa,* vol. 1, 7.
79 See pp. 54–55. P. H. Gulliver, in *Disputes and Negotiations: A Cross-Cultural Perspective* (New York, Academic Press, 1979), introduces the term "self-help violence" for the type of reprisals common to the Safwa. Legal anthropology here provides an apt typology, but it fails to catch historical processes and ramifications beyond the parties recognized judicially to be in direct conflict.

Bibliography

To underscore the way in which this volume draws upon clusters of first-person accounts, titles to published primary sources are presented first, followed by references to archival and secondary published works. I have erred on the side of inclusiveness in determining the limits of the published primary category, for example providing information on the German as well as the English version of Msatulwa's autobiography. Also to be found are supplementary titles of life stories, often of men, that have not been referred to directly but reflect the same general circumstances of nascent Christian communities at the turn of the century. Where a personal narrative is buried in a more general work, it may be cited in an independent entry.

Published Texts and Participant Observation
Arnot, F. S. *Garenganze: Or, Seven Years' Pioneer Mission Work in Central Africa.* London: Hawkins, 1889.

Arnot, F. S. *Bihe and Garenganze: A Record of Four Years' Work and Journeying in Africa.* London: Hawkins, 1893.

Baumann, O. *Afrikanische Skizzen.* Berlin: Reimer, 1900.

British Central Africa Gazette (official publication of the British Central Africa Protectorate, Nyasaland).

Bryan, M. A., ed. and trans., E. Kootz-Kretschmer, comp. *Stories of Old Times.* London: Sheldon, 1932.

Campbell, D. "An African Autobiography: The Story of Goi." Chap. 18 in *Blazing Trails in Bantuland.* London: Pickering, 1934.

-----. "Ten Times a Slave: The Story of Bwanikwa." Chap. 19 in *Blazing Trails in Bantuland.* London: Pickering, 1934.

-----. *In the Heart of Bantuland: A Record of Twenty-Nine Years' Pioneering in Central Africa among the Bantu Peoples,* 1922. Reprint. New York: Negro University Press, 1969.

-----. *Ten Times a Slave but Freed at Last: The Thrilling Story of Bwanikwa, a Central African Heroine.* Glasgow: Pickering, 1916.

Chisholm, J. A. "Notes on the Manners and Customs of the Winamwanga and Wiwa." *Journal of the Royal Africa Society* 9, no. 36 (1911).

Crawford, D. *Thinking Black: 22 Years Without a Break in the Long Grass of Central Africa.* New York: Doran, 1912.

Fortie, M. *Black and Beautiful: A Life in Safari Land.* Indianapolis: Bobbs-Merrill, 1938.

Fuelleborn, F. *Das Deutsche Njassa und Ruwuma-Gebiet: Atlas.* Berlin, 1906.

-----. *Das Deutsche Njassa und Ruwuma-Gebiet: Land und Leute.* Berlin, 1906.

Gemuseus, O. *Sakalija Mwakasungula.* Hamburg: Appel, 1953.

Hennig, P. O., ed. *Ambilishiye: Lebensbild eines eingebornen Evangelisten aus Deutsch-Ostafrika.* Herrnhut: Missionsbuchhandlung, 1917.

Kootz-Kretschmer, E. "Abriss einer Landesgeschichte von Usafwa in Ostafrika." *Koloniale Rundschau* 4–6, 1929.

-----. *Die Safwa, ein ostafrikanischer Volkstamm, in seinem Leben und Denken.* 3 vols. Berlin: Reimer, 1926–29.

-----. *Sichyajunga, ein Leben in Unruhe.* Herrnhut: Missionsbuchhandlung, 1927.

-----. *Tatu, das geraubte Muvembakind.* Herrnhut: Missionsbuchhandlung, 1927.

Livingstone, D. *Last Journals,* 2 vols. Edited by H. Waller. London: Murray, 1874.

Missionsblatt aus der Brudergemeine.

Mwashitete, M. *Ways I Have Trodden.* Trans. by M. A. Bryan. London: Sheldon, 1936.

-----. *Wege, die ich gegangen bin,* 3rd ed. Herrnhut: Missionsbuchhandlung, 1936.

Nigmann, E. *Die Wahehe.* Berlin: Mittler, 1908.

-----. *Schwarze Schwaenke: Froliche Geschichtchen aus unserem schoenen alten Deutsch-Ostafrika.* Berlin: Safari, 1922.

Northern Rhodesia Journal (NRJ).

Plymouth Brethren, "Family Relationships in Central Africa." In *Echoes of Service,* 1897.

Periodical Accounts (PA).

Roberts, A. D., ed. "The History of Abdullah ibn Suliman." *African Social Research,* no. 4 (1967).

Silanda, H.E. *Uzya Wakwe Mama Meli.* Lusaka: Publications Bureau, 1954.

Silavwe, Newton. "The Story of Mama Mary." Radio script, n.d., preserved in the Ethnography Collections, National Museum, Livingstone, Zambia.

Stephenson, J. E. *Chirupula's Tale: A Bye-Way in African History.* London: Bles, 1937.

-----. "Muhammedan Early Days in the Copperbelt of Northern Rhodesia." National Archives of Zambia, Occasional Paper 1 (1972).

Verbeken, A. Msiri, *Roi du Garenganze: l'Homme rouge du Katanga.* Brussels: Cuypers, 1956.

Verdick, E. *Les Premiers jours au Katanga (1890–1903).* Brussels: Comité Spécial, 1952.

Unpublished/Archival Sources

Berlin Mission Society (BM), Berlin

German East Africa, German Colonial Records group: National Archives of Tanzania (TNA), Dar es Salaam

London Missionary Society, Central Africa files: School of Oriental and African Studies Library, London. Houses the Congregational Church World Mission Archives (CCWM).

National Archives of Zambia (ZNA), Lusaka: British South Africa Company records; J. E. Stephenson Papers

National Museum, Livingstone, Zambia: Marshall Papers; Ethnographic Archives

White Fathers' Archives (APB), Rome

Published Secondary Works

Chanock, M. Law, *Custom and Social Order: The Colonial Experience in Malawi and Zambia.* Cambridge: Cambridge University Press, 1985.

-----. "Making Customary Law: Men, Women and Courts in Colonial Northern Rhodesia." In *African Women and the Law*, edited by M. J. Hay and M. Wright. Boston: Boston University Press, 1982.

-----. "Neo-traditionalism and the Customary Law in Malawi." *African Law Studies*, no. 16 (1978).

Cooper, F. "Indigenous Slavery, Commentary Two." *Historical Reflections*, no. 6 (1979).

Douglas, M. "Matriliny and Pawnship in Central Africa." *Africa* 34 (1964).

Eastman, C., "Women, Slaves, and Foreigners: African Cultural Influences and Group Processes in the Formation of Northern Swahili Coast Society," *International Journal of African Historical Studies* 21, no. 1 (1988).

Fetter, B., *The Creation of Elisabethville*, Stanford: Hoover, 1976.

Finley, M. I. "Slavery." In *Encyclopedia of the Social Sciences*, vol. 14. New York: Macmillan, 1968.

Gray, R. and D. Birmingham. *Pre-Colonial African Trade in Central and East Africa.* London: Oxford, 1970.

Haberlandt, M., "Dr. Oskar Baumann, Ein Nachruf." In *Abhandlungen der K. K. Geographischen Gesellschaft in Wien* (Proceedings of the Imperial Geographical Society of Vienna), Bd. 2 (1900).

Harwood, A. *Witchcraft, Sorcery and Social Categories among the Safwa.* London: Oxford/International African Institute, 1970.

Hay, M. J. and M. Wright, eds. *African Women and the Law: Historical Perspectives.* Boston: Boston University Press, 1982.

Iliffe, J. *German Colonial Rule in Tanganyika.* Cambridge: Cambridge University Press, 1970.

Jewsiewicki, B. and H. Moniot, eds. *Dialoguer avec le léopard? Practiques, savoirs et actes du peuple face au politique en Afrique Noire contemporaine.* Québec: Safi, 1988.

Johnson, D. H. "The Structure of a Legacy: Military Slavery in Northeastern Africa." *Ethnohistory* 36, no. 1 (1989).

Kalinga, O.J.M. "The Karonga War: Commercial Rivalry and Politics of Survival." *Journal of African History* 21, no. 2 (1980): 209-18.

Kopytoff, I. "Indigenous African Slavery, Commentary One." *Historical Reflections*, no. 6 (1979).

Lovejoy, P. "Concubinage and the Status of Slaves in Early Colonial Northern Nigeria." *Journal of African History* 29, no. 2 (1988).

-----. *Transformation in Slavery*. Cambridge: Cambridge University Press, 1983.

Marks, Shula, ed. *Not Either an Experimental Doll: The Separate Worlds of Three South African Women*. London: Women's Press, 1987.

Martin, B.G. "Muslim Politics and Resistance to Colonial Rule: Shaykh Uways B. Muhammad Al-Barawi and the Qadiriya Brotherhood in East Africa." *Journal of African History* 10, no. 3 (1969): 471–86.

Mbilinyi, M. "Runaway Wives in Colonial Tanganyika: Forced Labour and Forced Marriage in Rungwe District, 1919–1961." *International Journal of the Sociology of Law*, no. 16 (1988).

Miers, S. and I. Kopytoff, eds. *Slavery in Africa: Historical and Anthropological Perspectives*. Madison: Wisconsin University Press, 1977.

Miers, S. and R. Roberts, eds. *The End of Slavery in Africa*. Madison: Wisconsin University Press, 1988.

Minnesota Personal Narratives Group, ed. *Interpreting Women's Lives*. Bloomington: Indiana University Press, 1989.

Mirza, S. and M. Strobel, eds. and trans. *Three Swahili Women: Life Stories from Mombasa, Kenya*. Bloomington: Indiana University Press, 1989.

Moore, H. L. *Feminism and Anthropology*. Cambridge: Polity, 1988.

Morrow, S. "Policy and Practice: The Economic Role of the London Missionary Society in Northern Rhodesia to 1914." *Zambia Journal of History* 1 (1981).

Moyse-Bartlett, H. *The King's African Rifles: A Study in the Military History of East and Central Africa, 1890–1945*. Aldershot: Gale & Polden, 1956.

Nieboer, H. J. *Slavery as an Industrial System: Ethnological Researches*, 2nd ed. The Hague: Nijhoff, 1910.

Nigmann, E. *Geschichte der Kaiserlichen Schutztruppe fuer Deutsch-Ostafrika*. Berlin: Mittler, 1911.

Obbo, Christine. *African Women: Their Struggle for Economic Independence*. London: Zed Press, 1980.

Patterson, O. "On Slavery and Slave Formations." *New Left Review*, no. 117 (1979).

Perbandt, C. von, et al. *Hermann von Wissmann: Deutschlands Groesster Afrikaner: sein Leben und Wirken unter Benutzung des Nachlasses*. Berlin: Schall, 1906.

Pottier, J. *Migrants No More: Settlement and Survival in Mambwe Villages, Zambia.* Manchester: Manchester University Press, 1988.

Poewe, K. O. *Matrilineal Ideology: Male-Female Dynamics in Luapula, Zambia.* London: International Africa Institute, 1981.

Prince, Magdalene von. *Eine Deutsche Frau im Innern Deutsch-Ostafrika.* Berlin: Mittler, 1903.

Redmayne, A. "Mkwawa and the Hehe Wars." *Journal of African History* 9, no. 3 (1968).

Riesman, P. "The Person and the Life Cycle in African Social Life and Thought." *African Studies Review* 29, no. 2 (1986).

Roberts, A.D. "Pre-Colonial Trade in Zambia." *African Social Research,* no. 10 (1970).

-----. "Nyamwezi Trade." In *Pre-Colonial African Trade in East and Central Africa.* London, 1970.

-----. "Firearms in North-eastern Zambia before 1900." *Trans-African Journal of History,* no. 2 (1971).

-----. *History of the Bemba: Political Growth and Change in Northeastern Zambia Before 1900.* Madison: Wisconsin University Press, 1973.

Robertson, C. C. and M. A. Klein, eds. *Women and Slavery in Africa.* Madison: Wisconsin University Press, 1983.

Scott, R. J., et al. *The Abolition of Slavery and the Aftermath of Emancipation in Brazil.* Durham: Duke University Press, 1988.

Sheriff, A. *Slaves, Spices and Ivory in Zanzibar, 1770-1873.* London: James Currey, 1987.

Smith, Iain. *The Emin Pasha Relief Expedition.* Oxford: Clarendon, 1972.

Strobel, M. "Slavery and Reproductive Labor in Mombasa." In *Women and Slavery in Africa,* ed. C. C. Robertson and M. A. Klein. Madison: Wisconsin University Press, 1983.

Thelen, D. "Memory and American History." *Journal of American History* 75, no. 4 (1989).

Watson, W. *Tribal Cohesion in a Money Economy.* Manchester: Manchester University Press, 1959.

Weidner, F. *Die Haussklaverei in Ostafrika.* Jena: Fischer, 1915.

Whiteley, W. H. *The Bemba and Related Peoples of Northern Rhodesia.* London: International African Institute, 1951.

Wright, M. "Autobiographies, histoires de vie et biographies de femmes africaines en tant que textes militants." *Cahiers d'études africaines* 38, no. 108 (1988).

-----. "Chirupula Stephenson and Copperbelt History." *African Social Research,* no. 14 (1972).

-----. "Family, Community and Women as Reflected in Die Safwa by Elise Kootz Kretschmer." In *Vision and Service: Papers in Honour of Barbo Johansson,* ed. B. Sundkler and P. A. Wahlstrom. Uppsala: Nordic Institute, 1977.

-----. *German Missions in Tanganyika: Moravians and Lutherans in the Southern Highlands, 1891–1941.* Oxford: Clarendon, 1971.

-----. "Nyakyusa Cults and Politics in the Later Nineteenth Century." In *The Historical Study of African Religion,* ed. T. O. Ranger and I. N. Kimambo. London: Heinemann, 1972.

-----. "'Tambalika': Perspectives on a Colonial Magistrate." *African Affairs* 85, no. 338 (1986).

-----, ed. *Women in Peril: Life Stories of Four Captives.* Lusaka: Neczam, 1984.

Wright, M. and P. H. Lary, "Swahili Settlements in Northern Zambia and Malawi." *International Journal of African Historical Studies* 4, no. 3 (1971): 547–73.

Index